25¢

ALSO BY DAVID H. FREEDMAN:

Brainmakers: How Scientists Are Moving Beyond Computers
to Create a Rival to the Human Brain


ALSO BY CHARLES C. MANN:

The Aspirin Wars:
Money, Medicine, and 100 Years of Rampant Competition
(WITH MARK L. PLUMMER)

Noah's Choice: The Future of Endangered Species
(WITH MARK L. PLUMMER)

The Second Creation:
Makers of the Revolution in Twentieth-Century Physics
(WITH ROBERT P. CREASE)

# AT LARGE

## THE STRANGE CASE OF THE WORLD'S BIGGEST INTERNET INVASION

### DAVID H. FREEDMAN

### CHARLES C. MANN

Simon & Schuster

SIMON & SCHUSTER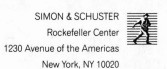
Rockefeller Center
1230 Avenue of the Americas
New York, NY 10020

Copyright © 1997 by David H. Freedman and Charles C. Mann
All rights reserved,
including the right of reproduction
in whole or in part in any form.

SIMON & SCHUSTER and colophon are registered trademarks
of Simon & Schuster Inc.

Designed by Karolina Harris

Manufactured in the United States of America

1  2  3  4  5  6  7  8  9  10

Library of Congress Cataloging-in-Publication Data
Freedman, David, date.
At large : the strange case of the world's biggest Internet invasion /
David H. Freedman, Charles C. Mann.
p.   cm.
Includes bibliographical references.
1. Computer crimes—United States—Case studies.
2. Computer hackers—United States—Case studies.
3. Internet (Computer network)   I. Mann, Charles C.   II. Title.
HV6773.2.F74   1997
364.16′8′0973—dc21                                              97-960
CIP
ISBN 0-684-82464-7

This book is dedicated to
Donald Schuyler Mann,
and to the memory of
Marilyn Jewel Freedman.

# A NOTE TO THE READER

This is a work of nonfiction. The story is true; the people, real. At their request, we have changed the names of a few characters— the members of the Singer family and a man we identify as "Riley."

# CONTENTS

# PROLOGUE

San Diego, California
April 1995

Several hundred people sit restlessly in a windowless conference room at a Hyatt hotel on Harbor Island. In appearance, the group is homogeneous, almost improbably so: white, male, and pale; beepered, cell-phoned, and laptopped; a preponderance of facial hair—the gestalt of the computer-industry entrepreneur or technical manager. The group is attending the first annual summit of the Internet Society, a small organization that is as close as the vast global computer network comes to having a government. With the Internet exploding at an extraordinary rate, the Society has decided to go public—to meet and greet the businesses that are flooding on-line, and to work through some of the inevitable difficulties.

At the head of the room, clutching a cordless microphone, is Jeffrey I. Schiller. He's untanned, not terribly tall, on his way to joining the ranks of the formerly thin. Short corkscrew curls explode from the top of his head. His features are dominated by a long but fragile mustache, which he has waxed into two slender prongs that

13

curve out from his upper lip like the horns of a toy antelope. In deference to his speaker's role he has upgraded his attire from his customary rumpled T-shirt to an oxford-cloth shirt that seems, in its unnatural crispness, to have been extracted minutes before from its cellophane wrapper. Schiller is the network manager for the Massachusetts Institute of Technology, which means that he is more or less in charge of designing, building, and maintaining one of the world's bigger and more renowned computer networks. Because the celebrity of the MIT system has attracted electronic break-in artists since the dawn of computer networking, Schiller has been forced, to his chagrin, to become an expert in computer security.

Ebulliently striding beneath a banner with the emblem of the Internet Society, Schiller is a fine public speaker who retails jokes in a distinct Boston accent. Today, though, he is in apocalyptic mode. He is trying to convince the crowd that computer security is not a threat looming in the distant future, it's a crisis right now, and it's much worse than people realize. At MIT, he explains, we *assume* our computer networks are being monitored by elements hostile to us. He says, Thousands of people eavesdrop on computer networks every second of every hour. He says, Going after these guys ends up being like stomping cockroaches. It makes you feel good, but there's always more of them. He says, The problems are getting worse by the day.

His audience is less than bowled over. Although attendees laugh politely at the funny bits, they don't appear to be engaged by the substance. Part of the reason is that the conference is nearing its end. Outside, there's glittering water, boats flashing in the San Diego sunshine, and terrific Mexi-Cali food in beachside stands; inside, there's more thin hotel coffee, clip-on name badges, and technical speeches under long, wandlike fluorescent lights. But another part of the reason seems to be that many of his listeners are resolutely uninterested in hearing what he has to say.

The Internet Society summit is aimed at the commercial enterprises that sell access to the Internet. Unsurprisingly, these Internet service providers—ISPs, as they are called—are not eager to tell their customers about the dangers of cyberspace. They want families to feel comfortable and safe as they surf the World Wide Web. They do not want to hear why some security people consider hooking a modem to a computer to be a dangerous act.

Schiller has addressed enough conferences to know when he is losing his audience. So he tries to regain it by pushing a little harder. He keeps talking cheerfully, but his voice grows louder and his gestures become more emphatic; maybe he leaves the confines of his prepared speech. He ticks off a monitory catalog of computer-penetration terms like "Trojan horse," "sniffer," "stringing the binaries." The reaction doesn't seem to satisfy him. He's ringing the bell, but everyone in the room is stubbornly asleep. Hey, out there, are you *listening?*

The inattention is exasperating, given what's at stake here. This isn't about digital pranks or purloined credit card numbers. Using the speed of computers and the astonishing reach of the Internet, a small group—even a single person—could slowly explore the nation's electronic infrastructure, invisibly seizing command of point after point, until all fell under their control. And not only Internet computers are vulnerable—any computer that can be connected to a telephone is at risk. The incursion could knock out a nation's electrical-power grid, telephone network, and air-traffic control system at a stroke; Wall Street and the banking system could fall, too. On an individual level, criminals could reach into hospital networks and change records, causing nurses to give patients the wrong medications. Or they could wipe out credit records and bank accounts. They also could be more indirect: someone could simply set all the traffic lights in Manhattan to constant red at rush hour—and do it every day for a month. In some sense, though, what worries Schiller most is the threat to the Internet itself. A passionate believer in the ability of computers to contribute to human welfare, he fears that a few big, dangerous security incidents may scare people away from the possibilities of the digital era, leading society to turn its back on the promise of the future.

Given this increasing threat, people like Schiller are appalled that the Internet as a whole may well be getting less, not more, secure. The reasons are several: the underlying software can never be made entirely loophole-free; the network has grown so fast that the average level of experience of its administrators has declined; and many Internet companies, such as the ISPs whose managers are listening to Schiller, brush off security concerns for fear of alienating their customers. But the greatest danger is people's reluctance to believe that something as faraway as Information Age crime can affect them. Small example: no matter how many times Schiller and other experts beg computer users to pick passwords that can't easily be guessed, many always choose something on the order of "hello." It takes only one fool with "hello," Schiller points out, to compromise a computer with thousands of users. Eighty, ninety percent of the systems out there, it's a no-brainer getting into them, if you have a little time. The crime is easy to commit, and the potential consequences are huge. A bad combination.

The audience still seems unmoved. Frustration is evident in Schiller's face as he wraps up with a few remarks on ways to protect against intrusions. Even as he speaks, most of the ISP managers are reaching for their leatherette laptop bags, preparing to make a fast getaway. Several rude souls are already striding toward the exits, snapping open flip-phones with one hand as they push through the doors with the other. Schiller thanks the audience, the lights rise, and everyone who hasn't already left files out. Everyone, that is, except for a handful of people who push toward Schiller with mumbled questions about security problems that have afflicted their companies.

Schiller dispenses advice with every appearance of enthusiasm until one of the group blurts out: Why should we get all upset about computer intrusions? We've heard the worst of it—Kevin Mitnick, the Masters of Deception, the Legion of Doom. Who cares if a few exceptionally smart teenagers crash a couple of systems or steal a few files?

Look, Schiller says, sharply. Look . . .

But then he stops and pushes his hand through the tight curls of his hair. It appears that there's something he wants to say, but he's hesitant to come out with it. Finally he mutters: Well, why you should be scared is because . . . You want to know why you should be scared?

His audience gives him an expectant look.

If you truly want to know why you should be scared, Schiller finally says, I have a story for you.

The story, as it turns out, involves what was almost certainly the biggest attack on the Internet in its history. An attack that reached into every corner of the sprawling global network, and hence potentially into almost every corner of life in the industrialized world. An attack whose enormous scope was matched in shock value only by the nature of the perpetrator. Yet the affair never made the newspapers, television, or the on-line discussion groups; the only articles about it were published in school newspapers at St. John's College (New Mexico) and MIT, and, for fear of compromising the investigation, distribution of the MIT report was limited. In fact, Schiller, although he was both one of the victims and a member of the nationwide team that traced the attack for almost two years, still didn't know its full extent, or much about its perpetrator. Like everyone involved in the affair, Schiller rarely spoke of it, and never in detail.

He sometimes called it the scariest story he ever heard.

And he didn't know the half of it.

# 1

# BUSY SIGNALS

**SEN. SAM NUNN:** There are some who believe we are going to have to have an electronic Pearl Harbor, so to speak, before we really make [computer security] the kind of priority that many of us believe it deserves to be made. Do you think we're going to need that kind of real awakening?

**CIA DIRECTOR JOHN M. DEUTCH:** I don't know whether we will face an electronic Pearl Harbor, but we will have, I'm sure, some very unpleasant circumstances. I'm certainly very prepared to predict some very, very large and uncomfortable incidents.

—U.S. SENATE COMMITTEE ON GOVERNMENT AFFAIRS, SUBCOMMITTEE FOR PERMANENT INVESTIGATIONS, *VULNERABILITY OF UNITED STATES GOVERNMENT INFORMATION SYSTEMS TO COMPUTER ATTACKS,* HEARINGS, JUNE 25, 1996

Portland, Oregon
March 1991

Janaka Jayawardene hit the steps to his office at the crack of noon. Having been forced by hurry to skip his customary wake-up jolt of caffeine, he was not at his best; driving to work in the drizzle —he lived in Oregon, it was early March—had not improved his mood. He had the proverbial Monday-morning blues. Monday afternoon, now. A few blocks to the north rose Portland's new postmodern skyscrapers, gray and cheerless with rain; five hundred yards to the south thrummed the main highway to the Pacific beaches, still windswept and gloomy this time of year. At the moment, both the dark buildings and the cold sand seemed more appealing to Janaka than climbing the wet, moldy steps that led from the basement parking garage to his office.

Jammed into a hill by the Willamette River, the Portland Center for Advanced Technology was an almost windowless two-story rectangle, sheathed in brickwork painted in two shades of dull, ceramic blue. At its heart was an atrium with two shallow concrete basins intended to hold water; people were supposed to congregate about them on sunny days. It being the Pacific Northwest, the requisite sunshine was rarely present. But even if it had been, the students and faculty in the building would never have gathered around the water. The Center housed Portland State University's computer-science and electrical-engineering departments, and no one affiliated with either of them spent much time outdoors. This included Janaka, the Sri Lankan émigré who maintained the electrical-engineering department's computer network.

Janaka exited the stairwell, turned right, went through the glass door, proceeded along the corridor that edged the atrium, then left into Room 136. Because the hour was still early, all movement was entrusted to autopilot. Shut door . . . move paper off swivel chair . . . switch on twenty-one-inch computer monitor . . . switch on second, equally large monitor on the other side of his workspace . . . momentarily consider cleaning up infestation of clutter . . . scroll through morning's supply of electronic mail (fifty messages, all claiming to be urgent) . . . contemplate attractiveness of coffee-pot steaming in next room . . . remember that past coffee abuse trashed GI tract, forcing reliance on Mountain Dew, the soft drink that computer jocks had discovered to be laced with caffeine. . . .

Even in his sleepy state Janaka had noticed one of the student assistants waiting for his arrival. Spotting Janaka, the assistant had scurried away, mouse-style, eyes fixed on the lint-gray squares of the linoleum. Moments later, Janaka heard raised voices in the room down the hall where the heart of the network resided. If people were shouting at each other there, it meant trouble of some sort. Extraordinary: the first minutes of the first day of the workweek, and trouble already. He wondered how long it would take to find him.

Room 136 was a rectangular space perhaps twenty feet on a side that contained several desks, half a dozen computer terminals, many yards of fat electrical cable sheathed in gray plastic, and a long, parti-colored heap of pizza boxes, soft-drink cans, and snack-food wrappers. Curiously, the mess was all on one side of the room —the side in which Janaka was sitting, reading his e-mail. The other side belonged to Trent Fisher, the administrator for the computer-science network and a man whose personal style was to Janaka's as matter is to antimatter.

Janaka worked late, irregular hours, often staying with a problem until his eyes got baggy and his thick, curly hair flopped over his forehead and even the loudest death-metal rock failed to revive him; Trent came to work at seven every morning, his long, straight hair tidily ponytailed, plugged his headphones into a boot-leg tape of Bob Dylan, and began working down his to-do list. Janaka covered the walls near his desk with a constantly changing gallimaufry of Dilbert cartoons, tabloid clippings about Elvis, UFOs, and reincarnation, and drawings of robots by his adored seven-year-old son, Christopher. He loved bustle and activity and the sound of people having fun. On the other half of the room, Trent liked the lights down and the computers quietly running and the music clearly audible. In his small, precise handwriting, he had filled a whiteboard by his desk with numbered instructions about rules to follow in his absence.

Orderly, almost fastidious, Trent acted as if life could be treated like a problem in computing—establish procedures correctly the first time, stick to them carefully, and everything will work out automatically. If randomness were kept out of the system, administrators wouldn't have to come up with ad hoc schemes to solve problems and everyone would be better off. Janaka, too, acted as if life were like computing. But in his view computers were prone to failures too unpredictable for anyone to anticipate. Following procedures, though important, was no substitute for being ready to solve unexpected problems when they arose, as they inevitably would. In practice, the only way to plan everything at the beginning was to restrict the users to a setup determined by the administrator, which was too sclerotic for Janaka's taste; indeed, some students referred to Trent's half of the room as East Germany. Given that the electrical-engineering network and the computer-science network were intimately entwined, the two men had a hard time not antagonizing each other.

About five minutes after Janaka entered the office, his doorway was filled by half a dozen undergraduates—computer-science or electrical-engineering majors who helped run the networks. Janaka stretched back in his swivel chair, making the springs creak, and presented the group with his avuncular smile. Yeeessss?

They all began to talk at once. Whoa, whoa, Janaka said, still leaning way back in his swivel chair, as if pinned by the verbal blast. Maybe if just one person talked. . . .

Wendy Wilhelm took the lead. She had a round face, dark hair cut straight across the back, and a direct, cheerful manner of speaking that suggested healthful formative experiences; she communicated equally well in person and via e-mail, a more unusual trait in digital circles than one might expect. We've been broken into, she said.

The swivel chair snapped to its upright position.

The students, Wendy explained, had been in the Center last night, working on the burdensome shroud of unfinished administrative tasks that always envelops computer networks. At a certain point they had noticed that an unusual volume of calls was coming through the university's rack of modems to a small, little-used computer on the periphery of the electrical-engineering network. Modems are small devices that transform the electronic signals understood by computers into the kind of signals transmitted through telephone wires; the university kept a dozen or so operating twenty-four hours a day. Surprised at the traffic, the students inspected the computer—lifted up the hood, so to speak, and looked at the engine. And inside they found someone who called himself "Phantomd."

By itself, the odd name set off no alarms—something about computers seems to invite people to come up with bizarre handles like Zyzzx, MegadOOd, and DeathStar. Phantomd sounded typical; the user list identified the account as belonging to one "Phantom Dialer." Phantom Dialer, in Wendy's opinion, was just the sort of dopey, immature moniker that would appeal to a college student. But this particular dopey name did not belong to any legitimate user at Portland State. Phantom Dialer, it appeared, had simply made himself an account.

This was dismaying. Under most circumstances users couldn't create an account—they didn't have the power. Which meant that Phantom Dialer had become something known as "root." In practice, anyone on a computer network is either an ordinary user or root. Ordinary users can't do much on the network except work with their own data and execute their own programs. Root, by contrast, has almost limitless power. Root has root access, in the jargon, which means that root can go anywhere, read any file, execute any program. Root users are sometimes called wheels or superusers, but the idea is the same. "God = Root," according to a sticker sometimes found in computer-terminal rooms.

Root access was invented to let network administrators fix problems from their desks without having to travel to wherever the problem is physically located. Root access lets managers control networks by preventing anyone but root from creating new accounts on the system. Root access ensures that the administrators alone have the ability to adjust the programs at the heart of the network —unless the wrong people become root, which was apparently what had happened at Portland State. The system had a new supreme deity.

Talk to me, guys, Janaka said to the students. What did you do about it?

They'd panicked, Wendy admitted. Crackers—she knew better than to call them "hackers," a term of respect in heavy-duty computer circles—had invaded on the students' watch and they hadn't known what to do about it. Some wanted to comb through the network logs for clues to Phantom Dialer's identity. Others wanted to shut down the entire network until it could be made secure. Still others, Wendy among them, wanted to do nothing until the problem had been assessed. If somebody broke into your house, she argued, you'd first find out how bad the damage was before you went burglar chasing.

Guessing what was coming, Janaka was hit by the abdominal sinking that is the advance guard of dismay. Even as they argued about the correct course of action, the students had been reading files and executing programs, which disturbed the electronic scene of the crime. Some of the group assailed the competence of the student who ran the attacked machine, who responded by blaming the student in charge of the modems, who in turn yelled at the student in charge of maintaining the software, the whole devolving into a knot of recrimination. By the time they spoke to Janaka, they had already been up all night arguing and were, he observed, one severely pissed-off group of modern American youths.

Setting aside their clash in style, Janaka and Trent moved to their keyboards. The first order of business was to find where Phantomd had been. What computers had he visited? What files had he read? What programs had he executed? And how the *hell* had he gone root?

Obviously, Janaka thought, something had failed; it had best get fixed ASAP. But as he hunched into the enormous monitor, his stubby, nail-bitten fingers flying, he had no notion how difficult the task would be or how widespread the break-in would prove. Nor did he know that he was launching a bizarre two-year hunt that would sweep up hundreds of people across the United States and involve half a dozen branches of the federal government. All he knew was that his hankering for a Mountain Dew had entered a critical stage.

Washington, D.C.
June 1991

As usual, the afternoon rush hour traffic was thick from downtown D.C. to suburban Alexandria, Virginia. Jim Settle played with the radio, hoping to come across a station that wasn't playing rap or grunge. He finally settled for a talk show. It felt good to let someone else do the talking. He'd spent the day, as he'd spent many other days in the last year, trying to convince his employer, the Federal Bureau of Investigation, that the growth of computer networks had created vast new opportunities for crime and destruction. For three hours that afternoon he'd warned an FBI–Secret Service interagency committee on telecommunications security of the troubles to come, only to realize that the eyes of his audience were covered with a cataractous film of incomprehension.

Settle turned up the A/C; the Washington sun, already vicious in June, was beating through the windshield. It didn't help that he was, as he was quick to admit, a touch heavy. He'd starved himself for three months to make the FBI entry requirements, and had been overweight on every monthly checkup in the nineteen years since. An agent's weight—that was the kind of thing the Bureau concerned itself with. Not what was actually happening beyond the stately brass doors of the J. Edgar Hoover Building.

In his frustrated mood he was content to let the talk-show host hector his guests. Anyway, the news would soon come on.

The D.C. spot news still gave Settle a vestigial tingle. It came from having served for almost a decade in the Bureau's metropolitan Washington field office, where he had worked the robberies, murders, and kidnappings that were the lifeblood of local news. When caught by the cameras at some particularly ghastly crime scene, Settle always tried to utter the clichés expected from a good company man without coming off like Agent Boo-Boo Bear. In the background the other investigators would be hopping around, trying not to get their shoes in the blood.

Oddly, though, the very hairiest episodes—the ones in which Settle had come closest to being shot or having his head kicked in— never came from the sociopaths. Those guys knew how the game was played: when the feds came to your door, you were caught, and you gave up without making a fuss. Settle had once learned that a multiple murderer had escaped from prison and was hiding out at an aunt's house in the city. He telephoned the aunt, who cheerfully informed him that the escapee would be back in an hour; if Mr. Settle would leave his number at the FBI, she'd make sure her nephew rang him back. The murderer was a monster: he'd burned his victims to death without compunction. Nonetheless, he returned Settle's call. Settle made an offer: Turn yourself in tomorrow morning and I'll take you in without handcuffs. When the man showed up, on time and sober, Settle rewarded him with a handcuff-free trip to the station. Half a block away from their destination Settle apologetically snapped on the bracelets to make the capture look official.

In Settle's experience, the dangerous ones were the confused amateurs who had never imagined they would get into trouble. Deserters were the worst—real pains in the patoots. They had absolutely no sense. To evade capture, they would jump out of third-story windows, thinking they were in the movies. Someone would have to peel them off the sidewalk. Settle had once picked up a deserter with a cast on his neck, which apparently he'd broken in his flight from the military. Sitting in the backseat of Settle's car as they roared down the highway, the fool unlocked the door and rolled out, broken neck and all. God only knew whether he ever made it out of the hospital.

The newscaster's voice, resonant and powerful yet curiously characterless, cut in with the four o'clock news. Settle desultorily cocked an ear, trying to predict what would come next: *Drug deal gone bad in . . . Drive-by shooting leaves . . . New charges against Congressman . . .*

Then he almost drove off the road with surprise.

The top story on the afternoon of June 26, 1991, was that the central telephone network in Baltimore had blacked out at eleven that morning. The outage had spread through Maryland and Washington into parts of Virginia and West Virginia, leaving six million phone lines as useless as so much string. Police, fire, and ambulance services were interrupted; the federal government was in irons. No one knew when service would be restored. On top of that, the central telephone network in Los Angeles had crashed just about an hour ago, at two o'clock eastern standard time, knocking out another few million lines on the West Coast.

Settle experienced a momentary difficulty with reality. He had been trying to convince his bosses that massive telephone collapses could occur at the same time that exactly such a collapse was occurring. And, beautifully, the outage had nuked Washington, D.C. That meant national television and irate members of Congress. Best of all, it meant headlines in the *Washington Post*. Settle had observed that the higher echelons at the Bureau lived and died by *Post* headlines.

If L.A. had gone down at 2:00 eastern time, Settle realized, it had crashed at 11:00 A.M. Pacific time. Eleven in the morning was the same local time that Baltimore had been hit. It was as if an electronic time bomb had been set to explode at the same hour in both cities.

Settle drove the last ten minutes to his house in five minutes. No one but the dog was around. His wife, Judy, was at work; his two grown children were at their own homes. Once in the living room, he stood for a moment, excited but unsure of what to do next. Finally he grabbed the phone and called the Department of Justice. Fast busy signal.

The implications went beyond the phone system, he thought, redialing. Although the phone disaster would attract attention, it was only a stand-in for the real problem: computer networks. The telecommunications system was vulnerable not because saboteurs could cut fiberoptic cables—the companies had backup systems that would handle the traffic—but because it depended on computer networks. Not only telephone companies were vulnerable. Utilities, insurance firms, and governments depended on computer networks, too. All were at risk.

Last winter, after months of agitation, Settle had been asked to produce a report on the threat, and what the Bureau needed to do to be ready for it. He recommended creating a squad of agents

focused on computer networks. The report had been officially approved—whatever that meant—in May. But nobody seemed ready
to do anything. Now maybe this was the incident that would make
people wake up.

Another fast busy signal. Settle muttered to himself. He began
to try a third time, then dropped the receiver on the hook, feeling
stupid. He had forgotten: the phones were down.


Cambridge, Massachusetts
Spring 1991

At the edge of the Massachusetts Institute of Technology is a
nine-story structure known as Building NE43 or, more colloquially,
545 Technology Square. Across its facade march rows of windows
with rounded frames that recall the shape of computer screens—a
bald architectural metaphor, for 545 Technology Square is the site
of two institutions that have made signal contributions to the digital
age. They are the Laboratory for Computer Science, which occupies
the bottom four floors, and the Artificial Intelligence Laboratory, on
the top floors. In fine academic style, the two labs have been feud-
ing for decades. As a nod to the vendetta, one of the two groups
that neutrally employs researchers from both departments is
known as the Swiss Project. Its computers are decorated with Swiss
flags.

The other group that balances between the two labs is the Free
Software Foundation, an unusual gathering of anarchic programmers that emerged from the AI Lab but is physically based in the
Laboratory for Computer Science. In the spring of 1991, its staff had
just moved into two small offices on the fourth floor, having spent
years working on tables crammed into a corridor. They were small
in number but had lofty goals. The Foundation sought to nudge
society toward a utopia of sharing by creating computer programs
that unlike ordinary software could be freely copied and passed
around.

It was no accident that the Free Software Foundation arose
from MIT in general, and the Artificial Intelligence Laboratory in

particular. Since its founding in 1972 the AI Lab had acted as a proselytizer for computers. In the days when computers were big, costly, and used mainly by coteries of obsessed engineers, this meant giving almost any interested party a guest account on the machines. As long as the tourists didn't disturb other users or consume too much computer power, they were free to do whatever they wanted. Indeed, staffers were delighted when new people wanted to learn about the amazing devices they were inventing.

Much as Berkeley, Columbia, and Michigan incubated one strain of American society in the 1960s and 1970s, MIT—and especially the AI Lab—was the Petri dish for another strain. And just as the counterculture spread from enclave to enclave, the attitudes at MIT replicated themselves in computer centers across the nation. In many ways, especially their emphasis on personal freedom, the two cultures were surprisingly similar, although one arose in the very mathematics and engineering departments picketed by the other during the Vietnam War. Berkeley, Columbia, and Michigan helped create the potent mix of sex, drugs, amplified music, and grassroots activism that has characterized the nation ever since. The MIT computer culture took longer to swim into public view, but in the long run may have had even more impact.

At Tech Square, programmers traded their work back and forth without restraint, often throwing the latest incarnation of a program into a wire basket in the AI Lab for the next round of modifications and improvements. All parties contributed to the common pursuit of better, more efficient, and more elegant means of computing. As software grew into big business in the 1980s, the old openness was difficult to sustain. Programs became encrusted by copyrights, patents, and trademarks; software, from the MIT perspective, was expensive to obtain, difficult to work with, illegal to improve. MIT types were stunned to learn that programmers could be arrested for tinkering with a program and passing the fixed-up version to friends. Imagine it—laws that stopped people from enhancing the use of computers! The Free Software Foundation was founded to preserve the spirit of joyful inquiry that had marked the

AI Lab. Funded by donations and user fees, it produced software that people could freely copy and change.

The Foundation's tradition of unbounded exploration had long extended beyond Tech Square. In 1972 MIT became the second site on the East Coast to connect to the experimental national computer network that would develop into the Internet.* Although warnings about network security appeared as early as the next year, the AI Lab ignored them. In its view, the act of securing machines—closing them off from the outside world—was antithetical to the spirit of networking, which was intended to open computers to the outside world.

As the Internet expanded from its original audience in academia and the military, much of MIT rethought its policy of open access. Passwords appeared, along with codes of computer conduct. But the Foundation kept its computers available to anybody on the national network who wanted to use them for any purpose, provided that their activities did not interfere with the work of the Foundation itself. A certain sector of the emerging Internet society found this liberality attractive in ways not intended by the Free Software Foundation. Using its computers as a headquarters, some Internauts broke into other networks and tried out new tricks on them. Then they would report back to their friends via the Foundation computers. At any moment dozens of people might be on the system, all happily anonymized by their computer monikers, chatting about secret ways of breaking into systems.

Tiresomely, the invaded networks kept bleating in the direction of Cambridge about the electronic slumber party at Tech Square. They were not happy to hear that the real problem was their desire to lock out people. Why not just give the intruders accounts? Foundation staffers asked. We let them freely use our systems, and they often become good users. We don't try to control anyone.

---

* The first was Bolt Beranek and Newman, a Cambridge-based engineering firm founded and largely staffed by former MIT faculty. BBN built the first Internet-capable computers; the emerging network was then called the ARPANET, after the Advanced Research Projects Agency of the Department of Defense, which funded much of the initial research into computer networks.

You're maintaining a public nuisance, other network adminis-trators charged. The whole insistence on security is counterproduc-tive, the Foundation replied. You are busy locking the door, which prevents you from hearing what other people are up to. We can assure you that the people outside your locked doors are talking to each other. Your very insistence on maintaining "security" is doom-ing you to a race you cannot win.

In the hubbub on the Foundation network, few paid attention to the arrival that spring of a visitor who called himself Phantomd. Phantomd had set his sights on another Foundation visitor, a break-in artist who styled himself Grok, after a term in the science fiction novel *Stranger in a Strange Land.* An elusive figure who was fanatically careful about concealing his tracks, Grok was renowned for his encyclopedic knowledge of the software flaws that permitted unauthorized access. He had briefly encountered Phantomd in a chat session—a sort of Internet party line.

On-line, Grok apparently made the mistake of telling the inex-perienced Phantomd that he was often at the Foundation, with the result that Phantomd followed him there, constantly pestering him for tips. Every time Grok worked on the Foundation computers, his would-be friend was waiting with more questions. Grok invariably blew him off, which didn't in the least deter Phantomd, who seemed to be extraordinarily persistent. Indeed, as Grok—and, later, many others—would discover, the persistence of Phantomd was like noth-ing they had encountered before.

# 2

# CRAZY HOUSE

The thing is that the really, really good ones no one knows about. I mean, they may be kicked off systems, but they're never caught. Most of the time you don't know who they were, by any name.

**—DAN FARMER, AUTHOR OF THE SECURITY PROGRAMS COPS AND SATAN**

Birmingham, Alabama
July 1991

Beth Barnett read the teletype message in her hand for the seventh or eighth time. Report to Washington, D.C. Expected Monday, July 8.

She was being TDY'd—removed from her current assignment and placed on temporary duty.

Twenty-four hours earlier, she'd received a call from headquarters: Michael Gibbons in the Bureau's intelligence division. Gibbons, whom Barnett knew slightly, asked if she were interested in coming to D.C. to investigate last week's telephone outages.

Sounds fascinating, she'd replied. It would be delightful to work on the outages—in three months. At the moment, though, she was in the middle of a difficult corruption inquiry that she wanted to take through to the end. Finishing the case would be the best way Barnett, a young agent, could develop as an investigator. Okay, that's the way it is, Gibbons said, as she later recalled it.

Twenty-four hours later, she looked up to see the ASAC—assistant special agent in charge—drop a teletype on her desk.

She called up Gibbons. Not to be irate, but hadn't she made it clear what she wanted? Which was not to be transferred to the Beltway? Plus she had friends coming to Birmingham to stay with her for the Fourth of July. Was she supposed to pack while they were visiting?

Gibbons was contrite. As the apologies issued from the receiver, she sorted through the paper on her desktop. We need your skills, he was saying. There simply aren't that many agents with master's degrees in computer science.

But I don't *have* a master's degree in computer science, she said.

You *don't?* Clearly, this was embarrassing. The master's degree, he told her, appeared on the Bureau's skills-evaluation database.

Nonplussed, Barnett explained that she had completed an undergraduate degree in computer science and had worked as a low-level programmer, but that by now her last contact with the electronic world was three years ago—a lifetime in computer terms. It was like having a degree in physics from before the invention of the atomic bomb. On the other hand, the FBI was so far behind, electronically speaking, Barnett might be the closest thing it had to an expert. And she had known that sooner or later she'd be pulled into some sort of computer work—it was a big reason the FBI had accepted her application.

Bored and unfulfilled as a programmer, she had been considering law school, thinking that she might become a prosecutor. Something about *investigating* appealed to her. She liked the idea of picking apart nasty circumstances, unraveling the factual skein, identifying the guilty party. Then she learned that prosecutors did little more than negotiate with other lawyers and present facts in court that had been gathered by the police and FBI, who did the actual investigatory work. The Bureau was almost impossible to get into, but computer jocks had a leg up on the competition. Trying to increase its expertise in technology, accounting, and foreign languages, the FBI was placing applicants with backgrounds in those fields in special pools with lower entrance requirements. It was affirmative action for geeks.

After sweating through the torturously hot summer of 1988 at the Bureau's training academy in Quantico, Virginia, Barnett was thrown in with the regular applicants anyway. This was a compliment; her scores were high enough without help. Her first assignment, unusually, was a TDY. She was sent to the Washington Metro field office to help with the wiretaps in Operation Illwind, the inquiry into Pentagon procurement fraud. You're going to love it, an instructor told her at Quantico. Wiretaps are a lot of fun.

In this way Barnett learned a valuable lesson about the Federal Bureau of Investigation: never believe anything said at Quantico. Illwind was boring beyond belief. She pored through thousands of pages of transcriptions of wiretapped dialogue, almost all of it banal. And that was the *interesting* part; most of her time was spent photocopying those transcripts and performing the clerical jobs needed to support a wiretap operation, with its tidal wave of legal and procedural requirements. By contrast, low-level programming was a giddy roller coaster of excitement. She felt like a secretary, but she reminded herself that she was paying her dues. The good jobs would come later. Besides, she managed to make a few contacts in Washington, Mike Gibbons among them.

After two months with Illwind, Barnett went to her first real assignment. At Quantico, fledgling agents are usually presented with two options. The first is moving to one of the hundreds of tiny "resident" offices that the Bureau maintains as satellites to the main offices in big cities. The resident offices are one- or two-person shops that have little independent activity. The other option is New York City. Most agents choose the resident office. The Big Apple, in Bureau folklore, is the sewer of all assignments. It has the highest cost of living and an unending stream of crime. The only reason some graduates pick New York is because after their stint in the city they probably won't ever have to return. Meanwhile, the agents who picked resident offices often end up in New York on their second assignment.

Raised in a small midwestern town, Barnett had no desire to immure herself in the nation's premier semibankrupt metropolis. She asked for a regional office, which, she knew, almost certainly meant the Deep South. That was the routine for midwesterners. If she had been raised in the South, she would have been given a small midwestern town. The geographical shuffle was the Bureau's notion of broadening agents' horizons. Barnett moved to Birmingham, Alabama.

There Barnett was put on white-collar crime, which included corruption, bank fraud, money laundering, and—the bane of new agents—background investigations of FBI applicants. In larger offices, greenhorns sometimes do little but applicant investigations. Happily, the Birmingham office was too small to stick agents with a single task. Indeed, Barnett found herself occasionally pulled away from the plodding inquiry that characterizes white-collar cases into reactive work—the adrenaline-surging madness of a kidnapping or bank robbery.

Almost none of the job involved computers. She supposed that would come later, maybe her second assignment (ugh, probably New York). Which would be fine with her. She had clocked enough time in front of the monitor in her pre-FBI life to enjoy being away from its cathode-ray glow for a while.

In addition, she liked Alabama. She had a nice apartment and a short commute. The food was sweet and mushy and nobody got too excited about dressing for success. The office, like the Bureau itself, wasn't exactly crawling with women, but the guys treated her fine, although they kept telling her she looked like a sixteen-year-old. It was true; even at thirty, she could still pass for a high-school senior with her straight blond hair, shy smile, and big, porcelain-blue eyes.

And then, this teletype message.

She didn't want to leave the friendly people in Birmingham. She remembered what people in Washington were like. She remembered what summer in Washington was like.

Obviously, though, this TDY wasn't negotiable. The FBI wasn't known for giving new agents a big say in what they did.

It could have been worse. They could have been sending her to New York.


## Portland

Many people regard computers as frightening, remorselessly logical machines that coldly grind out numbers without human intervention. In truth, behind the apparently automatic responses of every console on a computer network is a system administrator—"sysadmins," as they are called. What sysadmins do is simple to describe but hard to understand: they run computer networks.

The profession of sysadmin came into existence because computer networks have transformed society but still do not work very well. In 1925 the United States already depended completely on the automobile, but drivers expected to break down at least once in the course of a hundred-mile trip. In those days every new car came with a tool kit to fix the problems that inevitably developed on the road. Now, more than seventy years later, automobiles are much more reliable; computers have taken over their role as pivotal but unstable ingenues. They constantly misfire, exhibit mysterious behavior, suddenly cease to function altogether. Their manufacturers equip them with tool kits, but most people don't understand the tool kits. When things go wrong, they summon a sysadmin.

Janaka was the sysadmin for the electrical-engineering network at Portland State University. Like a doctor, Janaka had to know the solutions to a staggering number of problems. He had to know the quirks of dozens of types of computers and programs, many of which in his opinion didn't work well even when they were running perfectly. Like a doctor, he had to be patient when hypochondriacs told him that something was terribly wrong and had to be looked at *right now*, and then it developed that the hypochondriacs hadn't known that pressing the D key would delete their e-mail. He had to pretend not to be gritting his teeth when told that someone wanted to attach just *one* more new machine to the network, I know you've never heard of this brand but the department got it for next to nothing . . . hey, uh, can you make it work because I don't understand it myself, actually?

Unlike doctors, though, sysadmins are not respected figures in society. Nor are they especially well paid. Because human beings generally do not want to think about their computers until they go wrong, sysadmins in most organizations are usually associated with catastrophe, and everybody dreads their appearance; they're the disheveled folks who seem to be taking forever to fix whatever the problem is. Positive reinforcement from the user community is infrequent.

Networks arose when computers were scarce resources that had to be parceled out among hungry users. To keep the books, users were given accounts identified by their names; every time they began using the system, they logged on—that is, they typed in their names and passwords—which signaled the network to start running the meter. Although processing power is much cheaper today, the system hasn't changed. Every program and data file on the network is still labeled with the name of its owner—the accounts permitted to use it. As a rule, only the owner of a program can execute it; nobody else has permission. Only the owner of a file can read it; nobody else can take a peek. (Root, usually reserved to sysadmins, is the exception; root can read and examine everyone's files.) And when users log into a computer network, their every move is automatically monitored: time of entry, programs used, machines contacted, duration of computer session. In this way computer networks are a combination of libertarian dreamworld (every byte privatized, every second of computer-processing time allocated and paid for) and Orwellian nightmare (every byte subject to recording, every second of computer-processing time held accountable).

Unauthorized users are trespassers. They are random elements in the complex systems that people like Janaka spend their days nurturing. If sysadmins are jugglers, keeping the pins of a hundred users in the air, intruders are spectators who suddenly throw their own pins into the mix. Unauthorized users read mail that doesn't belong to them, execute programs that aren't theirs, alter files that are owned by someone else, crash the whole system, then walk away. They are not accountable. To people like Janaka, they violate the Aesthetic of the Network.

That was why he was upset by the arrival of Phantom Dialer.

Phantom Dialer had entered a computer called Serena that belonged to the computer-science department. (All computers on networks are given names so that sysadmins can distinguish them.) Serena was a NeXT, a trendy but financially unsuccessful brand of computer. Sitting at his keyboard in Room 136, Janaka, who had root access, electronically stretched across the building and performed the digital equivalent of exploratory surgery on Serena. With Trent's help, he examined the computer's inventory of approved users. Phantom Dialer was on the list, exactly as Wendy had said.

Janaka tapped through the rest of the user list to see if anything else looked—wait. Tucked into the list was an account named Power. Power had no password. When Serena asked for a user name, anyone who typed "power" was in—just like that. What could Power do? It turned out Power owned just one program, which was also called Power. The program activated a routine that switched off the computer. Power made it easy to shut down Serena in an emergency. From any computer in the network you simply contacted Serena, typed "power" to get in, then typed "power" again. No muss, no fuss, no nonsense about passwords. Janaka realized that one of the sysadmins—possibly himself—must have installed the account for some reason that doubtless seemed plausible at the time.

Alas, the Power account had root access, which meant that anyone who logged on as Power had all the capabilities of root. Power could create a new account in any name—Phantomd, for instance.

This carelessness was inexcusable, in Janaka's view. Not only had the sysadmins left a door open for intruders, they had rolled out the red carpet.

There was more bad news.

When users work on several computers in a network, they get tired of having to enter passwords every time they switch from one machine to another. As a convenience, sysadmins can set up a special file—its name is .rhosts (pronounced "dot-are-hosts")—which permits the people registered in the file to jump freely among certain machines. (The initial dot in .rhosts indicates, more or less, that the file should be looked at only by sysadmins.) When users contact a computer with a .rhosts file, in other words, it first checks to see if they are listed in the file. If they are, it lets them in forthwith; if not, they must provide a password.

Serena's hard drive contained a .rhosts file. One of the computers in it was Jove, a powerful box made by Sun Microsystems. Serena, in the jargon, "trusted" Jove with the users listed in .rhosts and accepted them without question. The system was more useful, Janaka and Trent knew, if the trust went both ways—that is, if Jove also trusted Serena, so that users who could jump freely to Serena could also return freely to Jove. To trust Serena, Jove would need its own .rhosts file. Did it have one? Yes. Certain users on Serena could switch to Jove without hindrance, including anybody with root access. Power, for instance.

This discovery caused Janaka to look at Trent, and Trent to look at Janaka. They felt exceedingly stupid. That crackers could surreptitiously obtain root access on Serena was annoying, but not much damage could be inflicted from such a small, peripheral machine. Root access on Jove was a different matter. Jove was a central file server, which meant that it was a computer with big hard drives that contained much of the data on the network.* If someone in the computer-science department had information worth stealing or wrecking, it would probably reside somewhere on Jove. If the information were elsewhere, anybody with root on such a central computer would quickly be able to get to it.

---

* All personal computers are alike, but computers on a network are of two basic types: servers and clients. Servers contain the files and programs that lie at the heart of a computer network and are shared by its users. As a rule, ordinary users don't work directly on the servers, but on smaller, less powerful computers—clients (or, sometimes, terminals)—which are linked by copper wire or fiber-optic line to the servers. A single server may have dozens or hundreds of clients, depending on the network. As computers have become more powerful, the distinction between clients and servers has lessened in importance but not disappeared.

Although the computer gurus at Portland State prided themselves on their savvy, they had—idiots! idiots!—managed to set up
the network in such a way that the red carpet led directly from
Serena to Jove. All an intruder needed to do was find Serena, claim
the identity of Power, thus grabbing root access, and hop to Jove as
root. Shazam! Instant network deity.

Luckily, Trent pointed out, the intruder seemed not to have
done any damage. Apparently no files had been tinkered with.

We better make sure of that, Janaka said.

How?

This question touched a sore spot. Computers are like crazy
houses whose owners at any moment can move the walls or add
new corridors or knock out rooms. Even if anyone wanted to try,
keeping track of the alterations would be a full-time job. On top of
that, the networks—the neighborhoods of interconnected computers—are also in constant states of change, like suburbs at the edges
of rapidly growing metropolitan areas. When the office needs more
computers, somebody buys the cheapest ones available and plugs
them in any which way. Often sysadmins discover the additions
only when they receive a frantic message that the boxes don't work.
As a result, computer networks tend to be bricolages of different
machines and software, wired together in haphazard mad-scientist
fashion. The Portland State computer-science department was
small by most standards: about 250 boxes. But even Trent and
Janaka didn't know exactly how they were connected or what was
on them.

In their endless debates, Trent told Janaka that the best way
to oversee a system with a natural tendency to architectural randomness was to restrict the users from the beginning to a minimal
set of programs that the sysadmins completely understood. Because
the Portland State network had not been assembled in this fashion,
Trent was confronted with hundreds of crazy houses that might
have any number of rooms and anything at all in them—exasperating! Phantom Dialer could be hidden anywhere in the shambles.

By contrast, Janaka thought that griping about the futility of
working in chaos was itself an exercise in futility. People wanted to

use their computers the way they wanted to use them, not the way that was most convenient for administrators. Concerning Phantom Dialer, all that could be done was to poke around as thoroughly as possible, which Janaka planned to do.

After a few hours of searching, Trent drifted off to work on something that he felt was more likely to be of positive value. Meanwhile, Janaka paddled through the thousands of files and directories in search of—what? Something that looked odd. It was hard to figure out what strange things Phantom Dialer had left behind and what strange things had been created by the students' blundering chase after him. The students hadn't written down in any coherent way what they had done. By opening files, they had inadvertently erased the record of when the file had been opened before that, which might have provided useful information. They had deleted the password file with the Phantomd account. And they hadn't—but what was the point in berating them? The main fault, in Janaka's view, was his. Someone had stolen into his network, and taken advantage of sysadmin tools—the very files (like .rhosts) and programs (like Power) that he had created for his own convenience and control. By leaving these tools accessible, he had been negligent, foolishly naive.

Shamefacedly, Janaka expunged the Power account and deleted every .rhosts file on the network.

Later, Janaka would wonder if he had been too hard on himself. Such accounts and files were standard practice in 1991, when the Internet was new. Astonishingly, though, such red-carpeted paths for intruders remain common to this day.* For instance, many machines are still shipped from the factory with preset passwordless accounts, in order to let repair teams log in without having to bother the uncertain purchaser about setting up a new account. Unless these accounts are specifically deleted, they remain open doors to crackers.

---

* The much-ballyhooed attack—apparently by the infamous cracker Kevin Mitnick—on the personal network of security maven Tsutomu Shimomura in 1995 had as its target Shimomura's .rhosts file, which the intruders altered to permit free entry.

Sysadmins concerned about security have always looked for such invitations to trouble and eliminated them. But as the Internet grows, the number of sysadmins with the experience to identify and expunge the holes is not keeping pace. Many sysadmins don't know of the problems; some believe the added convenience of shortcuts like .rhosts files outweighs the risk of attack by the likes of Phantom Dialer; others intend to disable them when they have nothing else to do. One bromide among computer-security experts is that every new entrant on the Internet, without exception, is grievously vulnerable.

The effects of lapses by manufacturers and sysadmins are amplified by the computer underground. Through their many covert channels of communication—channels with no counterparts in the world of legitimate computer users—crackers constantly trade news about the most recently discovered security lapses. By assiduously exploring this hidden society, the novice cracker could leverage a startling array of tools to breach the flimsy defenses of the Internet.

Which, though Janaka didn't know it at the time, was exactly what Phantomd was doing.


Before going home Janaka e-mailed a note about the incident to the Computer Emergency Response Team, established by the Department of Defense at Carnegie Mellon University in Pittsburgh. Then he dodged the swarm of midnight skateboarders in the Center's parking garage and headed for his bedroom in suburban Beaverton, west of town. The next morning he found a response from Kenneth R. van Wyk, the CERT technical coordinator. "Thank you for the report on the break-ins which you have experienced," van Wyk wrote. "If you figure out where the intruder was coming from . . . we would very much like to know."

Me, too, was Janaka's reaction. Meanwhile, he intended to get some work done. Spring vacation was in a week, and he wanted to be away from the office.

Instead, on the first Monday of vacation he was summoned

back to the Technology Center. No new accounts were in evidence, but the students had discovered other problems. First, users had ignored Janaka's instructions and reinstalled their .rhosts files. Second, the cracker had broken in and, taking advantage of the reinstalled .rhosts files, jumped all over the network, putting in programs that gave root access to ordinary users.* Amazingly, he had inserted them throughout the network. Dozens filled directories in crazy profusion—they were everywhere. What kind of boneheads would scatter around a hundred obvious copies of a program when they needed only a single well-hidden copy to get root? Some of the programs were in the electrical-engineering network, so it was apparent that both networks had been compromised. Phantom Dialer and his friends now had access to everything in the Portland Center for Advanced Technology.

Stomping on the programs, Janaka thought, would send a message—stay away. When the intruders returned to find their handiwork gone, they would realize that their entrance had been spotted. So he combed through the network and erased every trace of Phantomd's presence. (He also deleted the .rhosts files again.) When the rest of the vacation passed with no further sign of break-ins, Janaka allowed himself to hope that the message had been received and understood.

He returned to work on the next Monday. No student tumult this time. No sign of Phantom Dialer, either. But on a hunch Janaka looked for more of those programs—and found them, though not as many, and not in such easily spotted locations. Phantom Dialer was learning—a creepy thought. Reading the logs carefully, Janaka saw no evidence of illicit activity. Everyone who had dialed into the computer over the weekend was a legitimate user. So who were the crackers? How were they gaining access?

The only log entry that immediately stuck out was a long series

---

* In technical terms, the cracker had installed what are called "SUID" programs—the term stands for "set user identification." These temporarily endow ordinary users with some of the powers of root for specific purposes like changing passwords. Because SUID programs can easily be manipulated to create security holes, sysadmins nowadays are told to avoid them whenever possible, a warning that is often ignored.

of attempts to jump from Portland State to machines at MIT. In itself, this was nothing suspicious. Many legitimate users contacted other networks. MIT, in particular, had electronic libraries that were of interest to students and professors elsewhere. But these repeated attempts—dozens of them, some only a few seconds long—looked as if someone had tried to use Portland State as a springboard into the MIT Artificial Intelligence Laboratory, the Laboratory for Computer Science, and the Free Software Foundation. Sometimes this person had knocked on the door and failed to gain entrance, which was why those contacts were short. But other attempts had been successful.

If this scenario were true, Janaka realized, the intruder would have to be someone who was using the network at the time of the attempts on MIT. It would have to be a legitimate user or someone who had purloined that user's identity. Logged on during the attacks were accounts that belonged to a gaggle of kids who had taken to hanging around the terminal room. Janaka e-mailed the kids an invitation to Room 136.

A few days later he found himself speaking with Patrick Humphreys, a freshman. Patrick was a marketing major who had taken a computer class and become fascinated by the network; his username, Path (that is, Pat-H, an abbreviation of his real name), was scattered throughout the logs. Janaka reserved a soft spot for computer-smitten kids, having been one himself. On the other hand, if Patrick was Phantom Dialer. . . . Patrick was blond, soft-spoken, and looked as though he had never needed to shave. He was dressed in the digitally correct uniform of jeans and stained T-shirt, but Janaka had heard that Patrick's father was a lawyer and that his grandfather owned oil land in California.

Patrick denied that he had broken into the network. On the other hand, he said that he might know the culprit. Patrick had a friend from high school named Steve Singer. Steve had this strange brother, Matt, who was deep into computers. And Matt had been bragging about break-ins. Matt wasn't malicious, Patrick thought. But he'd had trouble with computers in the past. He lived with his mother in eastern Portland.

Janaka took the phone number. If Phantom Dialer was a harmless teenager, that was a relief.

Contacting the mother proved difficult. She was a city bus driver who worked from late in the morning to late in the evening—sysadmin hours. And Janaka and his wife, Pam, had managed to forget the phone bill at home for long enough that Pacific Bell had disconnected them. In the office, Janaka played telephone tag with Mom for a while, trading messages on answering machines, but then dropped the matter when he saw no further evidence of break-ins. He bet the kid had been given the holy flame by his mother.

As April turned into May and then June without evidence of further attacks, Janaka felt less threatened. One kid had come in, but why would anybody else invade? Portland State was hardly the sort of place that had valuable secrets. Maybe he'd overreacted to the whole thing.

Only later would he realize that these comforting suppositions were entirely mistaken. Indeed, Janaka had not begun to grasp the magnitude of his problem. He had never ejected the intruders from the network, because they had weapons he had never encountered. One of the simplest was a program called Crack, a program that guesses passwords.

In most networks the list of passwords is stored in scrambled form in a special file on a central computer—a server. To use an example supplied by Simson Garfinkel and Gene Spafford in their book *Practical Unix and Internet Security*, a user who chose the password "rachel" would never see the word "rachel" in the password file. Instead, it would be encrypted into "eH5/.mj7NB3dx." (Actually, every password, in a further refinement, can be scrambled in 4,096 ways, so two people who picked "rachel" probably would not end up with the same encrypted password.) Because passwords are stored in this encrypted form, computers do not directly compare the passwords typed in by users with the passwords in the password file. Instead, they scramble the password entered by the user in the same way and match the now-encoded result with the appropriate entry in the password file.

Phantomd broke the password file in classic fashion. First he copied Portland State password files to another network. There he ran the files through Crack, which laboriously scrambles and encrypts every word in a dictionary, checking the results against a password file. Because of the huge number of possible matches, Crack may need weeks to compare them all. Eventually, though, it will find the user who chose, say, "hello" for a password. (It will also find the user who picked "rachel"—*any* ordinary word or name is a bad password.) Running Crack for days, Phantomd had slowly discovered passwords on computers all over the university.

With access to so many accounts, Phantomd could log on in many guises. Once in the system, he watched the Portland State sysadmins pursue him. Like many members of the Internet confraternity, Janaka, Trent, and the students communicated mainly by e-mail. As these memos appeared on the network, Phantomd intercepted them. He sent choice excerpts thousands of miles to another computer network, where they sat, undisturbed, for years.

### Washington, D.C.

Jim Settle's father had been an FBI agent in Asheville, North Carolina. While other kids were playing baseball, Jim and his twin brother, John, kept the old man company, cruising the lazy, steaming back roads of the nearby Cherokee reservation in a Bureau car, a Nash that was nondescript in a way that screamed G-man to anyone who cared to notice. Settle's father never seemed overly caught up by the job, except when someone got killed on his watch. Jim knew when that had happened: his father would come home with a tight jaw and a silent glare. Usually there was another sign, too. He brought home the corpse's soiled clothes and hung them on the clothesline, where they dried out before being shipped to the Bureau's crime lab. Playing tag in the yard, Jim and John dodged around the bloody, bullet-holed shirts and underwear of killers and stoolies.

Although the brothers were fraternal, not identical, twins, they were uncannily hard to distinguish. Strangers called to them in the street, mistaking one brother for the other. The brothers were close, as twins often are. Together they played high school sports and chased girls. Together they attended Presbyterian College, a tiny institution in Clinton, South Carolina. And together they were swept up into the Vietnam War, although neither actually saw combat. John served his time in Korea. Jim was stationed in Fort Bragg, North Carolina—couldn't make it out of the Carolinas, he liked to joke. He was made commander of an administrative battery charged with tracking and distributing ammunition, supplies, and payroll. It was a low-morale unit, filled with sullen college kids who wanted to be anywhere but Fort Bragg. Settle found he had a knack for working with misfits, though; he could meld them into a team that excelled. Part of the reason for his success was that he secretly thought of himself as a misfit, too. He always took on the oddball assignments.

He didn't *look* like a misfit. He was a tall man with a sharp, almost birdlike nose. His posture was stiff, almost military; when he walked, he swung his arms in short, choppy arcs. Just enough North Carolina twang remained in his voice to establish his bona fides as a good ol' boy. He had a thick torso that suggested, correctly, that he was on friendly terms with the business end of a beer bottle.

Growing up, Settle had always intended to go to law school. But by the time he left the military, he was supporting a family. He had married his college sweetheart; their daughter was now eighteen months old. Settle found himself thinking, Well, Dad has a steady paycheck from the Bureau. The nation's not going to run out of crime in the near future. And the FBI liked legacy kids—they knew Bureau culture. He joined in 1968.

In 1979, after a decade in the streets of Washington, D.C., Settle was asked to join a group of Department of Justice attorneys on a task force investigating federal procurement scams. Most agents avoided this sort of gig—procurement fraud was not the kind of crime that sparkled on a résumé. Try telling your next supervisor that while the rest of your office had been taking down murderers and extortionists, you'd been going *mano a mano* with government waste.

Settle was intrigued, though, because the case involved computers. In the army his brother had been assigned to missile-control systems, which acquainted him with this new technology; Settle had learned a bit, too. Now John was doing well in Hartford, Connecticut, as a computer manager for Traveler's Insurance. Given the opportunity, Settle liked the idea of learning more about these putty-colored boxes that had taken over his brother's life. It would be pleasant, he thought, to spend a little time working with a staff that could put together two consecutive English sentences.

The task force was going after the Computer Sciences Corporation in El Segundo, California, which sold the government time on its mainframe computers—and, according to investigators, overcharging Uncle Sam by millions of dollars. Settle spent months paging through financial records before he figured out the scheme. Washington bought so many services from the firm that as a practical matter it couldn't audit them all. The General Services Administration—the branch of the government that controlled billing—used an accounting program that spot-checked a few items, in much the same way that light-bulb manufacturers test only a few bulbs from every batch. By reading the code, Settle concluded, a Computer Sciences vice-president had figured out which services were being audited and jacked up the prices on the others. (After a three-year legal battle, Computer Sciences settled for almost $3 million but did not admit guilt; the vice-president pleaded no contest to two charges and was fined $20,000.)

Settle was fascinated. Just by deciphering the gibberish in a computer program, an executive had bilked Uncle Sam out of millions. He had stolen in a single year much more money than a bank robber would take in a lifetime of theft, and he had done it from the air-conditioned comfort of his office. When word of this got out, Settle realized, it would change the face of crime. Why would criminals risk their lives mugging people at gunpoint if they could make much more by reaching through the Internet to steal corporate information from an office on the other side of the country? If one wanted to look at crime in business terms—a natural stance for a career FBI agent—then computer misuse was going to be the criminal growth industry of the future.

Was the FBI prepared for a wave of digitally adept bad guys? Not a chance, Settle believed. If he was among the most computer-savvy agents in the Bureau, the agency was in trouble. It didn't have the experience, it didn't have the expertise, it didn't have the awareness.

Settle didn't have much chance to act on these ideas until 1987, when he returned to Washington, D.C., as a supervisory special agent. There he discovered that his boss, Bill Esposito, the head of the white-collar division, was also worried about computer crime. But despite this interest Settle saw no sign of response from the Bureau hierarchy until the day in November of 1990 when Esposito asked Settle to come into his office. The Bureau hit savings-and-loan fraud on the wrong side of the curve, he told Settle. We came in years after the stolen money had already been spent and the banks were going under. Wouldn't it be novel if the FBI got into something *before* it was a national disaster? With the approval of management, Esposito asked Settle to put together a team to write the long report that would, among other things, articulate the reasons for creating a computer-crime squad.

Although writing the report at first filled Settle with optimism that the FBI would move fast on computer crime, it hadn't led to any action—until the double phone crash in Washington and Los Angeles on Wednesday, June 26. By that Friday Esposito had told Settle to set up a seven-person task force to work with the Secret Service on the outages. Congress was screaming for action, so the task force would have to work fast.

The pressure increased on Monday, July 1, when another dual blackout occurred. At eleven in the morning eastern standard time —that time again!—the phones in Pittsburgh went down. For six and a half hours, millions of people lost communication with the outside world. Police, fire, and ambulance services were again thrown into chaos. San Francisco blacked out, too, at eleven in the morning Pacific standard time. Alert technicians managed to route around the problem in a few minutes, though.

The digital age suddenly seemed less abstract to the Bureau higher-ups, Settle observed, when members of Congress realized that computer problems meant no 911 service in their home districts. Six and a half hours was a long time for voters who couldn't report that their houses were on fire.

Strangely, the blackouts bore every sign of malicious intent, but the phone companies involved said they had received no demands for money. It was as if someone had been playing with them, showing off what could be done. Watch me throw this city into darkness over here, and then this one over there. Want to see me do it again?

On July 2 Pittsburgh crashed for the second time.

# 3

# CRASHING THE
# SHUTTLE

Whoever . . . knowingly causes the transmission of a program, information, code, or command to a computer or computer system, if the person causing the transmission intends that such transmission will damage, or cause damage to, a computer, computer system, network, information, data, or program; or withhold or deny or cause the withholding or denial of the use of a computer, computer services, system, network, information, data or program; and the transmission of the harmful component of the program, information, code, or command . . . causes loss or damage to one or more other persons of a value aggregating $1,000 or more . . . shall be punished [for a first offense by] a fine under this title or imprisonment for not more than five years, or both.

**—18 U.S.C. 1030 (FRAUD AND RELATED ACTIVITY IN CONNECTION WITH COMPUTERS), SEC. (A)(5)(a)**

Cambridge
Late Spring 1991

The deletions at the Free Software Foundation had been happening for several weeks now, and people were getting upset. Every morning it was the same thing. Drift into work around eleven with a cup of herbal tea or a health drink, rubbing red-rimmed eyes after a

night of pounding code. Take a seat at whatever computer was available. Look around at people's faces to see if it had happened again.
It had, of course. Check one's own work. Gone. Someone had wiped
the disk clean. Again. Noah Friedman, the sysadmin, was reloading
the system with a backup tape, too tired even to curse.

Usually staffers at the Foundation would gossip, put on some
music, check their e-mail, gradually work in to the day. But the
routine—insofar as a group of anarchists can have a routine—had
been broken for weeks. Day after day, people trashed the network.
The vandals worked methodically, marching from machine to machine, blanking each one in turn. One of them kept e-mailing and
telephoning the Foundation, calling himself The Wing, and taunting
the Foundation with its inability to stop him. To the programmers
the attack was painful and bewildering. They put up no barriers to
entry. Why would anyone do this? What should be done about it?

The simple answer—set up security routines—elicited vehe-
ment protest. Most of the objections came from Richard Stallman, a
medium-sized thirty-eight-year-old man with very long and very
dark hair who had been working at MIT since 1971. Stallman didn't
own a suit jacket or a dress shirt or even a tie; when he stayed in
hotels, he was sometimes questioned by detectives because he
walked around the lobby at night in his socks. If a computer programmer can be famous, Stallman was famous; he had written several programs that were essential to the functioning of many of the
world's computer networks. The year before, in 1990, he had become the first programmer to win one of the grants from the John D.
and Catherine T. MacArthur Foundation known, to Stallman's embarrassment, as "genius prizes." Most important in this context,
Richard Stallman was the founder and president of the board of the
Free Software Foundation.

Stallman had established the Free Software Foundation because he regarded proprietary software as unethical. Proprietary
software is software copyrighted by a commercial enterprise—programs that cannot be copied without permission. Because the fundamental act of friendship between computer programmers,
Stallman thought, was to share programs, proprietary software was

inherently anticommunity. If Stallman received a commercial program from a friend, he was legally forbidden to give a copy to another
friend. This, in Stallman's opinion, violated the Golden Rule. Worse,
it restricted human freedom. The stated goal of the Free Software
Foundation was to create software that users could copy and
change without hindrance.* Stallman's larger purpose was to use
computers to increase freedom for humankind.

A programmer by vocation, Stallman was an anarchist by
conviction. Many people think of anarchists as bomb-throwing
lunatics, but Stallman fell more within the tradition of nineteenth-
century prophets of mutual cooperation like Pierre-Joseph Prou-
dhon and Pyotr Kropotkin. He had a summa cum laude undergraduate degree from Harvard in physics, but his real collegiate
passion had been working as an unpaid volunteer at the other end
of Cambridge, in the MIT Artificial Intelligence Laboratory. At the
AI Lab nobody had private desks or private phones; nobody's work
was more important than anyone else's. Every person who wanted
to use a computer was given a terminal if one was available, no
questions asked. No passwords, no log-ins, no security. No root—
nobody had special privileges. People told AI Labsters they were
crazy to live and work that way, but they did it through the 1970s.

That was how Stallman wanted the Foundation to operate, too
—deletions or no deletions.

By that spring, though, the attacks had been going on long
enough that Stallman's insistence on open access was brewing revolt. I can't go on this way, Noah the sysadmin said. We're dealing
with unbalanced people here. You don't know what it's like to have
this Wing guy call every day. And we're losing incoming e-mail, especially reports of bugs in our software—reports we really need to
improve it.

We can take ourselves off the Internet altogether, Stallman

---

* Free software was not necessarily given away gratis. Stallman didn't mind charging
for manuals and disks; the income was a major source of support for the Foundation.
The kind of freedom that concerned him was intellectual—the freedom to use ideas
without restriction.

said. He had a quiet but flatly definitive manner of speaking that charmed some people and irritated others. That way we're not preventing anyone from gaining access, he argued, because the access will no longer exist.

We need the Internet to get e-mail, Noah and most of the staff said. How else can we get bug reports and fixes?

Use the post office was Stallman's response. If we cut ourselves off the Internet, we will not be doing anything to others that we are not willing to do to ourselves.

Why not simply register the users? That way we will know who is on the system and can finger the bad actors.

If you start getting involved with security, Stallman said in his soft, stubborn way, you start spending time being a policeman. He said the word "security" with a kind of audible curling of the lip. Are you going to spend all your time checking to see who is authorized and who is unauthorized? Are you going to kick out unauthorized users even if they've done nothing wrong? If so, you'll be punishing people not because they've done something bad, but because they've violated a rule. Well, I think rules *should* be violated.

They've been wrecking our system every night for weeks, Richard.

The debate continued until Stallman recognized the imminence of a mass exodus of staff. In the first few days of June the Free Software Foundation without warning cut off outside access to unregistered users. At a stroke, thousands of people lost their electronic home. (In solidarity with the new class of digital homeless, Stallman denied himself remote access to the network of his own Foundation.) The members of this displaced horde wandered about the Internet, wailing and gnashing their virtual teeth, vainly seeking each other in the wilderness. It was the Expulsion from the Garden.

The expulsion apparently caught the legendary cracker Grok by surprise. He knew some idiot had been hassling the Foundation, but evidently he had never imagined that Richard Stallman, the most intransigent idealist on Earth, would give in. When the doors shut, Grok lost his home base. Where would he operate from now? What his temperament required was a place that would let him work unsupervised. But that was hard to come by; the Free Software Foundation was one of the few sites on the Internet that had made a point of accommodating guests without questions or hassle.

Which seems to have led him to recall the greenhorn Phantomd. He often came to the Free Software Foundation from a university in Oregon. Any network that would let somebody like him run around freely was worth inquiry.

Grok broke into Portland State and created an account with an inconspicuous name. As he had suspected, Phantomd had stumbled across the perfect network: a system with full Internet connectivity whose sysadmins, despite their evident competence, were touchingly naive about security. In a way, Phantomd was training them. They hadn't yet realized that he had created half a dozen accounts for himself and was brazenly copying their e-mail and storing it on another machine at MIT. Kind of funny, watching an utter amateur nail the pros.

Then Grok got nailed, too. He was changing his account name —a precaution to avoid having too much activity associated with a single user—when Phantomd unexpectedly asked the Portland State machine what programs were running. Discovering the name-changing program, Phantomd correctly reasoned that because ordinary users had little reason to change their account names, the other person must be a cracker. To his mortification, Grok received a cheerful message: Hey, there! I see you!

Grok ignored him.

Who are you? Phantomd asked.

No response.

I see you, Phantomd wrote. You can't hide from me.

Grok gave up. The novice had whacked another expert. Now Grok could either acknowledge the call or log off the network. Logging off would be too humiliating. Make a sign, he wrote.

It was an elite way, Phantomd knew, of saying: Speak to me.

Who is this? Phantomd wanted to know. What are you doing? What are you up to?

The chagrined Grok told him the truth.

Phantomd was overjoyed. At last he had the attention of the celebrated Grok! Grok, caught, launched what was in effect a tutorial. Although sometimes slow to pick up things, Phantomd proved an eager student. In fact, his fervor alarmed Grok, who wondered what force he was unleashing on the world.

## Washington, D.C.

In a bureaucracy, Jim Settle knew, it was important to run several schemes at once. Wanting to alert the FBI to computer crime, he had managed to become one of the coleaders of what was being called Telecommunications Task Force. But that had not stopped him from pursuing a second case. Southwestern Bell, the regional telephone company, had discovered a gang of teenagers called the Masters of Deception in its networks. It had traced the intruders to New York City and reluctantly called the FBI. Settle asked agent Jim Kolouch to follow up the lead. Kolouch went to Manhattan in mid-June—not a moment too soon, as it turned out.

Within hours of his arrival, Kolouch learned that the New York office of the Secret Service—which shared, under vague and sometimes contentious terms, responsibility with the FBI for computer crime—was already snooping around the Masters of Deception, as well as a related gang, the Legion of Doom. Why hadn't the Bureau been informed of the Secret Service's investigation? The special agent in charge (SAC) of the FBI's New York office had long ago told his Secret Service counterpart that the Bureau had no interest in computer crime, and that the Service had the field to itself.

Settle was not exactly surprised to hear this. Still, it exasperated him. The biggest Bureau office outside of Washington, and its SAC couldn't wait to rid himself of the crime of the future!

I want you on this case, Settle told Kolouch. I don't care what the SAC says.

Kolouch, Settle knew, didn't mind bending the rules.

Like many agents, Kolouch's interest in law enforcement derived from a youthful fascination with riflery. He had spent his adolescence in marksmanship competitions in New England. At Northeastern University he was president of the rifle club. The varsity rifle team outshot West Point, the Coast Guard academy, and MIT—the last being especially satisfying, because in those days MIT awarded scholarships and fancy Anschutz rifles to expert shots.

Wanting to join the FBI, Kolouch had chosen the college major most likely to gain him admission: accounting. Kolouch's plan was derailed by marriage; to his surprise, he ended up actually becoming a CPA. For five years he worked for one of the predecessors of what is now the accounting conglomerate of Ernst & Young. He applied and was accepted to law school, but decided that corporate law was a boring way to make a living—and distastefully manipulative, to boot. Returning to his original plan, he joined the FBI in 1972. He was twenty-eight.

After working on the fringes of the Watergate scandal in the Washington Metro field office, he moved to management in Bureau headquarters in 1977. He arrived on April Fool's Day—an omen, he later decided, because he ended up on one of the few FBI beats duller than corporate law. He performed financial and operational audits, postmortems documenting that agents hadn't violated laws, regulations, or procedures. Sick of what he regarded as dronelike paperwork, Kolouch returned to the streets in 1980.

Two years later, Kolouch committed professional hara-kiri. He joined the least desirable section of the entire Bureau: counterintelligence. Although chasing foreign spies has a glamorous image, FBI agents disdain it. Counterintelligence works in secret, rarely attracting the favorable press coverage that ensures promotion. And the work is boring, because agents spend most of their time reading documents at their desks. If they're lucky, they escape their offices for surveillance, which usually translates into waiting in parked automobiles while suspects eat lunch.

As far as Kolouch was concerned, though, his six years in counterintelligence were the best of his career. He loved matching wits with his foreign counterparts; he didn't care about the secrecy, the desk work, and the lack of promotions, if it was for a good cause.

In 1985 he and another agent arrested navy spy John Walker, the man who had turned his family into an espionage ring. To Kolouch's disgust, the pudgy, balding Walker had corrupted his brother and son to support his houseboat and his platoon of wan-witted girl-friends. Kolouch and another agent arrested the spy at gunpoint in the hallway of a Ramada Inn. While the other agent snapped on the handcuffs, Kolouch had the pleasure of checking for hidden razor blades by ripping the toupee from Walker's head.

In 1989 an assistant special agent in charge at the Washington Metro office asked Kolouch to explore a new area: computer crime. Sure, said Kolouch. Why not? Tackling a fuzzy new area was just the sort of thing he would do. To brush up his accounting, he had learned something about mainframe computers. Now, he discov-ered, networks were the coming thing. He picked up technical tips at CERT, the computer-crime information center in Pittsburgh. Washington Metro, he concluded, should become a national clear-inghouse for computer-crime investigations.

Bureau higher-ups—the thickheads, to use Kolouch's term—rejected the scheme. Some rejected the notion of computer crime itself, because it was based on the means of the offense, rather than the end. The FBI didn't categorize malfeasance in terms of "gun crimes," "car crimes," or "pen crimes"; the agency used terms like "blackmail," "rape," and "murder." Why care, the thickheads asked, if someone used a computer to commit theft? It was still a theft, wasn't it? Yes, Kolouch fumed, of course it was a theft. But computer criminals cannot be caught by conventional investigative tech-niques, so their deeds should be treated as a separate category. Maybe so, the thickheads said, but who cares if some wonk-a-lator leaves a network open to teenagers? Excuse us real men while we go out and kick down some doors.

In addition, Kolouch's opponents said, where was the mass of computer-crime cases screaming for justice? Few such incidents had been officially reported. The agency allocated staff and funds according to the number of known crimes of each type. With few reported incidents . . . well, Kolouch could connect the dots. To him, this was like arguing that counterespionage was worthless because not many government agencies reported their secrets stolen. In fact, he argued, the paucity of known incidents merely reflected how often the victims of computer crime never learned of their loss. When companies did discover a break-in, most firms wouldn't report it because they feared the bad press that would come from admitting their networks had been insecure.

In the end, Kolouch's efforts to establish the FBI in computer crime fizzled. If anything, he thought, the Bureau's anticomputer bias got worse. Field offices were filled with gung-ho types who would be quick to trade a computer for an extra ammo clip. A few agents were willing to crank up a word processor, if only to save time writing reports. But the thickheads looked so askance at computers that these agents often hit the keyboard only after their bosses left for home.

Having stuck his neck out for computers before, Kolouch was an obvious candidate to go to New York City to chase the Masters of Deception. The next step, though, was to ask the court for permission to emplace a wiretap—exactly the kind of bureaucratic rigmarole Kolouch abhorred. He called Settle to say that he didn't want to wade through the paperwork by himself.

In Washington, Settle promised that he would send some backup. There was an agent named Barnett down South who was one of the few agents with a master's degree in computer science.

Grok could do things that amazed Phantomd and often didn't mind Phantomd following along while he did them. They exchanged messages for hours, Phantomd vacuuming up the other's knowledge, scribbling down the answers in his notebooks or on any scrap that came to hand (papers, it subsequently turned out, that ended up being read by a surprising number of people).

Much of the conversation occurred on a branch of the Internet called Internet Relay Chat. On IRC, many people in different places could conduct on-line conversations simultaneously, sending typed messages back and forth to each other in disconnected streams that looked like dialogue from a screenplay about a cocktail party of technoweenies. Five, ten, fifteen people might be on at once, all emitting short, cryptic messages, sometimes talking to the group at large, sometimes directing their remarks to one participant alone.

Most chat channels have names that begin with a pound sign; Phantomd was drawn to #hack (pronounced "pound-hack"), where the Grok and the rest of the elite went to meet and greet. He watched, fascinated, as American gangs like the Legion of Doom and the Masters of Deception leaped onto his screen, their braggadocio punctuated by quiet questions from experts in Europe, Australia, and Israel. Or the #hack crowd would talk about Kevin Mitnick— Teal, as he called himself on-line—who had just emerged from prison for committing a series of now-infamous exploits.

Many of the #hackers gave Phantomd a hard time. They called him a wannabe, a lamer, a poser. They said he was stupid. Grok, by contrast, treated Phantomd as a youthful version of himself, an aspiring colleague, an open vessel in which to decant knowledge. He provided Phantomd with some programs—fifteen minutes' work for Grok, but a life-changing event of importance for Phantomd. The programs were the electronic equivalent of power tools. (The Crack program was an example, although as it happened Phantomd had already found it himself on the Internet.) Without them Phantomd was no more than the lamer derided by the crew at #hack. Tools in hand, he was the functional equivalent of Grok. His lack of knowledge didn't matter; if he pushed the right buttons, the programs would do all the work for him. Phantomd was enormously pleased by these Pygmalion-like gifts.

Grok wasn't always friendly. Sometimes he got in a bad mood and treated the importuning from Phantomd as an annoyance. But he was like a grumpy adult confronted with the demands of a two-year-old—destined to lose. The two-year-old, its attention focused only on its small number of concerns, watches for any opportunity to pursue its agenda; adults, distracted by the other things in their lives, inevitably provide them. Wherever Grok turned, Phantomd would be pinging for his attention, asking him for software, beseeching him to share his knowledge. Grok would be working on something interesting, Phantomd would show up, and then good-bye concentration. Almost always Grok irritatedly gave in. It wasn't worth the trouble of resisting.

Phantomd didn't mind the occasional displays of pique. Lying low, he used one of his Portland State accounts to hop to MIT. There he read faculty e-mail he had learned that professors often wrote their friends or students something like, "I'm going to be away for two weeks, so if you want to use my account the password is . . . " He also checked whether MIT staffers had accounts on other networks; not wanting to memorize multiple passwords, people frequently used the same one for all their accounts. Incredible how far you could go with a few tricks that even he knew to be beginners' stuff—he got to networks in Italy and Switzerland.

The best stuff came from .rhosts files. In one MIT scientist's account, Phantomd discovered a .rhosts file with an entry for another network, which let him enter that network, where he found —yes!—a passwordless root account, which allowed him to comb through the second system until he found a .rhosts file that led to a network at the National Aeronautics and Space Administration. Climbing the ladder of trust, he visited the NASA site. Quickly he learned that NASA had an enormous computer system, a veritable network of networks. Writing in his small, erratically angular handwriting, Phantomd happily mapped the interconnections. He couldn't find any passwordless root accounts. But there was something else just as good.

Many of the boxes in NASA were the powerful, network-ready personal computers—workstations, as they are called—made by Sun Microsystems. As Phantomd had learned from Grok, many Sun computers came with their directories marked as "world-exportable," which meant that their files could be sent to any computer at all, even computers not on the network. What Phantomd quickly discovered was that directories throughout NASA were still world-exportable—including the directories with password files. Skipping from subnetwork to subnetwork within the vast NASA system, he copied password files, added some passwordless root accounts for himself, and replaced the old password files with the new, doctored versions.

Sometimes the machines wouldn't let him replace password files, because the files were world-exportable (they could be copied) but not world-writable (they could not be changed). When that happened, he had an alternative: breaking the password file with Crack, the password-guessing program. To do that, Phantomd copied the password files to a little-used workstation at MIT. As with the Portland State password files, he ran the NASA files through Crack. After Crack ground through the files, it usually decoded a few passwords, enough to let him tunnel further into NASA. By June of 1991 he was deep enough that Grok, to whom he reported his exploits, told Phantomd to be careful.

Don't worry, Phantomd replied. No way was he going to crash the space shuttle, ha ha.

Grok wasn't amused. Presumably NASA took precautions against damage from intruders. On the other hand, the agency was supposed to be preventing people like Phantomd from getting in at all. And NASA was involved in so many fields, from medicine to microwaves, that the potential consequences of security breaks were huge.

Phantomd had no intention of stopping. He had heard that NASA had some of the nation's biggest supercomputers—speedy machines that he hoped could overcome the limitations of Crack. Although the program guessed hundreds of passwords a second, it needed weeks to generate the millions of possible matches needed to break a password file. Practically speaking, this was a big problem, because even the least alert sysadmins noticed when somebody ran a program for a week. But if Phantomd could gain access to NASA's supercomputers, he could grind through the calculations in a few hours. He could knock off password files like a factory assembly line, spitting out passwords in a routine fashion.

That would give him access to important places. Places that nobody at, say, #hack had ever reached.

# 4

# S U - Q V T

The only system which is truly secure is one which is switched off and unplugged, locked in a titanium lined safe, buried in a concrete bunker, and is surrounded by nerve gas and very highly paid armed guards. Even then, I wouldn't stake my life on it.

**—GENE SPAFFORD, DIRECTOR, COMPUTER OPERATIONS, AUDIT, AND SECURITY TECHNOLOGY (COAST) PROJECT, PURDUE UNIVERSITY**

Portland
June 1991

Paul Mauvais was sitting in Janaka's office when the students appeared in the doorway, shifting from foot to foot with the characteristic undergraduate mixture of abashment and impatience. Paul was experiencing a bit of impatience himself. Although his official position was at the central campus network, he was working that Thursday in the Center for Advanced Technology. In a not uncommon situation, the unplanned growth of the university's networks had ended up endowing Portland State with several overlapping networks. Three of them, to be exact—the computer-science and electrical-engineering networks at the Center for Advanced Technology, and the central university system on the main campus. Part of the reason Paul spent much of his time in the Center was that the three networks, once separate, had more or less merged, and administering one necessarily involved helping out with the other two. But the other part of the reason, Paul conceded, was that he liked hanging around with Janaka and Trent, especially Janaka, the more easygoing of the two. The only trouble was that students—an occupational hazard of all educational establishments—kept interrupting the conversation. Already they had barged in at least four times with questions and complaints.

Something's wrong with the network, the students said now.

Vague complaints that something was wrong with the network ranked high on Paul Mauvais's list of least favorite forms of user feedback. It was like dropping off an automobile at a repair shop with the instructions, "Broke—please fix." After being asked for more specific information, the students revealed that they were having trouble logging on. They typed in passwords and the computer rejected them. When they tried again, the passwords were accepted.

So you actually can get into the system, Janaka said. Once you're in, does everything work?

Yes, everything worked. But every time they logged in, the network first refused to take their passwords.

Paul was skeptical. Countless times students had rushed to him with the claim that something was wrong with the system, and then he'd find out that they didn't know how to run some program and hadn't even tried to read the manual. In those cases, exasperated sysadmins sometimes answered with the curt acronym RTFM —read the fucking manual.

Well, he said, let's test it out.

He sat down at Janaka's workstation and logged onto the computer they were complaining about: EECS, a big server made by Sequent Computer Systems, a high-end manufacturer based a few miles away in Beaverton. EECS functioned as a bridge between the electrical-engineering (EE) and computer-science (CS) networks. As it was supposed to, EECS asked him to log in. Paul typed his account name, "pmauvais." Then it asked for his password. Paul typed that in, too.

Login incorrect, EECS said.

Maybe, Paul thought, he hadn't entered his password correctly. To prevent people from reading passwords over users' shoulders, the log-in program did not show them on-screen. If users made a typing error, they wouldn't know until the password was rejected. He tried a second time.

**Login:**

Paul again typed in his account name. The computer responded with:

**Password:**

Paul typed his password slowly, careful about hitting the correct keys.

**You have mail**

the computer informed Paul. Then EECS printed the date and time of his last log-in. Below that was the "prompt," the symbol indicating where the user should type commands. In most personal computers, the prompt is a greater-than symbol (>). Computer networks usually have two prompts, a greater-than symbol (or, alternatively, a percentage sign) for ordinary users and a pound symbol (#) for root. On-screen, both are often preceded by the name of the computer. Paul had root access on EECS, and thus saw a pound symbol:

**eecs#**

Everything seems fine, he told the students. He ran a few commands and observed their execution. I'm not seeing the problem, he said, producing a murmur of protest.

Humoring them, he logged out, then immediately returned. Demonstrating his extreme care to the spectators, he typed in his name and password.

## Login incorrect

Despite the impatience of the students, who sensed that EECS had done something unusual, Paul let his eyes grow vacant behind his black-framed glasses as he thought about the situation. Two possibilities existed. A sysadmin could have fiddled with the log-in program, perhaps attempting to fix a bug, and introduced the problem accidentally. But if that were the case, Janaka would know about the work.

The other possibility was that someone had slipped into the Portland State network, deleted the log-in program, and inserted a different program in its place. The replacement would look the same as the original while secretly performing actions never intended by the program's authors. Such modified programs were called "Trojan horses," because of the unpleasant surprises hidden inside them. In the jargon, Portland State had been Trojaned.

What do you think, Janaka? he asked in his quiet voice. Looks to me like we've got a cracker.

Trojan horses and other cracker tools are rife on networks connected to the Internet, largely because most of these networks are based on software called Unix. Unix is an operating system, the most fundamental type of software on a computer. A computer's operating system defines what services programs can ask of it—services like adding two numbers, or moving information onto a hard disk, or making letters and numbers appear on a monitor. Like a telephone switchboard, an operating system directs requests for these services to the hardware that performs these requests, including the keyboard, monitor, printer, disk drive, microprocessors, and so on. Operating systems also include collateral programs that perform necessary housekeeping functions like copying, moving, and deleting files.

Many different operating systems exist. Two of the best-known are MS-DOS—the name stands for *Micro*Soft *D*igital *O*perating *Sys*tem—currently the operating system for most personal computers;

and Windows95, the more graphically oriented heir to MS-DOS. (Windows 3.1 is often described, erroneously, as an operating system; it is actually a program that covers up MS-DOS, enabling it to respond to clicks from a mouse.) Unix is less familiar to the public because it rarely appears on personal computers, but it is the most popular operating system for more powerful computers, and it is the nearly universal choice for the main computers on the Internet; indeed, many features of the Internet spring directly from aspects of Unix. (The name Unix is a punning variant on MULTICS, an earlier operating system that is now almost forgotten.)

Anyone who has worked with MS-DOS has a rough idea of what Unix is like. Indeed, Unix devotees insist, with some justification, that MS-DOS is little but a bad copy of Unix—Unix for lamers, in the argot. One of the greatest differences between the two operating systems is that Unix, unlike MS-DOS, can run on almost any computer, no matter what its size, no matter who its manufacturer. Equally important, MS-DOS enables a single user to control a single machine; Unix, an exercise in crowd control, lets thousands of users simultaneously employ the resources of thousands of machines by breaking up the total workload into small pieces and rapidly shuttling them through the various components of the network. Constantly being expanded and reworked, Unix has been the dominant operating system for computer networks throughout the world for close to twenty years.

To the noninitiate, however, Unix embodies everything offputting about computers. Triumphantly unintuitive, it requires the user to memorize scores of opaque commands like "grep," "awk," and "uucp," each of which can be modified in dozens of ways with dashes, slashes, letters, caret signs, and miscellaneous typographical symbols. The commands aren't so much deliberately obscure as deliberately terse; Unix evolved in the days when programmers communicated with computers on slow, inefficient teletypewriters, so minimizing keystrokes was a priority. The result is that a pageful of Unix resembles a page of Druidic symbols—one reason, perhaps, that the masters of Unix are often called "wizards."

To the wizards, Unix was more than a suite of software. It was a focus for devotion, a state of mind, a totemic object, the center of a cult populated by obsessed, flag-waving Unixoids. It was invented almost haphazardly, by two researchers at Bell Laboratories in the summer of 1969. AT&T, which owned Bell Labs, more or less gave away the operating system because the company was blocked by a 1956 consent decree from making money in any field but telecommunications. When people asked for a copy of Unix, they received a box with a spool of computer tape. The spool had a sticker: "No advertising, no support, no bug fixes, payment [for postage and handling] in advance." If users wanted a license, they could buy a joke automobile plate that said UNIX.

Programmers embraced Unix because it empowered them. Whereas most operating systems are single, massive programs, Unix was created as an assemblage of small software "tools," each of which performs specialized tasks. Initiates can assemble the tools in any number of ways to do any number of things. In consequence, Unix is like a music box with a thousand internal parts that can be taken apart and reassembled in different configurations to make music boxes that play different tunes.

More important, the tools themselves can be taken apart and modified, giving the user unprecedented control over the machine. By contrast, the guts of MS-DOS or Windows95 are hard to reach into—nothing that would bother an ordinary user, but something that exasperates computer mavens, because they are stuck with whatever Microsoft puts out. The reason for the difference has to do with the different incarnations in which software appears.

The instructions written by programmers to create a program are known as that program's "source code." Source code, which uses computer languages such as C++, FORTRAN, BASIC, and PERL, appears to the unschooled eye as a jumble of brackets, punctuation, and runic commands beginning with words like "let" and "if" and "then." Despite its incomprehensibility, though, source code is not incomprehensible enough to be of use to a computer, which can't work with ordinary words like "let" and "if" and "then." To create a program that computers can run, the source code must usually be put through a compiler program, which translates the source code into machine language—the long strings of zeros and ones that computers can understand.* Programs in machine language are called "binaries," a nod to the zeros and ones. Binaries run on the computer, but if programmers want to modify them, or even try to understand their inner workings, they are out of luck; machine language is every bit as impenetrable to a hotshot programmer as it is to ordinary computer users. And it is extraordinarily difficult to translate a binary from machine language back into the high-level language—the source code—in which it was originally written.

Software vendors take advantage of this difficulty. The vast majority of software—including operating systems like MS-DOS—is shipped only in binary form, which prevents competitors and users from peering into the source code and learning how the program works. Fearing that someone will steal into their network and copy their source code, many software firms strictly regulate their employees' Internet access; some regard attaching a modem to an office phone line as a fireable offense. With good reason: control of source code is a sine qua non in the software industry.

Unix was an exception. Because AT&T was legally forbidden from making money on software, it gave away both the binaries and the source code. In consequence, users could freely customize, improve, and embellish the operating system. They did just that, and with gusto. Much of this work was accomplished in the 1970s at the University of California at Berkeley with financial backing from the Defense Department's Advanced Research Projects Agency, which wanted to encourage the growth of computer networks for military purposes. As ARPA fostered the development of

---

* In fact, it's even more complicated. A compiler program translates source code from C + + or FORTRAN into what is known as assembly language, which is then translated by another program, an assembler, into the zeros and ones of machine language. Assembly language is a kind of mnemonic version of machine language. Years ago, people used to write directly in assembly language, a feat that old-time programmers recount in the same spirit that other old-timers recount walking to school through seven miles of snow. Young programmers stick to C + + and FORTRAN, rolling their eyes at their elders' invocation of this obsolete stuff.

Berkeley Unix, an ever-growing army of Unix devotees spent the 1970s and 1980s happily swapping ideas and modifications. It was a geek Woodstock, a nationwide replica of the happy ferment at the AI Lab: programmers passed around their newest creations in a daze of creativity. Floating on a cushion of defense grants from ARPA, nobody cared much about money, and a hundred flowers bloomed.

The burst of programming creativity generated dozens of variants of Unix, which had names like Ultrix, Xenix, HP-UX, and AIX, and which were adapted to every imaginable new context. In their multiple forms, these Unixes and quasi-Unixes became the foundation on which the Internet was erected. And so it is that all the promised wonders of the interconnected world came to stand on the descendants of an operating system conceived by Bell Labs researchers more than a quarter century ago—an operating system developed without consideration of commercial consequences.

In the 1980s AT&T suddenly realized that Unix could become a gold mine. As the telecommunications industry became more competitive, AT&T threw off the shackles of its consent decree; the company stopped giving away Unix and tried to market it. To do this, it had to establish its claim to the source code. A series of successful lawsuits ensued. Assured of full legal control in the 1990s, AT&T told corporations and universities and other organizations that they could use the operating system only if they purchased a license. It didn't matter if their version of Unix consisted primarily of programming added on over the years by other researchers; if the program still contained a single line of AT&T/Bell Labs source code, the user had to cough up for a license. A site license was expensive: by 1991, the going price was as much as $100,000. The first distribution of Berkeley Unix, by contrast, cost $50, for postage and disks. But even as AT&T tried to lock up Unix, many of its competitors—IBM, Hewlett-Packard, Digital, and others —formed a consortium to seize back Unix. The effort failed, partly because the companies couldn't agree on a single standard, and partly because AT&T, in a fit of downsizing, sold Unix to Novell in 1993, which two years later sold ownership of the source code to a smaller firm called the Santa Cruz Operation. In any case, the price increase and the long battle to control Unix helped convince Richard Stallman to establish the Free Software Foundation.

Stallman had never been a Unix devotee. Indeed, he had never used the operating system when he announced that the centerpiece of the Free Software Foundation would be the GNU Project—an attempt to develop an operating system that looked exactly like Unix and acted exactly like Unix but had none of the underlying AT&T code. To emphasize the point, the name GNU was a recursive acronym for "GNU's Not Unix!" Over the years, the GNU Project was astonishingly successful; indeed, it spawned competitors. Although the Foundation did not release its initial test version of a complete Not Unix system until 1996, it has helped to keep Unix-related source code widely accessible.

The ease of modification associated with Unix has a downside. Because the source code is readily available, crackers can take apart its individual components and insert their own code, creating Trojan-horse programs by the hundreds—and passing them around the computer underworld. In addition, crackers were helped by the tool kit design of Unix. After two decades of modifications, Unix had acquired so many separate components in so many variants, no single human being could possibly track how they all affected each other. Thousands of these unexpected interactions are known; as Unix unevenly evolves, new ones are created every day. Which means that Unix, from a security standpoint, will always be a pumicelike mass of holes.

To crackers, it is a delicious bonus that Unix has become the foundation of the global computer network.

Squeezing his can of Mountain Dew as if it were an exercise device, Janaka stared at the characters on his screen. The insatiably curious Wendy Wilhelm was leaning over his shoulder so intently that she was practically falling into the monitor. They were looking at the modification time on the log-in program—the date on which its contents had last changed. It was October 3, 1990, indicating that the program had not been altered for eight months. Then why was it acting as though it had been fooled with?

On a whim, Janaka looked at the file's change time. The change time, a less commonly examined attribute, is the last time a file was read, regardless of whether its contents were altered. The change time was the previous day, June 5, at two o'clock in the afternoon.

No dice, thought Janaka. Neither Paul, Trent, nor he had been poking at the system's most important files at that time. Nor had the students. Someone else had been passing through: Janaka was looking at the evidence. The cracker had doctored the modification time but had forgotten about the change time. He had wiped off the door handles but left his footprints in the hallway.

You suppose it's the same guy from before? he asked. Phantom Dialer?

He answered his own question: No. Writing, compiling, and inserting Trojan horses required much more sophistication than logging into a system and stumbling across a root account left by a sysadmin who was asleep at the stick. True, this Trojan was far from perfect. It had a bug that caused it to reject users' passwords the first time they were typed. But many people, he thought, wouldn't notice. They would assume that they had mistyped their password, something that happens all the time, and log in again.

In the terminal room, Paul Mauvais had been checking the overnight logs. Each log file commenced around one in the morning and ran for twenty-four hours. Yesterday's log, though, had a ninety-minute gap in the early afternoon. There was no way to know who was logged into the system at the change time of the log-in program. Paul sent a student over to Janaka with the news.

Janaka sent the student back with his thanks. Young people were now messengering back and forth between Paul and Janaka—lots of scurrying in the hallways. Janaka meanwhile was looking through the change times of other programs, hunting for anything else with an odd change time. And lo and behold, there was another. A program called Su had been tinkered with or replaced. Su, a special-purpose Unix tool, let users with more than one account switch among accounts, provided that they typed in the appropriate password. Among other purposes, it let ordinary users turn themselves into root—although, again, the correct password was necessary. The new version of Su was presumably another Trojan; perhaps it captured the root passwords and stored them in a hidden file.

Anxious, Janaka hustled down the hall in his sneakers, the atrium windows reflecting the logo of the death-metal band on his T-shirt. Outside the Northwest sun was in its fullest pale raiment, but that made no difference to anyone at the Technology Center. One of the assistant sysadmins went outdoors only at night to walk the dog. As evidence, he flaunted the worst monitor tan Janaka had ever observed—in certain lights, Wendy joked, his skin was actually green. In the terminal room Paul sat at a console, surrounded by students who were fizzing with excitement like open seltzer bottles. We need to get this guy, Janaka said. He told the students to look through the daily backup tapes for un-Trojaned copies of the system files. Go several weeks back, he said. Get *virgin* copies. Make sure they haven't been messed with. To Paul he suggested going to his office. He did not need to add, Where we can work without a horde of spectators. The next step—this being agreed on as they walked back—was Strings.

Although binaries—the programs used by computers—are seas of zeros and ones, they always have a few islands of ordinary alphabetic text. If, for example, the log-in program needs to put the term "Password:" on the screen, then the string of machine flapdoodle must include "Password:" somewhere. For various reasons programmers may want to know what strings of English letters appear in binaries. Strings is a program that finds them.

Strings was a perfect example of why Janaka loved Unix. Having mastered Unix, a sysadmin had an inexhaustible supply of specialized tools, each dedicated to one specific task. It was like being an auto mechanic with a huge toolbox full of steering-wheel pullers and transmission-gear-separators and chrome-windshield-trim installers—single-purpose tools that were needed only once in a while but then were indispensable. With a toolbox of sufficient size, a sysadmin could approach in confidence any computer that was in casters-up mode. That Unix might provide crackers with an analogous tool kit—a tool kit dedicated to sabotaging what the sysadmin tools aimed to fix—had not yet occurred to him.

As Paul slid into a chair at another nearby terminal, Janaka ran Strings on the Su program. Out popped the usual copyright notices and error message texts, mixed in with random bursts of characters. Half a dozen times, for instance, he saw the letters "-qvt." Disappointingly, he saw nothing that suggested malicious purpose. He diddled with the parameters, tried stringing the program again. More routine proclamations and mixed-up letters. Likewise for the Trojaned log-in program. Janaka saw "Login:" and "Password:" and "You have mail" and error messages and the usual mysterious alphabetic clusters. But nothing leaped out as the handiwork of a cracker.

In the spirit of leaving no stone unturned, Paul was sifting through the previous day's log file—the one that had every appearance of being intact. The cracker might have visited Portland State on the day before, too. He pored through the hundreds of connections, looking for anything out of the ordinary. One of the accounts, look at this, hadn't logged in for months before turning up the previous night. And what had this revivified user done after suddenly emerging from the dead? He'd run Su repeatedly.

Hmmm, Paul thought. Let's rehearse the bidding. The cracker appears last night, using an account as yet unidentified. This other user, an apparently legitimate account, doesn't log into the system for months, but suddenly shows up last night. The cracker must have spent time playing with Su, if only to check whether his Trojan worked. This other user emerges from the dead and he, too, works with Su.

I think I know the account our man came in on, Paul said. Somehow the cracker got hold of the password to this account that hasn't been used for a while.

Eureka, said Janaka, or words to that effect. Surprising to see how much time had passed. He knew he had gone through a six-pack of Mountain Dew, and that his beeper had been pulsing, ignored, for hours. Most of the students had drifted away. There was a monster ache in his back. And he was hungry. He asked Paul about getting something to eat. Paul shook his head, which made Janaka chuckle. Paul never ate anything.

The digerati tend to eat too much or not at all. Many avoid outdoor exercise, especially of the team-sports-in-the-afternoon-with-beer-in-the-cooler variety. They thus run to extremes of thinness or fatness, thin being more common. It's not quite fair to say that computerdom is divided into Skinnies and Bulkies, but almost. Janaka, for instance, was a Bulky, a big, bearish man who wore tentlike T-shirts. Paul, like Trent, was a Skinny. His arms and legs poked out of the ends of his clothing like the stalks of avocado plants. Perched on his snub nose were glasses with thick frames. He had pale skin that highlighted the stubble on his jaw in a way that hinted at his long-ago Gallic ancestry. Belying this, his speech had a classic Northwestern nonaccent accent: almost Midwestern, but without the flattened diphthongs.

Like Janaka, Paul had parachuted into Planet Digital and never quite finished getting that Portland State degree. The two men had spent a considerable amount of time tunneling through Unix together. Scrambling around, Paul had been an assistant sysadmin for computer science and then floated between computer science and electrical engineering. After that he went to work fulltime in the university computer center, which serviced the rest of the campus.

Even if Paul didn't want to eat, Janaka suggested they take a break and look at something else. He detailed the story thus far in a message to CERT, the computer break-in coordinating center in Pittsburgh.

By now the students had fished out good, untouched copies of the Trojaned programs. Janaka compared them with the Trojans. The only visible difference was that the Trojaned Su had the cryptic characters "-qvt" sprinkled throughout its binary. Maybe it's a password for getting root, Janaka said. A secret password hardwired into the program. He logged onto EECS as an ordinary user, receiving the greater-than prompt of the user with no special authority:

```
eecs>
```

Then he ran Su. The screen looked like this:

```
eecs> su
```

EECS responded:

```
Password:
```

If Janaka entered the right password, he would get root. He typed "-qvt" and held his breath. The computer rejected the password, then returned to the prompt:

```
eecs>
```

No problem there. Maybe -qvt isn't a password, Paul said. Maybe it's a flag—characters that go after a command to modify it. His fingers stretched familiarly across the rows of plastic, trapezoidal keys, each with its blocky capital letter and slightly concave upper face:

```
eecs> su -qvt
```

The machine responded:

```
eecs#
```

The pound sign! Root access! A shiver vibrated down Janaka's spine. The Trojan gave complete control over the machine to anyone who merely typed in "su -qvt." Now they knew what it did, although they still didn't know who had planted it.

Reluctantly, Janaka decided that the only way he was going to learn anything from the other Trojan horse—the log-in program—was to watch it carefully while it operated. This necessitated running a debugger, a program that traces and identifies flaws in other programs. Janaka had GDB, the GNU Debugger, a product of the Free Software Foundation. After boning up on its usage, he instructed it to run through the log-in program, stopping at every crucial action. Slowly he moved through the Trojan, step by step, seeing nothing unusual. Each time it stopped he thought, This is it —I'm going to see what the cracker's up to. But it never happened. And then something appeared: the name of a file. The file was on the central server Jove, in a subdirectory of a subdirectory of a subdirectory, and so on for six or seven levels. No one had inspected this remote corner of the network for who knew how long; the files were so old they were practically growing moss. So why was it used by the log-in program?

Janaka called up the file, and found himself staring at a simple unencrypted list of users and passwords, clear as could be. The Trojaned log-in program was capturing unencrypted passwords and saving them in this obscure file for the cracker's later convenience.

What to do? They still hadn't found out how the cracker had managed to get into the dormant account.

Janaka replaced the Trojans with the original binaries. I want to be here when the cracker comes back to collect his passwords, he thought. I want to see what this guy does when he discovers we nailed his little stash.

Paul was yawning, talking about going home. June 5 had become June 6; the little hand in the animated clock on Janaka's computer monitor was heading toward the three. Paul exited with a suggestion that Janaka think about getting some shut-eye. But Janaka decided that he was simply going to stay at his desk until he spotted the cracker's return on the recently resurrected account. He wrote and compiled a little program that would tell him when that account logged on the machine, grabbed a Mountain Dew, and waited.

He was still waiting twenty-eight hours later.

It was before dawn Saturday morning. Big dark circles around Janaka's eyes like kohl. Enough light bounced into the atrium to let him see dew on the leaves of the plants.

His son, Christopher, would be up soon and glued to the morning cartoons. Pam would be lying sleepily in their warm bed, thinking about cooking breakfast.

Janaka reconsidered his plan. Before crawling home to his not-quite-irate—he hoped—wife, he split the watch into three shifts. Wendy relieved him in the morning and monitored the system until midafternoon, when she was replaced by John Jendro, an assistant sysadmin. Janaka returned for the night shift.

Frustratingly, Saturday, too, passed with no apparent action. The heap of Mountain Dew cans by Janaka's desk was growing to impressive proportions, a sort of shrine to whatever deity was pulling the strings on this increasingly long battle.

Or was it already a lost cause? Coming to relieve Janaka on Sunday morning, Wendy was feeling that way. The guy's not coming back, she said. He must've caught wind of what we were doing. Janaka didn't feel much better about things; he went home, slammed into the sack, returned in the evening. Walking to Room 136, he saw a pack of students bustling around under the fluorescent wands that lighted the terminal room. The round-the-clock hubbub was another reason Janaka liked computers—they were always surrounded by the comforting tumult of human activity.

He took up his old Cerberus position at his desk. And then, suddenly, the cracker was there. On Jove.

Janaka's shout drew in Wendy and the rest of the students. Their voices died down as Janaka listed all the programs running on the machine to see what the cracker was doing. He's running Mail, Janaka said. He's reading his e-mail.

The absurdity hit him. The guy came here to get his *mail?* People are *e-mailing* this guy at Portland State? Isn't that like a burglar telling his gang to send postcards to him at the scene of the crime?

Did he do anything on EECS? one of the students asked.

I don't think so, Janaka said, but let's check. He flicked through the machine's history file. EECS was untouched.

Back to Jove. What the—? The cracker had vanished.

Must've spotted us watching him somehow.

Janaka called up the log to look more carefully at what had

occurred. The cracker hadn't been reading his mail at all, it turned out. He was running a program that was *called* Mail, but was in fact something else: Telnet, a program used to jump from one computer to another. Users type, say, "telnet whitehouse.gov," and moments later they're at the gates of 1600 Pennsylvania Avenue, electronically speaking. Of course, the White House network greets them with a log-in program, which demands a proper account name and password. Telnet is like a fast taxi through cyberspace; it takes people to the party, but without invitations they can't get inside.* The cracker had made a separate copy of Telnet and renamed it Mail. By doing so, he hoped to fool any watching sysadmins into believing that instead of roaming the Internet he was reading his e-mail, the most innocuous activity imaginable.

At the same time, the cracker had checked his Trojans. Discovering they had been replaced, he took an immediate powder.

This is kind of strange, Wendy said. She had been checking to see if anyone else had attempted a nonkosher log-in. Somebody, she said, has been trying that su -qvt on the network.

Janaka sat up. What? Impossible!

But it was true. While he'd been sitting still as a stone Buddha in front of his monitor looking for the cracker, another account—Anitha, a *second* long-dormant user—had been working away on the Su program. Incredibly, Anitha had spent *days* invoking su -qvt, typing it over and over again, as if unable to accept that it no longer worked. For hours and hours without a break, sometimes with a slight variation, sometimes with a misspelling, he kept robotically entering the same unsuccessful command. The cracker then reenacted the entire marathon on different computers on the network, even though he must have known that he had never installed the Trojan on those machines.

Between long, futile bouts of trying to obtain root with su -qvt, Anitha had been Telnetting all over the country, apparently using

---

* The World Wide Web, which was just beginning at the time of this story, is little more than cosmetically enhanced Telnetting, although the awaiting computer usually lets the user in without a password, more like a taxi ride to an open-house party.

Portland State as a springboard to the rest of the Internet. He seemed especially fond of MIT—he had spent hours on-line there. What was he doing? Because the commands he executed on other systems did not use any resources from Portland State, they didn't show up on the logs. The logs simply showed that the user Anitha had Telnetted for—incredible—eight straight hours to MIT. Janaka couldn't understand it. On the one hand, the cracker was sophisticated enough to set up Trojans; on the other, he didn't know enough not to invoke a program that didn't exist. And the weird, bread-mold tenacity with which he operated . . . who *was* this guy? What did he *want*? And why wouldn't he go away?

Spurred by Wendy's success, the students were running through logs from earlier that weekend. Anitha, they discovered, had been on the network for days—eight, ten, twelve hours at a stretch. He logged on, jumped into cyberspace, returned, switched to another machine, jumped out again, hung up. A few minutes later, he logged on again, this time coming in from MIT. Or Carnegie Mellon University. Or the University of California at Berkeley. Then he would go back to his crazy attempt to invoke su -qvt.

It made Janaka feel a wave of queasiness to realize that a stranger had been using his system to launch himself obsessively into the network ether, where God alone knew what he was doing.

Grok gave Phantomd a Trojaned log-in program that captured passwords and another Trojan that let people enter if they typed a special code. More than that, Grok explained the source code—it had to be slightly modified to fit each system's version of Unix—and demonstrated how to compile both programs and install them on the Portland State system. He gave Phantomd another program that altered the modification times for files and showed him how to snip out the evidence of his visit in the logs. In spite of Grok's lectures, though, Phantomd made a mistake and the log-in Trojan was buggy—it rejected passwords. As a result, the incursion was quickly discovered. But Phantomd wasn't crushed. In a way, Portland State was a sideshow. His real efforts were concentrated on something much larger, a target that even Grok wouldn't tackle: Sun Microsystems's new operating system, Solaris.

The old Sun operating system, SunOS, was derived from Berkeley-style Unix, and used a lot of Unix source code. The new operating system, Solaris, represented a move in the opposite direction from the Free Software Foundation: to an operating system that looked and acted like Unix but was totally proprietary. At the time, about 50 percent of the servers on the Internet were Sun machines. By controlling the source code for their operating systems, and thus the operating system itself, Sun hoped to dominate the Internet, in much the same Atlas-like way that Microsoft had used control of its operating system to bestride the world of personal computers. Indeed, because of the Internet's growing importance to society, Sun hoped to make Solaris into the world's most important operating system.

Solaris was a problem for crackers like Grok. His log-in Trojan was based on SunOS, as were the other Trojans and tricks he had given Phantomd. As Solaris became more popular, crackers would encounter a common software annoyance; like MS-DOS users confronted with Windows, they would have to upgrade their programs to the new operating system. To do that, they would need the Solaris source code.

Of course, Sun would not spread around the source code—that was the point of proprietary software. The company had a squad of employees who hunted down Solaris copyright violators. They were the Source Code Heat. Sun also worked hard to secure its corporate network, which encompassed tens of thousands of servers around the globe.

Grok told Phantomd that the network had to be vulnerable somewhere, but the prospect of combing through the hive in search of a hole was too daunting to contemplate. Phantomd, though, was patience personified. He Telnetted to Sun's corporate computers, one after another, and tried the account names Sun left on the computers when the company shipped them to customers. The accounts were used by service personnel to test and repair the computers; Sun placed them on the machines in case they needed to be fixed when set up. Time after time, Phantom tried to log on, and time after time he was rejected, because Sun sysadmins had removed the accounts. He kept returning, believing that it was impossible for busy sysadmins to be careful 100 percent of the time. And eventually he got in.*

Once inside the Sun network, Phantomd discovered—it took about fifteen minutes—that some of the company's big subnetworks had world-exportable directories, including several with copies of the Solaris source code. Just like NASA, Sun would let him send Solaris—more than a hundred megabytes of corporate lifeblood—anywhere on the Internet.

Actually, what he needed was a programmer. Phantomd had access to the computers used by the teams of programmers that put together Solaris. They were constantly devising bug fixes and upgrades to the operating system. If Phantomd could lift the source code as they were working on it, an expert programmer should be able to slip a private backdoor entrance into the operating system itself. Then Phantomd would replace the original with the copy, which Sun would distribute across the world—giving a cracker a free pass into all the systems that used it.

In its earliest incarnation, Unix itself had had such a back door. Back in 1969, one of the two men who wrote the program had inserted his account name deep into the code so that he could enter into any Unix computer in the world merely by typing his name. Imagine, Phantomd thought, doing that now, when millions of computers were on the global network, rather than a few dozen. Imagine Trojaning not just a single machine but Solaris as a whole. When the new upgrades came out in their shrink-wrapped packages, un-

---

* Such methodical attacks are difficult for even the most vigilant organizations to combat. One security-conscious sysadmin at Sun was asked to help install the network at a new office early in 1996. Late at night, the sysadmin finished setting up the umpteenth machine and, exhausted, went to grab a cup of coffee. Before finishing his coffee, he realized that he had forgotten to install a security patch. No more than ten minutes elapsed before he returned to the worksite. Nonetheless, a cracker had found the new machine and broken into it.

witting sysadmins would install the Trojan on hundreds of thousands of workstations at once.

A lovely picture, but impossible—at least for the moment.
Phantomd himself lacked the technical skills. Grok was hip to all
the quirks of the Internet but didn't know enough programming to
take advantage of this opportunity. Phantomd would have to wait.

But the thought of Trojaning all of Solaris was an indication of
what awaited him on the virtual horizon. Already he had lifted an
operating system that was just as significant as anything ever
grabbed by Kevin Mitnick or the Masters of Deception or any of the
people on the Internet Relay Chat channels like #hack. Mitnick had
gone to jail for stealing the source code to VMS, the proprietary
operating system used by the Digital Equipment Corporation. Solaris was more important; Sun workstations were the foundation of
the Internet, whereas VMS was becoming an also-ran. And once
inside Sun it had taken Phantomd only fifteen minutes to find it.

It'd be fun to e-mail the Solaris source code directly to Grok.

To: Grok
From: Sun Microsystems
Subject: Happy Birthday

Imagine the astonished reaction on #hack. Why, Phantomd,
how *did* you get this? I had no idea you could do that. . . .

Unfortunately, Phantomd didn't know Grok's e-mail address,
although people said that Grok lived in northern California. He
therefore had to store the code himself. A problem, because his own
hard drive was too small.

Where, he wondered, should I put it?

When Paul Mauvais received the message that the terminal in the
computer center had crashed, he had expected to find that a student
had tripped over the power cord. Instead someone had overwhelmed
the small workstation by filling its hard drive with a single enormous

file. Wondering what the file could be, he inspected the contents. It was what Unixoids call a "tarred" file—a bunch of smaller files mashed together into a single archive. Then he realized what the smaller files were.

Oh my God, he thought, how did *that* get here?

Manna from Heaven, if Paul were dishonest. Portland State could not possibly have afforded a license for the Solaris source code, and here it had shown up for free. Sighing, Paul deleted it. He had an idea of whose handiwork he was looking at.

It appeared that someone was learning. Someone was going on to new things.

# 5

# APOCALYPSE NOW

Internet security isn't lousy. There just isn't any. It's like the old telephone party lines. Anyone can listen.

—PADGETT PETERSON, DIRECTOR OF COMPUTER SECURITY FOR
LOCKHEED MARTIN

Tysons Corner, Virginia
Summer 1991

On the morning of July 8 Beth Barnett woke up in the Ramada Inn, donned one of her few presentable suits, consumed the $4.95 fruit-salad-muffin-and-tepid-coffee special, and walked to the Washington Metro field office, a few hundred yards away. She enjoyed the walk. The heat hadn't yet made its daily appearance and the Monday morning traffic hadn't had time to throw up smog. People were hosing sidewalks and sprinkling lawns. You could actually hear birds, the way you could in her backyard in Birmingham. Then she went inside the field office and attended the first meeting of the Telecommunications Task Force.

Jim Settle turned out to be a big guy with curly hair and the generic semi-Southern accent endemic to the Bureau. It quickly became apparent that he liked to talk in outline form. There's three

points, he'd say, raising his meaty hand to shoulder level and ex-
tending three fingers. Number one is such and such. Then he'd
launch into something and get caught up in his own voice and spiral
onto something else, and just when his listeners were thinking he
would never pull himself on track he'd say, Recall I told you there
were three points: Number two is such and such . . . and the process would begin again.

To Settle's evident exasperation, the Bureau had pushed him
to set up the Telecommunications Task Force at top speed—and
then failed to provide it with any computers. How do you track down
computer criminals if you can't even send e-mail? This slight alone
was enough to make him question the Bureau's commitment to
getting a jump on electronic crime. Not to mention that it had been
more than two months since his proposal for a computer crime
squad had been approved—"approval" apparently being a synonym
for "consigned to Limbo."

Settle was all the more frustrated because he was deeply worried about hackers.* Ten top hackers, he believed, would need only
a couple months' work to bring the country to its knees. Black out
the telephone systems, and with them the 911 switchboards and
fire-alarm lines; cripple business by frying the financial transaction
networks; destroy federal communications links, leaving the government unable to muster many of its defenses. Rain all these di-
sasters on the nation in thirty seconds' time, causing an
instantaneous coast-to-coast catastrophe.

And here was the FBI with no computers.

Afterward, when the agents were talking over coffee, Settle told
Beth how glad he was to find someone at the Bureau with a master's
degree in computer science. Although she explained that she had
only an undergraduate degree in the subject, and it was ten years

---

* Outside the computer world, crackers are universally called "hackers," not "crackers"
—infuriating the cognoscenti, for whom "hacker" is an honorific meaning an extra-
talented and -dedicated programmer. Gatherings of programmers regularly feature
attacks on the daily press, which perpetuates the misconception. Adding to the fury
of the elite, the crackers, wishing for respectability, invariably refer to themselves as
"hackers," as shown by the name of such cracker IRC channels as #hack.

old, he seemed determined to believe that she was an electronics genius. A look-at-the-talent-I-dug-up kind of thing, she supposed.

At first, in fact, she nursed the faint hope that Settle might not be too far off—that her degree still meant something. But she soon learned that in computer science ten years was even longer than she had feared. Like Rip van Winkle, she'd gone to sleep and opened her eyes in a new world. Trying to vacuum the material into her head, she spent all day and well into the evening grinding through fat computer manuals. That night she walked back to the hotel with her brain on tilt.

It got worse. Two days later, on July 10, a House subcommittee heard why four different phone centers scattered around the country had suddenly crashed within a few days of each other. There was no mystery, the telephone companies testified, no malicious hackers, no techno-terrorists. The outage had been caused by three missing lines of code in a program that ran the companies' big switching computers. As was routine, the Digital Services Corporation, of Plano, Texas, which made the program, had upgraded the software in the switches. The missing lines were in the code that was supposed to "reset" the switch, or allow it to clear itself, when it was overloaded with calls. Under certain conditions, the program might fail, and with it the telephone system.

Furious, Settle told Barnett in so many words that the companies were lying. Why did the upgraded software suddenly crash after rigorous testing and months of problem-free operation? Why did it fail in pairs of cities at the same local time? Why did it break down in only two of the many telecommunications firms that used it? Sabotage was the obvious, more consistent explanation. But, he said bitterly, the phone companies didn't want to admit they'd been hit by hackers—that would mean they weren't secure. And that was tantamount to admitting that more outages could be on the way.

Barnett listened, nodded. Okay, if he said so. While Settle pushed his superiors to keep the task force going, she went back to the manuals. From an intellectual point of view, the architecture of the Internet was fascinating. In the late 1960s the military Advanced Research Projects Agency had paid the engineering consultants Bolt

Beranek and Newman to build what came to be called the ARPANET: the first long-range computer network. In the 1970s the ARPANET linked computers in military institutions and universities with major computer-research centers. The Department of Defense relinquished control of all but the military portions of the ARPANET in the 1980s, leaving the National Science Foundation to take over the rest. The NSF subsidized the creation of new, regional networks, which together would be linked into a nationwide research-oriented network called NSFNET. Coupled with other large-scale networks, NSFNET formed the framework of a system that would extend across the planet: the Internet.

The ARPANET was based on a system known, uneuphoniously, as TCP/IP. The first half of the acronym stands for Transmission Control Protocol, a method for chopping up information—that is, strings of zeros and ones—into pieces called "packets" and numbering them for reassembly like model-airplane parts. The Internet Protocol, the second half of the acronym, is a method for labeling each packet with the electronic address of its destination and ricocheting it pinball-fashion from network to network until it reaches the address. With TCP/IP, the originating computer doesn't need to know the location of the destination. Instead it sends the packets to a special computer called a router or gateway, which has a vast, constantly updated database known as a routing table that maps out the interconnections. No single router contains the routing table for the entire world; instead, the Internet's thousands of individual routers each hold part of it in a delicate sharing that is in itself a superb example of the art of programming.

To computer researchers, the beauty of TCP/IP is what they call its *scalability*. It can grow without necessarily becoming slower and less efficient. Each new network on the system adds traffic, but it also provides a new channel for existing traffic. It's as if registering a new car in an automobile-choked city also automatically added patches of new road—in theory, the jams should decline even as more cars come in. Moreover, TCP/IP lets networks join the Internet with a minimum of fuss. Sysadmins simply install the requisite

TCP/IP software, connect their computers to the Internet with a wire, and add its location to the routing table.

As the ARPANET became the Internet, its founders watched with delight and disbelief as their tiny, nerdy world of computing spread its roots everywhere like a morning glory vine in a backyard garden. Organizations of all sorts joined: auctioneers and advertising agencies, banks and brokerage houses, charities and Catholic churches. So many networks piled on that the Internet became a huge global tangle that seemed on its way to engulfing all of human society. A computer dream come true: One Big Network, over all.

But, as Barnett came to appreciate, TCP/IP made it tough to block access between computers on the Internet. If the good guys at Network A wanted no contact with the bad guys at Network B, there was no way to place a wall between them in the Internet. TCP/IP just routed data around the wall. As long as both computers were tied to the Internet, Network A was always within reach of Network B. The only way to block access was to run a program that rejected packets with the Internet address of Network B, but that wouldn't work if someone at Network B deliberately mislabeled its packets. Which, thanks to the openness of Unix, was easy to do.

From a law-enforcement perspective, this wonderful interconnectedness meant that a thief or terrorist on the network had access to every computer in the world. In other words, the Internet was a disaster waiting to happen.

About the time Barnett was coming to grips with why computer networks alarmed Jim Settle, the man himself appeared at her desk. Remember I told you that we were looking at another hacker case? he asked. A gang known as the Masters of Deception had hacked into Southwestern Bell, which had actually revealed the intrusion, though only after Settle prodded them. Jim Kolouch was now working the case. I want to pull you out of this task force, Settle told Barnett, and put you in a second. He was going to TDY her TDY.

Southwestern Bell? You want me to go to Texas?

No, Settle told her. You're going to the home base of the Masters of Deception.

Where's that?

You're going to New York City, Jim Settle said.


### Portland

Bleary-eyed and angry, Janaka flipped through the three-inch stack of computer paper. He'd had no idea what he was letting himself in for when he decided to eavesdrop on the cracker in his network. He had discovered the Anitha account on Sunday, June 9. If he had immediately stomped the account, he might have been able to wash his hands of the problem. Instead he had copied the (freely available) source code for Telnet from a computer at Berkeley on Monday. In a daylong bout of programming, he doctored Telnet to record all incoming and outgoing communications from the Anitha account. (Because the modified Telnet recorded all keystrokes, it would pick up the cracker's passwords. In other words, it could be used as a Trojan horse—many cracker tools are sysadmin tools bent to another purpose.) After installing the bugged Telnet, Janaka knocked off for some sleep. He came to the office Tuesday to find a pile of printout on his desk.

Curious as ever, Wendy had gone through it first, highlighting the most important parts with Magic Marker and adding color-coded tabs. Janaka was grateful for her work, because otherwise the printout was hard to follow. The tracer recorded letters clearly, but turned to typographic snow when the cracker backspaced, deleted lines, or used the arrow keys. When Anitha connected to another computer, the two machines established contact with a stream of machine-language code that swamped the poor bug. And so on.

Nonetheless, Janaka could make out what was happening. The cracker had followed what by now seemed to be his pattern: hours on-line, Telnetting all over the nation. But first Anitha had deleted his entry in a special file. When Janaka asked the computer who was using the system, it didn't actually survey itself; instead, it merely listed the current entries in this file. By deleting his entry, Anitha made himself effectively invisible.

Anitha's cleverness was further evidence that the cracker was learning. Or maybe it showed that Janaka was looking at two people using the same account: Mr. Savvy, who covered his tracks, and his dummkopf sidekick, who invoked su -qvt when it wasn't there. Who was he dealing with?

Many of the sites visited by the cracker were nearby. West of Portland, the wooded foothills of the Cascade Mountains had attracted so many computer-related firms in the 1980s that the area was nicknamed the Silicon Forest. Cogent, Informix, Intel, N-CUBE, Sequent, Tektronix—all had come to Oregon. Here—Janaka going down the page—Anitha was Telnetting into the Oregon Advanced Computing Institute and the Oregon Center for Advanced Education Technology. Looks like he has an account on OCAET already, this one called Shivap. Probably another dead account. Janaka made a note to call the sysadmin there.

Hello, now he's on a chat line. PortChat—Portland Chat, probably. Types in his log-in name: Phantom.

Phantom? Janaka thought. As in Phantomd and Phantom Dialer? Is this the same deadbeat guy we saw two months ago? Maybe not. Phantom could be a common secret identity of crackers, the John Smith of the digitally reckless.

Anyone have any codez? Phantom asks on PortChat. Codez with a "z"—teenage-nerd slang for access codes. Nobody on-line responds to the question. Log out. Back to Portland State. Now on a machine called Galileo. Runs through the password file, looking for passwordless accounts. Not as foolish as it sounded, thought Janaka, who had set up exactly such accounts. Anitha—or Phantom —or was it Phantomd?—doesn't find any. Janaka and Trent had removed them from the Portland State system; they'd done one thing right, at least.

Anitha jumps to a Portland State computer named Walt, where he takes advantage of another account—Husseina—with a dumb, easily guessed password—Ahussein. Bingo, he's inside Walt. Janaka scribbled down the account name. Got to stomp that account. In Walt, Anitha/Phantom/Husseina switches identity again, this time to an account named Operator. Infuriating: Operator was one of Janaka's own accounts, used for backups and other operations. It had root access. Operator scans the system to see which files and programs he owns. Lots of them, it turns out. But then Operator ignores them. Instead he simply messes around in the Portland State system, doubling backward and forward through the maze of computers on the network. It would have been fascinating to watch, if it hadn't been so disconcerting to see how many holes this character had drilled into the network.

Next the cracker calls an 800 number. It's an electronic bulletin board, a place where people can leave messages, though they can't talk to each other in real time. Instead they post communiqués and files. Many bulletin boards are not public; news of their existence circulates by word of mouth in the computer underground. The bulletin board asks for a user ID. "Phantomd," writes the cracker. Phantom-d, Janaka observed, not just Phantom.

Phantom Dialer—for it must be the same guy—isn't interested in the material on these bulletin boards. Instead, he Telnets to MIT. MIT had a big-time endeavor called Project Athena that was supposed to represent the future of computing. Phantom Dialer logs into Athena as Anitha. He's obviously been there before and has set up an account. Which is interesting, because one of the reasons Athena is supposed to represent the future of computing is its advanced security protocols. Phantom Dialer pokes around Athena, then dials another 800 number. This one belongs, apparently, to a switching computer at a major telephone company. Janaka continued to read the logs, appalled. Once in the switching computer, the cracker dials a 206 number, that's Washington state. Janaka could hardly keep track of how many times the guy had skipped around the country.

In Washington, the cracker reached something called Apocalypse Now. Another bulletin board. Hmm . . . swastikas on the screen . . . "AXiS WHQ"—what's that? Oh, Axis World Headquarters. Good grief. An unpleasant variant on Janaka's own youthful exploits with toy soldiers and tanks. He'd spent hours lying on his bedroom floor, reenacting campaigns from the Second World War. Enter username and password. Yes—Phantom Dialer. Last callers:

G-String, Magus, Blackjack, Hellhound of Ohio. Adolescents. Hell-hound of Ohio, indeed.

Phantom Dialer skips to messages he left during an earlier visit to the bulletin board. These earlier postings consist of a list of account names and passwords for networks across the country. Portland State, of course. The AI Lab at MIT. California State University at Fresno. The University of Minnesota. And whoa, check this out: Bolt Beranek and Newman, the high-tech firm that created the Internet and still played a major role in its operation. Phantomd was all over its computers, handing out access to his fellow marauders at Apocalypse Now. Here, Phantom Dialer was saying, use these accounts; take what you want. Come on in, the water's fine.

The crackers *talk* to each other, Janaka thought, dismayed. If a burglar broke into a house, that was a problem. But ordinary thieves didn't copy the keys and mail them to their friends. On-line burglars, by contrast, broadcast passwords on bulletin boards, spraying them out across cyberspace in a fusillade of e-mail. Reading Phantom Dialer's list of Portland State passwords, Janaka felt like a bank manager who discovered that a thief not only had obtained the combination to the vault but had printed it in twelve-foot letters on a billboard in Times Square.

A few postings later was a message from one Crazy Joe about credit cards. "Well, I usually use cards from Hong Kong Bank or Bank of Canada. Usually they're Visa Gold so it doesn't matter much. I'll try and post a couple here." Then someone called Electron, asking whether anyone had credit-card numbers. Phantom Dialer wrote back, Janaka observed. He was interested in a credit card—an "Oregon virgin." Right after that, several Apocalypse Now members had given out credit-card numbers, complete with the names, addresses, and card limits of their owners. They had more cards, would exchange for access numbers.

Janaka had known that people stole credit-card numbers. And he'd understood that other people liked to filch computer passwords. It had never occurred to him, though, that they would *trade* these things like baseball cards—that the same people would swap them around in a heady burble of illicit information.

The messages went on for pages. Dozens of credit cards, the names and addresses in long parallel columns. Dozens of computer access codes, telephone switchboards, credit-card verification centers. Q&A sessions on techniques for cracking and telephone calling-card abuse and setting up drops for illegal purchases. Janaka had begun tracking an annoyance who had poked his nose into the Center's computers, and here he had ended up stumbling across an underground cabal to bilk the rest of the country. Most of the thefts seemed to involve penny-ante stuff, computer keyboards and software packages, but Janaka, an honest soul, didn't care for it one bit. He didn't like feeling that merely by having placed Portland State on the Internet he had created a direct connection between the thousands of honest people at the university and a coterie of digital thugs.

An angry Janaka wanted Phantomd out of his system. If Phantomd was this Matt Singer, as had been suggested earlier, then somebody should lean on the kid. Janaka began the process by deleting the bogus accounts and back doors from the Portland State system. He also got on the telephone. The first group of calls was to the sysadmins of the systems Phantomd had penetrated. The second group was to law-enforcement agencies: city police, state marshals, Secret Service, FBI. The last call was to Patrick Humphreys, the undergraduate who had told him about Matt Singer.


When Patrick heard that Matt Singer had left the house, he jumped into his car with his friend Alvin Cura and floored it to southeast Portland. Matt's brother Steve let them in. After a little back and forth, Patrick, Alvin, and Steve marched up the dark, crumbling stairs to the inner sanctum. Steve was nervously rubbing his pale, freckled hands together. Patrick was nervous himself. It was a strange errand.

The family had fallen out of the habit of going into the room when Matt was away, Steve said. And when he came back, they didn't resume. A kind of respect for privacy, Patrick guessed. He let

Steve go first, of course—Matt was his brother. Steve opened the door and Patrick and Alvin pressed in after him.

Summer sunlight pushed through the curtains; the air inside was hot, stultifying, bacterial. Spending time around computer people, Patrick and Alvin were accustomed to personal disarray. But this room was exceptional even by those standards. They made out the waxy gleam of pizza boxes, dark clothing in a heap on the bed, empty two-liter Coke bottles filmed with age, haphazard blocky piles of computer parts. An alpine landscape of paper covered much of the floor.

In a corner Matt's computer sat athwart a tiny desk with a wooden top that swung upward on hinges to reveal a compartment for pens and pencils, the kind of desk Patrick remembered from elementary school.

Beneath the smells of perspiration and rotting food was another smell, a faint, dusty odor that Patrick found oddly familiar.

A few days before, Patrick had been called by a student sysadmin named Mike Wilson, a big guy who had just gotten out of the military. Patrick had driven in from his summer job and met Wilson in the Portland Center for Advanced Technology. In Wilson's hands was a stack of computer printout underlined in Magic Marker—logs of cracker activity. A cracker named Phantomd was using the school network as a conduit for credit-card fraud, Wilson said. Janaka was furious. If Phantomd was Matt Singer, and Patrick was involved with him, Janaka would cancel his computer privileges for a thousand years and maybe get him kicked out of school to boot. The same went for his friends.

Patrick hardly knew Janaka at that point, but was aware of his reputation for amiability. The World's Nicest Human Being was angry at him. Plus losing access and being kicked out of school. That night, he asked Steve if his crazy brother were up to his old tricks. Oh, yeah, Steve said, as Patrick later recalled it. Matt has gotten into all this stuff. And then Matt got on the phone and said the same thing. Oh, yeah, he told Patrick, cheerful as always. I got into all this stuff.

The cheery tone ticked off Patrick considerably. You better stop him, he told Steve.

I can't, Steve said. I've tried and tried, but I can't control him.

If you can't stop him, Patrick told Steve, Alvin and I will want proof of what he's doing. We'll want to show Janaka it's not us.

To his surprise, Steve readily assented—he was usually so protective of Matt. You can come over anytime he's not here, he said. And a day or two later he had called to say that Matt was out. So here they were, ransacking the room.

What are we looking for? Steve was shuffling through a stack of paper by the desk chair.

I don't know. Anything that could show whether he's been invading Portland State's network. Janaka's on the warpath.

Patrick used his foot to push through some of the piles of Matt's junk. He knew he might be shoving Matt's stuff hard enough to annoy Steve, but Steve wasn't the one with Janaka breathing down his neck.

At the other end of the room, Alvin was watching Steve, who was trying to help Alvin and Patrick because they were his friends, while at the same time dragging his feet because they were trying to narc his brother. In helping, Steve might have been bowing to the inevitable—Alvin was not going to let Matt cause any more trouble. If need be, he would toss the guy down the stairs.

Alvin himself was in low water. He'd left home for good, his parents proclaiming that they would have nothing further to do with him, and dropped out of Portland State. These days he was camping out in the back of a friend's U-Haul and working the graveyard shift at a gas station in Crip Central up in northeast Portland. About the only bright spot in his life was that Janaka still let him work on the computers at Portland State, even though he had no official connection to the school. Alvin had come under a cloud during the last incident, because Phantom Dialer had used his account, along with the accounts of Patrick and some of their other friends. Because he knew Patrick, who knew Steve, who was Matt's brother, he was under suspicion. He wasn't going to let anything stand in the way of maintaining his access to the network.

Atop the bureau was what must have been every knickknack anyone had ever given Matt. Major packrat behavior, in Patrick's opinion. Definitely odd. Enough ancient food was scattered around that it later occurred to Alvin to be glad that Matt's diet apparently consisted mainly of dry foods; otherwise a new form of life would have evolved in that environment. Patrick was pawing through the clothing in the drawers. Touching the underwear and socks that Matt's mom had folded and put away, Patrick was flushed with guilt, as if he were a housebreaker. But he wasn't, of course. He was there with Matt's brother. The oddly familiar smell nagged at him.

He opened the closet. At first he couldn't identify what was inside. A huge, spiky object was jammed in the space beneath the pole—rustling when the door folded to reveal it. Whatever it was, it was the origin of the smell. Puzzled, he slowly reached in, patting at the shape. Something like stiff feathers scraped his palm and outstretched fingers. Then he made out the smell: pine needles. It was a Christmas tree.

Yuletide tinsel made thin, gleaming ripples in the silver-green light from the computer screen.

Alvin shook his head in disbelief.

Patrick shut the closet door. Needles rained softly onto the carpet.

Got a Christmas tree in there, Steve, he said. Steve didn't react. Maybe he was used to it.

Patrick had met Steve through Dragonfire, a bulletin board Steve had set up. Back then, Steve was at Madison High School in northeast Portland and Patrick was at Aloha High School, about fifteen miles west of the city. Both were seniors, bright kids with a tendency to lose themselves in computers. Only after they met did Patrick learn that Steve had created the bulletin board after he nearly killed himself in a bicycle accident and had to spend months at home recovering. He'd borrowed a computer from school and a modem from a friend. Sitting in bed with the keyboard on his lap, he had spent hours talking on-line, tapping out messages till the dawn birds sang. After Steve's friends told their friends, it seemed to Steve like every bright, computer-literate kid in town was clamoring to get on Dragonfire. One of them was Patrick. They'd hit it off right away, both on-line and then in the 3-D world, although in retrospect their relationship was marred from the start by competitiveness.

After graduation Steve attended Portland Community College for a year and then quit to work at Radio Shack to earn tuition. He had just lost his job and was having trouble meeting rent. He was envious of Patrick, whose mother's late-earned MBA had finally won her a job with a salary that let him attend Portland State. At first Patrick had been a marketing major, but that didn't last long. His mother suggested that he take a programming class—learn Pascal, something like that—so he could acquire a marketable skill. Patrick's father had split from the family when he was eight; financial circumstances had been shaky enough for him to understand his mother's wish for a fallback. The class worked on the ancient clunkers in the campus computer center, which was in the basement of a former public school. There Patrick learned from Alvin—his oldest friend, whom he'd met over a game of Dungeons and Dragons—that only a few blocks away at the Portland Center for Advanced Technology were systems with real computers. At the Center, he said, they have color monitors you can do real graphics on, not these cruddy-ass green-screen jobs in the computer center. With a few friends, Alvin persuaded the freshman and sophomore adviser to approve their request for accounts on the computer-science network. After Trent Fisher set up the accounts, Patrick, Alvin, and the gang spent most of 1990 hanging out in the white noise and blinking LEDs of the terminal room. Somehow marketing fell by the wayside for Patrick.

Hey, look at this.

Steve was holding up a stenographic notebook covered with Matt's angular scrawl. On one of the blue-ruled sheets was a list of the computers in the Portland State network, complete with notes about their individual vulnerabilities. Other pages diagrammed networks at MIT, Reed College, and the University of Michigan, the charts adorned with account names and passwords. NASA—he saw

passwords for the Internet address orion.arc.nasa.gov.* The same
for the National Institutes of Health—alw.nih.gov.

By the small notebook was another, bigger notebook, spiral-
bound, dog-eared, its pages spattered with phone codes, file names,
and modem lines. This notebook had clearly been appropriated from
someone else, perhaps Matt's younger sister; electronic addresses
shared space with mash notes to someone named Sky. The last
page, written in red ink, was an unfinished screed entitled "Unix
Attack Program."

> Try to login as uucp, bin, sys, adm, root, guest, public
> Once login is secured try the following:
> Check for write access to /usr/lib/ . . .

Stacked on the tiny desk were more notebooks, and piled hig-
gledy-piggledy around them were paper scraps, many of them torn
from newspapers and magazines, sorted into separate heaps according to some scheme of Matt's own. On them were log-in names,
passwords, lists of numbers that looked like they belonged to credit
cards. MIT again, Willamette University, a bunch of other places.
Lots of numbers with a 725 prefix—Portland State.

For his part, Alvin had come across a thick pad of computer
printout. Running down it was what looked like a sequential listing
of every phone number in Washington, D.C., with handwritten an-
notations: "2400 modem," "fax," "no answer." Amazingly, the guy
had been painstakingly working over the entire 202 area code, look-

---

* The designers of the Internet decided in 1986 to classify networks by types, awarding
each its own name—a domain name, as it is called. Thus, arc.nasa.gov is the domain
name for the Ames Research Center (arc) at the National Aeronautics and Space
Administration (nasa), a government agency (gov). Each box on each network has
its own address: orion.arc.nasa.gov was a computer named Orion at NASA-Ames.
Similarly, pdx.edu is the domain name for Portland State University, an educational
institution; cs.pdx.edu was the network at the Portland State computer-science department. (The name "pdx," incidentally, came from the three-letter symbol for the
Portland airport, because psu.edu, the obvious domain name, belongs to another
PSU, Pennsylvania State University.)

ing for numbers attached to computers. As Alvin flipped through the stack of paper, it was clear that Matt had found dozens of them, most of them attached, one presumed, to government machines.

Christ, he's been busy, thought Alvin. And then: He *can't* be doing this on his own. No one would do this much activity by himself, right?

*It was the strangest thing Rose Singer had ever seen. Her sons— Matt was three and Steve was five—were drawing on rocks and pretending they were computers. Crouched in the yard, they arranged their rock computers like dollhouse furniture. Even then, Steve was the leader in the game and Matt struggled to keep up.*

*After that, their father always seemed to make sure the boys had a computer. Steve had friends, but to Matt the computer was everything. The first one came when he was six: a Radio Shack TRS MC-10, with a tiny screen that could not show lower-case letters. To Rose it seemed useless, an ugly metal box that seemed to swallow the boys whole. They stared at it for hours while Steve typed in their programs. Matt didn't yet have the coordination to type in his own programs, but he was content to watch.*

*His first machine with a modem was a Commodore VIC-20. It connected Matt to computer bulletin boards—to another world. On the bulletin boards nobody knew if you attended a special school or lived on relief or had a stepfather who was going mad in the bedroom next door. You were as good as anyone else. Better, if you could do more tricks with your computer. Learning those tricks took him a long time, of course. But he knew that if he tried for long enough he would eventually reach his goal.*

*Sometimes it took a long time indeed—weeks, months, years. He learned to ignore the frailties of his own body, typing through the pains caused by his ineradicable hepatitis and the shortness of breath from asthma and the dimness of his bad eyes. By patient repetition, by trial and error, by persistently asking questions to other bulletin-board users and enduring the often sarcastic replies, by mistyping his way through the commands for hours at a stretch, he* gradually taught himself how to climb over the walls that separated one computer system from another.

It wasn't so much that Matt lived in his room; it was that he lived in the computer there. Off-line, he had never had a friend; on-line, he was part of a digital community, frequently teased and sometimes respected. Off-line, he was limited to his house. When he went outside, he couldn't go far without getting lost; the bright light hurt his eyes. On-line, he could explore freely without worrying about the consequences; he was a Magellan of cyberspace. When Matt attacked Rose, it was because she had committed the ultimate affront: she had yanked the plug on his computer. She was trying to make him go out into 3-D society—a place he had no desire to visit. But the police came, and Matt was committed.

At the Oregon State Hospital, Matt wasn't allowed near a computer, of course. But when he wasn't in solitary he slipped down the halls at night to a pay phone. Hunched over the receiver at the psychiatric unit, he broke into companies' computerized telephone systems, enabling him to call the voice-message exchanges created by phone hackers, or "phreakers," across the nation. The exchanges were his link to his real existence on-line. "Welcome to Phreaker Central," the opening message would say in the adenoidal rumble of an adolescent boy playing with his recently changed voice. "Eat shit and die, lamers."

Listening to the growly tones, he sagged against the wall, dissolving in the sound of freedom.

When he got out computers were outlawed at the halfway house, too. But when the house provided him with a job at the local Veterans Administration, he couldn't help noticing it had a small computer center. On his second day at work, he was caught in front of a monitor. He was trying to use the computer to dial an outbound line. What did they expect him to do?

# 6

# THE HACKER
# ETHOS

The term "hacker" has always been bedeviled by discussion.... Pranks have always been part of hacking. But the inference that such high jinks were the essence
of hacking was not just wrong, it was offensive to true hackers, whose work had
changed the world, and whose methods could change the way one viewed the
world. To read of talentless junior high school students logging on to computer
bulletin boards, downloading system passwords or credit bureau codes, and using
them to promote digital mayhem—*and have the media call them hackers* . . . well,
it was just too much for people who considered themselves the real thing. They
went apoplectic.

—**STEVEN LEVY, *HACKERS***

In Colombo, Sri Lanka, it rains ninety inches a year. From May
to October winds sweep across the great warm belly of the Indian
Ocean, gathering up moisture all the way, until the clouds are
stopped by the stone coxcomb of Pidurutalagala Mountain at the
center of the island nation. Halted, they spill water over the jumble
of Dutch churches and Buddhist temples and English raj buildings
that make up Colombo. Janaka Jayawardene grew up within a few
hundred yards of the beach, but he spent much of his time indoors,

reading, drawing, arranging toy soldiers, and making plastic models while rain hammered the roof.

At home his parents spoke English—so much so that Janaka stumbled over his country's native Sinhalese. He read in English, too: science-fiction tales, alternate worlds that appeal to boys uncomfortable in their own realities. When he went out, he preferred American movies to the other choice: Indian musicals. Later he said that he had somehow never been imprinted by his own culture.

His father was a mechanical engineer, part of the Anglophile middle class. Intent on his career, at home in the world of logic and objects, he paid little attention to the deepening shadows of societal unrest that crept across the country in the 1970s. When the unrest became riots, the Jayawardenes fled to the landlocked African nation of Malawi. Despite the move, Janaka's parents still expected him to be a good Sri Lankan son. He was to attend a prestigious British university and become a professional man. Then he would return to Sri Lanka, which was bound to have solved its ethnic problems. This plan had no appeal to the adolescent Janaka.

Janaka found himself envisioning a different life when the family was visited by an uncle who had moved, improbably, to Portland, Oregon. Although the uncle detested the United States, Janaka convinced his parents to let him accompany his uncle there. After landing, they negotiated the splines of freeway overpass along the Willamette River. The racing traffic and the sweeping concrete arcs of the off-ramps were just like in the movies. Janaka was wild with excitement.

He ended up attending Portland State University, a local school with a department of electrical engineering. By and large, electrical engineers are handy types who can make machines work. Janaka discovered that he was neither handy nor good at making machines work. Worse, engineers were required to take courses in computer science, and Janaka, despite his fondness for the imaginary computers in science-fiction novels, was terrified of computers in the real world. He was certain he would never understand them.

The course began with the computer language BASIC. As its name implies, BASIC was supposed to be for beginners. But to Janaka it looked like little more than an arbitrary mishmash of symbols—math without answers. He couldn't grasp it. Fearful of failing the class, he decided to spend an entire weekend working on BASIC. By Monday morning, he had not slept for sixty hours—but he understood BASIC. He also knew what he wanted to do with his life.

He spent the rest of the semester learning to program. Lunchtime would go by, dinnertime would go by, moonlight would be scumbling the dark clouds in Portland's sky, and Janaka would have his head thrust in the dusty, rounded rectangle of the computer monitor as he absently guzzled his twelfth cup of java. His face glowed in the light of the screen and was reflected in its glass: pug nose, a circle of thick curly hair at the top of his broad forehead, lips that looked like he was smiling even when he was serious. His skin was dark enough not to look ghastly in the blue-green light. He was learning to type like a computer jock, in short, inaccurate bursts of unbelievably rapid character generation punctuated by grunts of annoyance. Sometimes he didn't come home to his uncle's house until midnight. Sometimes he didn't come home at all. He was utterly content.

His family was horrified. Computers, Janaka's mother told him, were not fit for professional men. It didn't help when his grades dropped in negative correlation with his increasing interest in computers. In high school he had been a straight-A student. Now he spent so much time in the computer room that he was in danger of flunking out of school.

His academic fate was sealed when he discovered Unix.

Unix was completely accessible; everything was subject to the user's creativity. But because the little documentation AT&T provided was cryptic and incomplete, learning Unix meant nervously risking the wrath of the Skinnies and Bulkies by asking dumb questions and humbly accepting the terse, scornful replies. Slowly gathering a body of unwritten lore, the beginning Unix user felt like a young novice monk trying to learn Zen from short-tempered masters.

Janaka learned Unix thoroughly enough to turn his undergraduate career to ash. His stomach, too. Swearing off coffee, he kicked himself into action with high-test Jolt cola. When that, too, got to his stomach, he switched to Mountain Dew—caffeine in a sweet, digestible base. He didn't particularly care about his stomach lining; like his grade-point average, it had been sacrificed to Unix. Horrifying his mother, he formally gave up his status as a student in 1984 and moved to the electrical-engineering department as a full-time system administrator.

Sometime in the mid-1980s, a Unix wizard—a local Skinny— referred to Janaka as a "hacker." Janaka was proud. In computer parlance, a hack was a particularly clever and amusing trick; hackers were masters at confabulating such tricks. More than that, the term had become a stand-in for a way of life. Hackers didn't give a rap about money or status or academic credentials or middle-class propriety. Obsessions about race, nationality, class, or gender were beneath contempt. So was wearing a tie, participating in business lunches, or buttering up stupid people who happened to be powerful. Hackers loved complex puzzles and elaborate puns and clever mechanical tricks; hating the dull, indefinite tasks associated with ordinary existence, they let bills go unpaid and piled up paper in their offices and wore the same GNU Project T-shirt for three weeks in a row. Meanwhile, they worked fanatically hard on their code, honing every line to a Spartan aesthetic standard appreciated only by other hackers. The sodality of hackerdom embodied everything Janaka liked about what he was doing. He had no regrets about leaving the so-called real world—the SCReW—for Planet Hack. Cruising the university network, he felt fully at home for the first time in his life.

Which was why he was enraged when crackers—they didn't deserve the honor of being called hackers—invaded the system that he had loved and learned from for so many years.


By the end of July, Janaka Jayawardene had performed the following actions: he had called (1) the campus telephone company; (2) the Portland police; (3) the Oregon State Patrol; (4) the Federal Bureau of Investigation; (5) the Secret Service; (6) various other organizations of a less authoritative character. In the above-enumerated order, he received the following responses:

(1) An operator at the campus telephone company—Portland State ran its own "telco"—explained it was effectively impossible to trace incoming calls, because the operator would have to be notified that the cracker was dialing in, then pull all the lines in the network, one by one, to see which one was used by the cracker, causing an interruption-of-service scenario that the operator didn't want to consider for a single moment.

(2) After leaving several voice-mail messages on a number to which he was directed by the operator and never receiving a return call, Janaka was connected to an impatient Portland cop who directed him to the fraud squad, which never answered his messages, a lack of response that led Janaka to give up on the effort to enlist the city police department, even though many of the cracker's calls were apparently of local origin, and the Singers, whom he suspected, lived in the city.

(3) See (2) above, substituting "Oregon" for "Portland" and "state" for "city."

(4) In a tone that to Janaka sounded like that of someone attempting not to register boredom, an agent at the local branch of the FBI suggested that Janaka identify the crime being committed at Portland State, and after Janaka tried to explain how the Internet connected a single malefactor to institutions like banks and brokerage houses all over the nation, the agent explained that maintaining a connection was not a crime, after which Janaka desperately cast about for a plausible-sounding crime in noncomputer terms and said that the intruder was reading people's mail and maybe stealing credit cards, prompting the agent to suggest in an overtly uninterested tone that Janaka call the Secret Service, which was in charge of crimes involving the U.S. Postal Service and credit-card fraud.

(5) By now in a state that might be described as disexpectancy, Janaka dialed the Secret Service, and was surprised by the rapid response of two square-jawed types who explained that the Secret Service was trying to specialize in such crimes and that they were highly interested in reading Janaka's logs, which they called

fascinating, although they admitted that the mainstay of the local office, one Ron Peters, was back East on a big joint investigation with the FBI of some suspicious nationwide telephone outages, and asked Janaka to keep in touch, which he did after Patrick Humphreys showed up and to Janaka's astonishment dumped a thirty-gallon green plastic garbage bag full of paper onto Janaka's desk (making less a difference to the appearance of Room 136 than he really liked to admit), said paper taken by Patrick after a second, solo visit to the Singer residence, the paper being covered with cryptic markings of a suspicious nature that closely resembled the less cryptic but equally suspicious words from the Apocalypse Now bulletin board on Janaka's logs, not to mention credit-card numbers and passwords from networks all over the nation, all of which Janaka took to the office of the Secret Service, the interest displayed there raising Janaka's hopes that something would get done, except that the Secret Service now seemed to be saying that the Portland office had no real expertise except this Peters individual, and that he was concentrating on this big case back East, which involved a gang of hackers—Janaka winced at the word—and that Janaka should keep monitoring until he found evidence of something big, because, in fact, this by itself was not enough, which caused Janaka to remonstrate (unsuccessfully) that not paying attention when this guy was running around networks all over the country was like not doing anything to shrink Typhoid Mary's arena of action until it was demonstrably proven that she had killed a few thousand people with an epidemic.

(6a)  Meanwhile, Janaka had called MIT, one of Phantom Dialer's biggest playgrounds, and told the sysadmin, a fellow named Mike Patton, that the cracker particularly liked to break into a computer named Gaak, and thereby learned from Patton that Gaak was Patton's personal workstation—but to Janaka's shock Patton was only mildly interested to learn that a cracker was using it to jump God knows where—sure, he'd delete the account, thanks, talk to you later . . .

(6b) . . . an attitude that Janaka found replicated tenfold, then twentyfold, as he called sysadmins across the nation and discovered that the people in charge of maintaining the networks seemed all too often to think of security as something they didn't have to bother with and indeed they sometimes thought that security itself was just a way to keep people from using networks . . .

(6c) . . . which notion Janaka found peculiar, as he explained to Dan Farmer, the brilliant, talkative hacker—hacker now in the correct sense—at CERT who had written COPS, the security-checking software Janaka had been trying to get his student sysadmins to run ever since the first Phantom Dialer episode earlier that spring, because the same people who were trying to put the whole world on-line were in effect laying a trap for the masses once they arrived, an observation that prompted a laugh from Farmer, along with the request for more logs, which Janaka e-mailed him night after night, causing Farmer to shake his head in disbelief at what was rapidly blowing up into one of the bigger incidents anyone at CERT had ever seen.

This guy, Dan Farmer told Janaka, doesn't believe in the word "no."

## Washington, D.C.

With the phone companies denying that sabotage had occurred, the Telecommunications Task Force closed down at the end of July. Settle's agents returned to their offices of origin, leaving him alone in the makeshift war room. The modest space was now meticulously clean—the Bureau didn't like agents leaving the detritus of their investigations scattered around. Except for the low throb of the air-conditioning, the room was dead quiet.

In addition to catching whoever was responsible for the telephone outages, Settle had hoped the task force would demonstrate the need for a permanently staffed computer-crime squad. Instead, he ended up praying that the failure to prove hacker involvement had not derailed his plans completely. The irony was pretty thick, come to think of it. Settle could hardly buy a newspaper these days without reading that a tidal wave of information crime was inundating the United States. Anonymous surveys of corporations found that more than half had fallen prey to computer banditry; CERT reported fielding five or six new break-in reports a week; the underground bulletin boards constantly displayed postings about new escapades. Incredibly, the hackers were bold and numerous enough to hold *conventions;* one monthly gathering at a hotel lobby in Manhattan invariably ended up with the participants clustering around pay phones, placing bets on the rapidity with which they could break into telephone switching computers. And all of these things, Settle knew, were just the obvious exploits, mostly those of teenagers; Settle shuddered to think of what the grown-ups were doing.

The criminals were out there. But for now his best hope of proving it to his superiors lay with Barnett and Kolouch, who were working the Masters of Deception case in New York.

Things would have been going wonderfully for Phantomd if they hadn't been going so badly. He had made mistakes—so many mistakes!—and been spotted. And then Portland State started logging him. They wiped out his accounts, deleted his back doors, plugged his entry holes. Phantomd broke into Reed College, but they kicked him out, too. On top of that, Phantomd's brother had let his friends ransack his room and stuff his notes into a plastic garbage bag. With so much against him, it was almost impossible to accomplish anything. Late at night, he griped about the problem on #hack, the Internet Relay Chat channel where the crackers gathered, ten or twenty at a time firing messages across the wires.

    &lt;phantomd&gt; I think my account is being monitored
       [ . . . ] evertime i get into irc [Internet Relay Chat]
       it slows down all of a sudden like. I just think it's
       them monitoring what i am doing. It would not be
       the first time. . . . The admins are real sneaky

    &lt;Gnome&gt; phantomd: get another account, *grin*

<phantomd> Everytime i login they find the account
i am using . . . There is no more.

<Holmes> phantomd: Why would they bother?

<phantomd> Everytime I find a way to get root they
either close it off or soon after close it [ . . . ]

<Holmes> phantomd: I assure you that sysadmins
have better things to do than watch everything
their users do.

<phantomd> Holmes: I assure you these are not
normal sysadmins.

To avoid scrutiny, he dialed directly into MIT, where the sysadmins never noticed that bogus accounts were Telnetting for hours on end to the Ames Research Center at NASA. But spending so much time on-line in Massachusetts was building up a huge phone bill that he couldn't pay. When the phone company threatened disconnection, he looked for an alternative means of reaching MIT. He found it in a local office of the Boys' Club of America, which had a PBX telephone system. PBXes—the acronym stands for "private branch exchange"—are the small computerized switchboards that many organizations use to handle telephone and voice-mail service. Like many PBX owners, the managers of the Boys' Club seemed not to know that their PBX was preset to give an outside line to anyone who dialed in and entered an access number. Phantomd telephoned, got the recorded message about office hours, entered the code— bingo, a dial tone. Then he cut in his modem and called MIT. Although the Boys' Club picked up the cost, Phantomd's problems weren't over. Bounced through the PBX, the connection was terrible; his signal kept getting lost in static. He ended up slipping back into Portland State, never sure whether he was being watched.

<phantomd> Hey admins are you here?

<ganja> who are you talking to phantomd?

<phantomd> The people that might be watching me [ . . . ]

<Templar> *waves* to people watching phantomd

<ganja> phantomd: f*** 'em

<BiZap> *kicks* phantomd for being paranoid!

<phantomd> BiZap. You would think it to if every bug you found was fixed after you discovered it.*

The struggle to maintain his access was all the more maddening because he was on the verge of success with the supercomputer at NASA-Ames. Exploring the NASA network, he learned that the supercomputer communicated with the outside world through a Sun workstation, which fed programs to it and extracted the results. Late one summer night, Phantomd called MIT, Telnetted to NASA, transferred to the Sun box, and slipped Crack, the password-guessing program, into the queue.

He was stunned by the results. The supercomputer hadn't deciphered passwords any faster than the smaller, less powerful machines he had tried. He couldn't figure it out. Why wasn't NASA's supercomputer supercomputing?

The supercomputer was a Connection Machine—a beautiful machine, if computers can be beautiful. The CM-2, then the most common model, had two components: a set of four black metal cubes assembled into a square monolith nearly five feet tall, and a curved, almost featureless disk storage facility, also black, that resembled an upscale restaurant bar by a minimalist designer. Connection Machines were a product of Thinking Machines, in Cambridge, Massachusetts. Thinkco, as it was called, was down the street from Technology Square, home of the MIT Laboratory for Computer Science, the Artificial Intelligence Laboratory, and the Free Software Foundation. The proximity was not coincidental;

---

* Phantomd's "paranoia" was justified. These exchanges were monitored at Portland State, where they were the subject of considerable amusement.

Thinkco founder Danny Hillis emerged from the electronic petri dish at Tech Square. A classic hacker from his high-top sneakers to his passion for driving deactivated fire trucks, Hillis had come to believe that all previous superfast computers were inherently flawed. Because they executed a program in steps, one instruction mechanically following another, the latter part of the job always had to wait for the first part, which inevitably slowed them down. Hillis developed a way to lash together thousands of chips into assemblages that broke a problem into tiny pieces and worked on all of them at once. The difference between conventional computers and Hillis's "massively parallel" computers was the difference between having a car washed by one expert worker or by a team of a dozen less-trained people. Simultaneously scrubbing the hubcaps, wiping the windshield, and waxing the hood, the team will always outpace even the most skillful single worker. In the same way, massively parallel computers like Thinkco's Connection Machines would always outpace conventional computers.

In 1994, Thinking Machines filed for bankruptcy protection. One reason for its failure was that—as Phantomd had discovered—most programs in fact ran no faster on Connection Machines than they did on ordinary computers. To take advantage of parallelization, programs had to be "parallelized." That is, they had to be written in a way that permitted their individual components to be executed separately. Parallelization, as it turned out, was an arcane art. Not enough people were willing to master its intricacies to make Connection Machines popular.

Grok was among the refuseniks. When Phantomd asked him why the supercomputer didn't run Crack any faster, Grok told him about parallelization. Could you parallelize Crack? Phantomd asked. Grok would have nothing to do with it.

This unwillingness was no surprise—Grok had been avoiding him. The rift had occurred when he made the mistake of telling Grok about the loss of his notes. Instead of expressing sympathy, Grok had acted like he had betrayed them both. Since then, Grok had made himself scarce.

Making up for the loss, Phantomd had met a hacker named

Jsz on #hack. They hit it off in a way unlike anything that had ever happened to Phantomd. He never had to pester Jsz or hide out when he got mad; they were just friends. Jsz logged onto #hack from Israel, which was where he lived, apparently. Other than that, Phantomd knew nothing about him and didn't want to know. What was important to him was Jsz's life on-line, not the shadow person he was in the 3-D world.

Phantomd and Jsz were a great team. Jsz knew about programming, but he didn't know about security. From the point of view of a cracker, understanding C + + was all very well, but it didn't help you learn about the meaning of world-exportable password files. Or that older Sun machines came from the factory with a file called hosts.equiv—a cousin to the .rhosts file—that had a line with two plus signs (+ +). The plus signs allowed any computer on the Internet to log on without a password. Or that . . . Phantomd passing this knowledge to Jsz, experienced hacker to apprentice, just as he had been instructed by Grok in his turn . . . private exchanges on #hack, the two of them on their own time line, Phantomd working in his room with the first fingers of dawn pulling at his window curtains, the evening sun setting on Jsz somewhere in Israel . . . messages halfway around the world as they worked out a marvelous scheme.

I can parallelize Crack, Jsz explained. And with a supercomputer you could work with a huge dictionary, so that Crack would be checking for every name, term, and word in the English language. But in the long run we'll need something better.

Phantomd didn't understand what he meant.

Crack, Jsz explained, matches the encrypted entries on the list of passwords with words from a dictionary that have been encrypted in the same way. But if someone chooses a password that is not an ordinary word or variant of an ordinary word—G5&c@?xQ, for instance—Crack cannot decode it, because G5&c@?xQ is not in any dictionary. As a result, such passwords are invulnerable to Crack. Increasingly, sysadmins were forcing users to choose such un-Crackable passwords.

Jsz had an idea for breaking those passwords—one that took

advantage of Phantomd's extraordinary persistence. Abandoning the dictionary, he would write a program that would scramble and encode every eight-letter sequence from aaaaaaaa to ZZZZZZZZ, then match them against the encrypted entries in the password list. This brute-force approach would eventually get any password. The key word, though, is "eventually." Each character in a password has scores of possible entries—letters, numbers, punctuation, spaces, and control symbols (characters made by pushing the control key at the same time as another key)—and each password can be scrambled in up to 4,096 different ways. As a result, Unix can create more than 423 quadrillion unique passwords, too many for even a supercomputer to guess. But—and here was where Phantomd came in—several supercomputers attacking the same password file simultaneously stood a much better chance of guessing passwords in a reasonable time. If Phantomd employed his unmatched tenacity to penetrate many supercomputers, Jsz and he could link them together into a worldwide password-breaking matrix that could topple even the most impregnable passwords. No network anywhere would be safe.

Phantomd considered this scheme to have considerable merit. He knew, though, that most supercomputers were in networks with reasonably good security—NASA-Ames was an exception. To steal into other supercomputers, they would have to employ hacking methods that the sysadmins at these sites had never seen before.

Fair enough, Jsz in effect said. But where will we come by these special, never-before-seen techniques?

To Phantomd, the answer was obvious. The best hacking tools were in the hands of computer-security experts. And those were the people he planned to attack next—as soon as he figured out a better way of maintaining access to the Internet.

# 7

# THE TALE OF
# THE TAPE

The typical computer network isn't like a house with windows, doors, and locks.
It's more like a gauze tent encircled by a band of drunk teenagers with lit matches.

**—ROBERT DAVID STEELE, CHIEF EXECUTIVE OFFICER, OPEN SOURCE SYSTEMS,
FORMER CIA ANALYST AND DEPUTY DIRECTOR OF THE U.S. MARINES
INTELLIGENCE CENTER**

Portland

Radio Shack had discontinued the product. But the clerk told
Michael Gray that he was lucky—the store had a used one in the
back, which he would sell at a discount. Even so, it was surprisingly
expensive. Michael had to fill out the form and obtain a Radio Shack
purchase card to buy it. Disgruntled, he carried the gizmo to his car
and drove to Steve Singer's house.

Michael had met Steve through Patrick Humphreys, whom Michael befriended in a computer-science class at Portland State.
Steve was okay, in Michael's view; Matt was another story. Michael
had first met him at Steve's birthday party. This is my brother, Steve
said, making the introduction. Watch out—he does whatever he

wants. Steve was laughing and excited, his pale, open features maybe a little flushed from celebratory tippling. But Matt didn't say a word. When Michael reached out to shake his hand, Matt almost flinched. He looked at the floor, the walls, his shoes, anywhere but Michael's eyes. He does whatever he wants? Steve didn't offer any further explanation. There was a younger sister, too, who seemed normal to Michael—she had nothing to do with computers. Michael saw Matt a few more times, always finding him crouched in a corner, watching the action like a spider. He didn't learn what Steve meant by "whatever he wants" until he was summoned to meet Janaka in the spring. Turned out that because of Matt the whole circle was under suspicion of breaking into the university networks. After that, Michael had stayed away from the Singers. But he had come to like Janaka, and Janaka was so frustrated by his inability to get help with the current round of intrusions that Michael had decided to investigate Phantom Dialer himself.

In discussions with Patrick, Michael came up with the idea of installing a telephone accountant. A telephone accountant resembles a small adding machine, complete with a roll of two-inch paper. When spliced into a telephone line, it records the number and duration of every outgoing call, printing them on the paper roll with the merry mechanical galloping sound of an old-fashioned cash register. After many calls, a ribbon of printed numbers curls away from the top of the machine. Michael's plan was to have Steve install the device on the telephone line connected to his brother's computer.

Steve didn't know what to think of this request.

Michael understood the hesitation; he was asking one brother to inform on another. On the other hand, Steve was easy to persuade. He was a conciliator, Michael thought, a compromiser, someone who always went along with everybody else's schemes, no matter what his doubts. It was easy to imagine him racing with a pack of lemmings toward the edge of a high cliff, arms furiously pumping, asking, "Hey, guys, are you *sure* about this? Is this *really* the right idea?"—a constant stream of dismay that would continue even as the mass of furry bodies flung itself into the empyrean.

We want to know where he is going besides Portland State,

Michael was explaining. Stands to reason we're just one place he is using for access. Where *else* is he going?

Steve didn't know, of course.

Patrick said: You yourself have said that you thought what he was doing is wrong. You yourself have talked about how you can't tell him anything when he gets on-line.

It was true. When Steve warned him that breaking into computers was illegal, Matt spouted this stuff about how information should be free—the Hacker Ethos, according to him. No doors, no root; the whole party line. A bunch of nonsense, in Steve's opinion. Not that he was a great enthusiast for the government, but he didn't see how freedom of information justified the credit-card swap meet on Apocalypse Now. Steve had just received his first credit card—a big event to someone from a poor family. Trading Visa numbers wasn't like bilking telephone time from a giant conglomerate that wouldn't notice the loss. It was stealing from ordinary strugglers like Steve himself.

Patrick and Michael pressed on. Look, you know and we know that everyone who gets into computers plays around a bit. We all experience the dark side of the Force. But this Apocalypse Now is out-and-out fraud, Steve. People go to jail for it. There's messages on Janaka's logs about people renting post office boxes and reaching around to lift checks and credit cards from neighboring boxes. Doesn't sound much like the Hacker Ethos, now does it.

Since I told Matt about Portland State logging him, Steve told them, he hasn't returned to Apocalypse Now.

What if he's doing something else on a network other than Portland State? Something much bigger than credit-card fraud?

Spoken aloud, it seemed absurd to worry about a single individual seizing control of something vital. The image it evoked came from the movie *WarGames:* kid with home computer in Northwest seizes control of nation's strategic missiles. In fact the bulletin boards mocked the film for its inaccuracy. A real-life *WarGames* was impossible, they said, because, as everyone knew, the military never put computers with secret information anywhere near the Internet. Others weren't so sure. The economies of developed nations depended completely on networks that were always connected to other networks. As a result there was a plenitude of targets and many routes to attack them. Besides, in the mercenary climate of the post–Cold War world, the ability to obtain commercial information was arguably of greater strategic value than the ability to control a missile. Which meant that in a broad sense the thesis of *WarGames* had become truer than it had been in 1983, when the film was released. Nowadays someone with a computer could really wreak havoc. Of course it was ridiculous to imagine that that someone could be Matt. Right?

Steve wanted to know what his brother was doing and didn't want to know.

In the end, Michael thought, it came down to the ultimate persuader: You don't want us to lose access, he said. We could get kicked off the computer system. And then you wouldn't be able to use it, either.

From Steve's expression, it was clear that he understood the power of this threat. The need for access was hard to explain to noncomputer people. Being in such an intimate relationship to these powerful machines that would do exactly what you said . . .

Steve agreed to attach the accountant, tucking it behind the door to his bedroom.

Within hours Michael got a call from Patrick. Their attempt to play detective wasn't going well, because Matt was using a war-dialer. A war-dialer is a program that harnesses a computer's talent for exhaustive repetition to find telephone calling-card numbers. It tries random combinations of numbers, one after another, until it finds a valid card.* More than 99.99 percent of the attempts are

---

* Calling-card numbers consist of the owner's telephone number and a personal identification number, or PIN, which is usually four digits. The war-dialer program employs two series of numbers: a set of potential telephone numbers (for example, those in a single area code between 111-1111 and 999-9999), and a set of potential PINs (for example, the numbers between 0000 and 9999). These can be combined to generate all possible calling-card numbers within those ranges. The war-dialer program tells the computer to telephone a modem in another area code and to try paying for the call with one of the potential calling-card numbers. If the call does not go through, the

unsuccessful, but the computer doesn't care; it's just a computer. Eventually, the power of chance will turn up valid numbers, which the cracker can then use for long-distance telephone calls. Unfortunately, Patrick said, Matt's war-dialer was generating so much activity that the accountant couldn't keep up.

Swallowing his reluctance, Michael accompanied Patrick to the house where Steve and Matt lived with their mother. It was a scene, he thought. The kitchen linoleum was torn; pieces curled off the floor in stiff little waves. Opened cabinet doors showed a larder that was nearly empty. There was a hole in the stairs you could put your foot through. Then, upstairs, Matt's lair.

Disassembled computer equipment lay like broken bricks on the floor.

Steve's bedroom was next down the hall. He'd just lost his job and been forced to move back to the house. The three young men crowded into the bedroom, stepping around the boxes from the move, talking about how to stop Matt. Michael reset the telephone accountant and turned it on. Immediately it began spewing numbers—Matt was at work in the next room. Within minutes the machine jammed. They reloaded it, tried again; a second jam.

Matt's modem and the accountant were not synchronized, Michael realized. When the accountant heard a busy signal, it dropped the line and marked a call as incomplete. Unfortunately, the modem didn't hang up so fast. A second or so later the accountant would test the line to see if anyone had lifted the receiver—and find the phone off the hook with the same busy signal. This was too much for the poor telephone accountant. Unable to interpret the busy signal correctly, it would treat the continuing connection as an indication that the call had actually gone through. It would then print the number of the "successful" connection. Because Matt's war-dialer was calling the same number again and again, the ac-

---

program assumes that it has generated an invalid number and tries again with the next on the list. If the call goes through, the computer immediately hangs up and notes the successful calling-card number.

countant kept printing out that number, filling up the tape with identical lines of print until the inexpensive device jammed or ran out of paper.

When they looked through the tapes, the general outlines of Matt's scheme were clear. He wanted to access MIT's Laboratory for Computer Science—specifically to a server called Terminus—but he didn't want to pay for the call. Thus he was war-dialing into Terminus, looking for credit-card numbers to pick up the charges. More distressing still, Steve said that MIT wasn't the only target. Matt was also war-dialing into a modem bank at the National Institutes of Health. In fact, Steve thought that Matt had previously used the modem bank to gain root access on networks throughout NIH, which meant that his brother could alter or destroy one of the world's great storehouses of medical information.

Great—that was Patrick's reaction. Suppose he damaged important medical research data? What was Matt going to say— "Whoops, sorry about that clinical trial"?

God only knows what your brother's up to, he said to Steve. So what are you going to do about it?

## Pittsburgh, Pennsylvania

Since 1990, Dan Farmer had been one of the five members of the CERT incident-handling team, which meant that once a month he spent a week fielding every report of break-ins that came in to the agency. This was called being "on point." Because intrusions could happen at any hour, being on point meant more or less living at CERT headquarters for a week. Point week began with Farmer riding his motorcycle to the Software Engineering Institute of Carnegie Mellon University. CERT occupies two floors there, though it has little contact with either the Institute or Carnegie Mellon. Instead, CERT is as close as the global computer network comes to having a police force, which isn't very close. CERT doesn't investigate crimes, can't arrest anyone, and has no statutory authority whatsoever.* Once inside, Dan would spend point week guzzling institutional coffee, fielding phone calls, answering e-mail, and pacing the wide, carpeted hallways at midnight. After finishing his shift, he was responsible for following up the incidents reported to him during point week; he owned those problems, so to speak, until they were resolved.

If Janaka was a Bulky, Dan was a Skinny—a slim, blue-eyed, freckle-faced Midwesterner with a pierced eyebrow and chestnut hair that hung in reddish waves to his pierced nipples. On duty, he wore black motorcycle boots with clinking buckles and a black cotton shirt open to the navel; his small apartment was full of printed material about fine wine and bisexual sadomasochistic practices, about both of which he was a cheerfully vocal aficionado.

As an adolescent, Dan had paid little attention to electronics; his passion was reserved for the pool hall. He went to college but dropped out after a year and joined the marines. Lack of other career opportunities was not the reason for his enlistment. Dan joined because he wanted to learn how to kill people. "I was interested in implements of mass destruction—from an academic point of view," he once told the *San Jose Mercury News*, the house organ of Silicon Valley. "Being able to blow somebody's head off at 500 meters with an M-16, that's an interesting skill to have." After six years in the reserves, Dan changed his mind. He became a conscientious objector.

When he went back to school, he naturally found a home in computer science.

As his senior project he wrote COPS, a program that combed through a network in quest of security problems. He gave away COPS to anyone who asked, because that was the hackish thing to

---

* It also doesn't really have a name. Today CERT is called CERT/CC—CERT Coordination Center—but at the time of this story it was known simply as "CERT" or "the CERT." CERT originally stood for Computer Emergency Response Team, but now the center insists the letters don't mean anything at all; "CERT(sm) is a service mark of Carnegie Mellon University," warns one official document, "and should not be expanded into an acronym definition."

do. In a small way, the program made him famous. COPS also made him notorious, because some security mavens argued that freely distributing the program would let crackers use it to discover holes. When he graduated, he was invited to walk through the big brass doors of CERT headquarters.

Having received the original report of the Trojaned log-in program, Dan was Janaka's contact. From his point of view, Janaka seemed to be a capable hacker—in fact, Dan suspected he was underemployed at Portland State—but he was untutored in security. He had doubtless long thought of himself as something of a rebel. But to the underground, Janaka was the Establishment. It was a shock.

The computer underground was anything but news to Dan. Still, the cracker or group of crackers plaguing Janaka was bizarrely, unnervingly persistent. Most intruders would vanish upon detection, cockroaches running from the kitchen light being a common metaphor; Phantom Dialer kept returning. No matter how many broken accounts Janaka eliminated, his reappearance was as inevitable as the resurrection of the supposedly dead monster in a horror film. And the cracker worked at it all day long, running the same commands again and again in this strange, automatonlike fashion. Such persistence inevitably generated huge amounts of computer activity. When Phantomd hit his stride, Janaka and the student sysadmins had to abandon their ordinary work to keep track of the intrusion.

From Dan's perspective, the Portland State incident was both tedious and alarming. Tedious in an intellectual sense: considered purely as a hack, each of the cracker's tricks, like replacing the log-in program, was threadbare stuff. Indeed, the intruder frequently spent hours typing random combinations of letters in what looked like an attempt to learn Unix by brute force. But in a more important sense the incident was alarming, because the ancient tricks *worked*. Crazily resolute, the cracker eventually managed to get into almost every system he tried. When he appeared at a new site, he tried his store of tricks one by one on every computer in the network. Hours of stupefyingly dull work later, he found a box that some overworked sysadmin had forgotten to secure, and then he was unshakable. By sheer persistence, he managed to bludgeon his way into many networks that would have foiled a more skillful but less patient cracker.

Janaka was like a convenience-store owner who had been robbed a dozen times by the same slow, inept criminal. But there was a key difference: In the case of the convenience store, the police would make it their job to hunt the perpetrator.

CERT could not fill the gap. Despite the implicit promise of action in the name CERT—Computer Emergency *Response* Team —it was really more of an information-gathering operation than a cracker-hunting operation. CERT issued alerts about specific security problems in specific pieces of software and hardware, but only after they had been fixed by the manufacturers. In Janaka's case, the break-in was so technically unskilled that CERT could do nothing—it had issued warnings about those holes years ago. Making a fuss would be like issuing an emergency warning to U.S. drivers not to park their cars with the keys in the ignition and the motor running.

So—Janaka sounding amazed on the other end of the line— it's basically okay to break into other people's property, read their mail, steal their passwords, play games with their credit cards, and destroy their data? You mean, your position is effectively the same as that of the *Free Software Foundation*? If I get upset, I should turn off the modems and yank my network off the Internet? Otherwise I've entered some kind of no-privacy and no-property zone?

Not exactly. Dan suggested that Janaka stop wasting his time with the local branches of the FBI and Secret Service, which were unlikely to have any computer expertise. If he wanted help, he should contact FBI headquarters. The Bureau wasn't exactly crawling with rocket scientists, but Dan had spoken with at least one digitally savvy agent.

The guy you want, Farmer explained, is named Jim Kolouch.

When the phone rang for Jim Kolouch, he levered himself away from the desk and barked in mock fury at whoever dared to disturb him. This time it was some fellow from Oregon with an unpronounceable name who apparently had not heard that Kolouch was no longer in charge of any FBI computer-crime effort. As the guy droned on, Kolouch cast his eye around the room.

Barnett was in the next chair, working on the paperwork for the Masters of Deception wiretap request. One nice thing about working with female agents, Kolouch believed, was that they could type fast. Not that women couldn't do the rest of the job well, too. As Kolouch liked to put it, Barnett's genetic credentials couldn't be held against her. She hadn't chosen to be born with the chromosomal endowment that management was panting after nowadays.

Oregon had spent weeks monitoring the attacker. He had a three-foot stack of logs he could show Kolouch.

Great, Kolouch thought. More paperwork.

The windows were shut to keep in the air-conditioning. But the glass vibrated slightly from the constant fury of traffic below. Even inside, taxi horns were audible.

Barnett was still making the metal ball of the IBM Selectric whirl, the letters on its surface whacking into the carbon film ribbon. This was a tough assignment for her, Kolouch suspected. She was shy, a small-town girl who had hardly gotten over the thrill of being an FBI agent, and here she was thrown into New York with a cynical wise-ass like Jim Kolouch. She didn't get half his jokes, and didn't seem particularly thrilled with the half she did get—especially when the butt of the jokes was the Bureau itself, as was often the case. But she was loosening up a little, even starting to needle him back. A good sign.

Kolouch asked Oregon what sites had been compromised.

Oregon recited a long list of universities and colleges—sites with .edu in their Internet address. Among them was, of course, gnu.ai.mit.edu—the cesspool run by Richard Stallman at the Free Software Foundation. The caller obviously had no idea how many teenagers used that place as a launching pad. Nor did he seem to know whether his own university network contained anything worth stealing. Or that Kolouch was already eyeball deep in the biggest hacker case ever undertaken by the federal government.

We can't get him out of our network, the sysadmin was saying. He's blundering around all over the place and jumping everywhere you can imagine. Can you do something about him?

Don't get your hopes up, Kolouch said. There's a lot of people doing this. Look, most of them are kids.

I know that. But we think that he may be part of a group, or have an associate. . . .

Suppose you find him breaking into a government installation, Kolouch said. Suppose he does it across state lines, so there's no question that it's a federal offense. But you know what the penalty is? It's like a zero-dollar fine and no days in jail. For most federal prosecutors there are more important parking tickets—you know what I mean? This one guy breaking into your box is not something that will galvanize people into action, okay?

He saved his muttered imprecations until after he hung up. Then he turned back to the case at hand.

## Portland

Three thousand miles away, Janaka was stunned. Weeks of work had apparently been for nothing. Unless Phantom Dialer took down the stock exchange, Kolouch was saying, the FBI wasn't going to do anything about it.

Janaka wasn't going to pull any more all-nighters going through those logs, that was for sure.

At the same time, Janaka wasn't certain that Kolouch was wrong. Sometimes Phantomd seemed like nothing but a harmless incompetent. Logged onto the Portland State system, he kept invoking the Last command, which checks who recently came on-line. If he saw Janaka's name, Phantomd disappeared immediately. Once, Janaka, working with Wendy, saw the account belonging to assistant dean Richard Morris was active. Knowing that Dick Morris was in another building and not using the network, Janaka realized that

Phantomd must have broken into the account. Worse, he was running a file search in a way that was sure to snarl up the server—a beginner's error. Janaka sent a message: Hey Dick, what are you doing? Back came the furious response: *Don't call me names!* Wendy and Janaka exploded in laughter, Janaka leaning back in his chair with the trademark Janakian guffaw bursting from deep in his belly. How, he sometimes thought, could you worry about someone like that?

On the other hand, this person was on-line full-time—ten, twelve, fourteen hours a day. All that time, he was breaking into networks. Most of them were .edu sites, which were unlikely to contain valuable commercial secrets or secret government documents. But it was the nature of the Internet that university educational networks were connected to corporate and military networks. Inevitably, someone who nibbled around the edges of those other sites, as this cracker was doing, would find them. Letting Phantomd have root access to these systems would be like parking a car on a steep hill and letting a child fiddle with the emergency brake.

Then, in midsummer, Phantom Dialer performed his most surprising action yet: vanishing. For no evident reason, he stopped attacking Portland State. For months Janaka wondered about the cause of the silence. And then the press of business claimed him, and he stopped thinking about Phantom Dialer.

As a child Steve Singer had been full of rage but now he rarely lost his temper. Matt had driven him to it, though. He had shown his brother the tapes from the telephone accountant, hoping they would shock his brother into stopping. I know you're trying to get calling-card numbers, he had said. Do you have any idea what this could lead to? Like jail time? Instead of being cowed, his brother's sole reaction to the telephone tapes had been to dial MIT directly, not bothering with credit-card numbers, apparently to avoid the damaging strings of numbers that were evidence of war-dialing.

Half a dozen times they had scenes.

What else are you breaking into? Steve demanded. What are you doing?

Nothing. Stony-faced by the ever-present monitor light.

Matt, you're pushing me. I can't trust you anymore. I think you're breaking into a lot more places than you're telling me.

Maybe I am, Matt said. And maybe I'm not.

Are you fooling around with the military?

Very deliberately, Matt returned his gaze to his computer.

One night Steve waited until his brother left the room. This required a surprisingly lengthy period. It was well into morning when Matt went downstairs to fish something out of the pantry. Hearing the footsteps, Steve sat in front of the child-size desk. Matt had turned the box off, as he always did when not in the room. Steve switched it on. How could he have let this go on? Anxious, anxious; his heart was thumping.

Matt's machine asked for a password.

Stymied, Steve stared at the screen. He thought about shaking the password out of his brother.

You won't get in, Matt said. He was standing in the doorway. Even if you guess the password, I've got the hard disk encrypted.

Steve rose defeated from the seat.

As a final measure, he told their mother that Matt was getting himself in trouble with his computer. His mother, the free spirit, who hated all things digital. Armed with the telephone accountant tapes, he explained exactly what Matt was doing. Upset, she asked Matt if he were breaking into other people's systems. Matt looked her right in the eye and said that he wasn't. Steve couldn't believe it. Matt never lied, despite his secretiveness. And this was a direct lie. Naturally, she believed him—he'd never lied before.

Steve couldn't even get her to look at the tapes. I don't want to see them, she said. She kept formulating reasons why Matt could not be doing it. And looking at Steve like he was a monster for eavesdropping on his brother.

Look, Mom, Steve said, you try these numbers on the tape out and tell me what you get. This one here, when I tried it, I got some voice-mail number Matt pirated. You can hear his voice, Matt's voice, calling himself the Phantom Dialer. Do I have to explain more?

But she never called.

It's your responsibility, Patrick told Steve. Deal with it.

What am I supposed to do? Turn him in?

Hard to imagine calling the FBI. Growing up in the 1970s, Steve had accompanied his mother on protests against the war in Vietnam. As a three-year-old he'd been photographed in the local paper carrying an antiwar sign that he couldn't read. His folks had always imagined that the FBI was photographing them.

Steve didn't go for the party line anymore. But that didn't mean it was easy to contemplate turning in your brother. On the other hand, Matt might get into more serious trouble later if Steve didn't make the call now. Maybe Steve might be in that more serious trouble, too.

He picked up the phone before he knew what he was doing.

A receptionist put him on the phone with an agent named Rasmussen. Steve told him why he was calling. His voice shook as he said his brother's name. He was telling a federal agent to arrest Matt. How could he be doing this?

Rasmussen's pen scratched as he took notes.

The guilt was crushing for the first few days. But after a week with no fallout it had subsided substantially, and after a few weeks, when it seemed clear that nothing was going to happen as a result of his call, it had more or less faded. The FBI never called back.

He eventually confessed to Matt about the call. Matt laughed in his face, and Steve felt foolish. But he also felt more than a little relieved. His betrayal of his brother seemed to have no consequence.

No consequence at all—Matt was still active. Day and night, the plasticky clickety-clack of a computer keyboard came from the room next door.

What, Steve wondered, was he *doing*?


Throughout 1991 the cracker known as Grok spent time on the network at Reed, the small liberal-arts college in Portland that had put up one of the first Unix networks in the Northwest. For the most part, its sysadmins were almost as relaxed about intruders as those at the Free Software Foundation. Indeed, one of the student assistants, a man who shall be called Riley, particularly enjoyed talking to Grok. Grok was the only cracker that Riley had ever encountered who truly understood the Internet. He moved quickly and gracefully through it, and Riley could never find out where he was coming from —he suspected that Grok had tampered with the routing tables to disguise his whereabouts.

Strangely, Grok had chosen to hang out with Phantomd. Phantomd sometimes blundered into the Reed system—Riley couldn't figure out why Grok bothered with him. He would say that he liked teaching him, or that he found him amusing, or even that he wanted to keep him out of trouble. Riley never understood exactly what was going on.

And then, after a while, he noticed that Grok had shaken loose of Phantomd. At the time, Riley assumed Grok had become bored with his junior partner. Not till long afterward did Riley consider the possibility that Grok might have become scared of him.

# 8

# INFOMASTER

There is always at least one weak link in a site's security net.

**—MICHELE CRABB, FORMER PRINCIPAL COMPUTER SECURITY ANALYST,
NASA-AMES RESEARCH CENTER**

Fallsington, Pennsylvania
December 1991

In the end, Beth Barnett had come to realize, it all came down to kicking down doors. Fraud, kidnapping, computer hacking—it always ended with closed doors and cops who needed to open them. Accompanied by agents from the Philadelphia office of the Secret Service, she was heading toward the village of Fallsington, Pennsylvania. There she would crunch through the morning frost to the home of Allen Wilson, identified by the FBI as the notorious hacker The Wing, whose front door she would then cause to open.

From the start, they'd had the culprits dead to rights: Southwestern Bell had traced the intrusion to the hackers' homes. In addition, the two gangs—the Masters of Deception and the Legion of Doom—had boasted about their exploits on computer bulletin boards. One might think with such strong evidence that obtaining a wiretap would be easy. Instead it had been a headache.

From the way civil libertarians wailed about wiretaps, it was clear that they'd never tried to get one. To obtain permission, the FBI had to assemble a T-3. "T-3" was Bureau jargon for the affidavit required by Title III of the Omnibus Crime Control and Safe Streets Act of 1968, which laid out the procedures for obtaining permission to use an electronic listening device. Each T-3 had to be approved at many levels in both the FBI and the Justice Department. Almost thirty signatures were required—all before it arrived on the judge's desk. The T-3 had to show that the Bureau would use the wiretap to pick up information about a specific crime from a specific set of people without eavesdropping on anyone else. Then agents were allowed to install a bug, provided that they reported their findings to the judge every ten days.

In theory, the more evidence agents acquired before a wiretap, the easier it was to justify in the T-3; in practice, having a lot of evidence meant that the agents had to present a greater body of material. In this case, the justificatory evidence was so overwhelming that Barnett and Rick Harris, her opposite number at the Secret Service, spent a month assembling the brief.

As they put together the T-3, Settle was riding them. He called daily, urging greater speed. Barnett wasn't crazy about the pressure, but she could understand it. They were both frustrated when the judge took six weeks to approve the wiretap. When the approval finally came through, the Bureau installed her in a tidy efficiency apartment, complete with kitchenette, on the Upper East Side. She took the subway down to the suite at the World Trade Center where the investigation was headquartered.

The Bureau's Engineering Research Facility had crammed the suite full of custom high-fidelity intercepting gear—a monolith of cables and disk drives and needle-jiggling gauges. On the walls were shelvesful of Frisbee-like storage tapes. Tool belts clanking, a squadron of technicians kept the whole jury-rigged assemblage running.

In addition to Barnett, the FBI team included agents Jim Ko-louch, Levord Burns, and Dennis Kintigh. A mature, dapper figure with Johnny Carson–like good looks, Kolouch quickly figured out how much Barnett didn't know about computers. Despite his flip, sarcastic exterior, he went out of his way to help her catch up on the endless complexities of Unix and networks. Burns was a good-looking African-American, almost as much of a rookie as Barnett; before joining the Bureau, he had been a sysadmin at Rutgers University, which probably made him the most network-literate agent in the FBI. The close-mouthed Kintigh was an odd character. He had a Wild West look; cowboy boots were a major item in the Kintigh wardrobe. In terms of computer knowledge, Kintigh was second only to Burns; he had a master's degree in computer science—a real one, not the creation of an FBI database. He was a stickler for doing things right, which Barnett got to see up close.

When the equipment was switched on, it didn't work. Barnett, Burns, Kintigh, and Kolouch spent a week watching Engineering Research Facility technicians bend over their dials. They couldn't understand the problem—the equipment had worked perfectly at the lab. They had tested it, a technician explained to Kintigh, by connecting one of the laboratory computers to a modem and phone line and sticking a wiretap in the middle of the line. Everything had worked perfectly.

Kintigh had exploded. You have to do more than that to test a system that's going to tap calls from miles away with half a dozen different kinds of modem! What is the matter with you turkeys?

Kintigh was alarmingly red-faced; it looked as if three quarters of the blood in his body had rushed to his head. Barnett couldn't tell if he was about to cry, throw a punch, or both. Kintigh raged on for another minute before suddenly losing steam and stalking off, leaving the rest of the group in awkward silence. The Secret Service agents sat at their desks with their mouths agape. Even Kolouch couldn't think of anything to say.

A few days later Settle visited. He took Kintigh aside and asked him not to alienate the help. By that time, in any case, the intercept equipment was working.

The data rushed in at enormous speed. Mobsters, the usual wiretapping targets, tended to speak tersely on the telephone; they spent their days on the streets. By contrast, the hackers seemed to live on the phone. They would spend hours wriggling their way into networks, then call their buddies to report on their findings in minute detail. Two dozen Secret Service and FBI agents spent weeks collecting, transcribing, and analyzing data from the wiretaps until the prosecutor pronounced himself satisfied with the material. It was time to close down the Masters of Deception.

All of the suspects were to be served search warrants on the same day: December 6, 1991. Barnett rode with the group that went to Allen Wilson's house. In the 3-D world, Wilson was a geeky student janitor at Drexel University who lived with his parents. But on-line Wilson was The Wing, a fearsome member of both the Masters of Deception and the Legion of Doom.

When the agents knocked on the door, Wilson's mother answered. Confronted with a search warrant, she produced Wilson in a hurry. The suspect's bedroom was eye-opening. In addition to the standard desktop computer he had a stash of Bell Atlantic jackets, hardhats, and electronic gear. The agents found identification cards from the phone company, gasoline credit cards issued to the phone company, and portable electronic handsets belonging to the phone company. Wilson, quiet and clever, seemed ready to blend in with the gang around the water cooler at any Bell facility.

Facing the evidence accumulated by the FBI, he quickly began giving up the names of his friends. When the charges were filed, he was listed as an unindicted coconspirator. As a result, Barnett never found out for sure what he was doing with the equipment in his room, or even if he was the hacker who called himself The Wing as he trashed the Free Software Foundation.

Sometimes these uncertainties—the inevitable result of the kind of horse-trading that characterizes the justice system—left Barnett wondering how bad the perpetrator was. In this case, though, she had no doubt. Wilson gave her the creeps.

New York City

The press conference, held long afterward, was intended to emphasize the perniciousness of the Masters of Deception and the Legion of Doom. Staged in the lobby of the St. Andrews Plaza in Manhattan, U.S. Attorney Otto Obermaier spoke from a dais full of G-men, Secret Service agents, and Justice Department lawyers. This is the crime of the future, the dark-suited Obermaier said. As assistant U.S. attorneys guided reporters through charts of the hackers' exploits with laser pointers, the prosecutor painted a picture of brilliant but destructive young people run amok.

Slouched in folding chairs, the newspaper and television reporters studied the charts. And they noticed a curious thing—the Masters of Deception and Legion of Doom may have been brilliant and destructive, but they had not broken into any computer networks of value except those belonging to telephone companies.

A reporter asked where the damages came in.

A prosecutor explained that the phone companies had spent money fixing security holes.

Isn't that, the press asked, like charging the burglar for the bars you buy to put up on your windows?

Infuriatingly, the reporters didn't get it. The crime was not the cost to the telephone companies but the illicit power acquired by the hackers. Big pieces of the national communications network had fallen into the hands of juvenile delinquents; sooner or later, they would have realized the profit in, say, shutting down the telephone burglar alarms in businesses and homes.

In another sense, though, the skeptical reporters were right. Despite their technical savoir faire, the Masters of Deception and Legion of Doom had not understood the opportunities provided by the Internet. They had settled for playing with the phone company when the real opportunities were much larger. Which meant that Settle and his cohort had once again failed to find the perfect, gold-plated example of the hacker threat—the example that would demonstrate to a skeptical public how these seemingly trivial incidents had the potential to cross the line at any moment and turn into something very ominous indeed.

Portland
January 1992

Since high school Trent Fisher, Janaka's officemate and the sysadmin for the computer-science department, had been an exponent of Technocracy, Inc. Founded in 1918 by an engineer named Howard Scott, Technocracy, Inc., advocated letting an impartial intellectual elite replace the irrational free-market economy with a scientifically sound production and distribution system derived from the laws of thermodynamics. In this way humankind would be freed from toil and debt. At first Technocracy attracted intellectual figures like the social philosopher Thorstein Veblen, the statistician Leland Olds, and Charles Steinmetz, father of the alternating current. In recent decades, though, only isolated acolytes like Trent had kept the flame alive.

Janaka thought that Technocracy was an excellent example of how computers attracted smart but naive people who imagined that their expertise with these machines somehow translated into expertise in other fields, like politics and philosophy. Secluded in their semi-academic environment, the digerati passionately espoused ideas that in the real world wouldn't fool a cow. The Internet was chockablock with screeds in favor of some completely crazy scheme like solving the population problem by recording human personalities in digital form, transferring the recordings to a computer, and then killing the meat bodies, thereby eliminating the need to grow food. Then these ideas would be savagely ripped into by those who believed that the real solution was to build tiny nanotechnological robots that would construct foodstuffs molecule by molecule, inaugurating an age of unmatched prosperity for Earth's billions. The personality recorders would attack back, and the debates would go on acrimoniously for weeks.

Not that Janaka was fully grounded himself. His hackish pursuit of the immediately interesting meant that he was always falling behind on conventional organization. He'd been immensely grateful last summer when Wendy Wilhelm, the preternaturally energetic student sysadmin, had announced that his office was a disgrace to the human species and had taken charge of cleaning it up. Out went crates of computer manuals and ancient science-fiction novels and tapes of horror-film soundtracks that Janaka could not remember recording, let alone listening to. When she was done, Room 136 had acquired a floor.

Flushed with success, Wendy had argued that the confused hunt for Phantom Dialer had demonstrated the need for a systematic approach not only to security, but to sysadmining itself. Portland State needed to assign specific tasks to student sysadmins, rather than relying on the hackish method of letting people volunteer to solve problems. Goaded by her good-humored nudging, Janaka and Trent put together a series of not-for-credit hourlong lectures on Friday afternoons. By the end of two semesters, attendees would know something about running a network. The program was embraced by Trent, who had spent months compiling a detailed guide to Unix; Janaka, for his part, laboriously struggled to put together a curriculum. Wendy herself did not attend, because she had graduated and gone to work at Intel, twenty miles away.

After two months of lectures, Janaka realized that the best students were dropping out. They didn't want to wait two semesters to get to the boxes. Recalling his own memories of bonding with the machines, he concluded that there was no substitute for hands-on experience. To Trent's exasperation, Janaka spent the Christmas break performing what he called a "brain dump" before student volunteers. For four or five days he spoke for eight hours, pouring out a torrent of digital lore until he was too hoarse to talk. Then he put the students in front of a workstation and told them to make the box work. The students would load the operating system, Janaka expected, bollix the job, reload it, and so on, failing time after time until, in an epiphanic moment, the box suddenly came to life. Those who succeeded could join his team. Meanwhile, the annoyed Trent continued giving lectures on Friday afternoons. The remaining students formed a group around Trent that developed careful procedures for logging reports of problems.

Janaka's students—Patrick Humphreys, Alvin Cura, and Michael Gray among them—were thrilled by the Promethean challenge of giving life to a machine. Immersed in the problem, they became One with the Box. Those who passed through the experience should form a special cadre, Patrick suggested. We'll call ourselves the Systems Hackers In Training—think of the T-shirt possibilities! I think not, Janaka said. How about CAAT, another student proposed. Computer Action/Alert Team.

Maybe just CAT, Janaka said. Computer Action Team.

Rowdy and cocksure, the CAT took over a small corner office, which became, of course, the CAT house. Janaka set them to monitoring the system and fixing problems; they fell to with a will. After twelve hours on shift Janaka would shoo them home, where they logged on remotely, aching for action.

They got it on January 15, when a CAT member noticed an oddity on a little-used Sequent box in the computer-science department. When anyone logged into the machine, it responded:

Login:

After the user typed in the account name, the machine answered:

password:

Inexplicably, the "p" had switched from uppercase to lowercase. Computers cannot make such changes by themselves. Ergo, somebody had been fooling with the log-in program. The box had been Trojaned.

Janaka and half a dozen alarmingly eager CAT volunteers searched through the network; Trent and his group stood back disapprovingly from the fracas. To the cracker hunters' amazement, the system was riddled with Trojans. Moreover, the cracker had not confined himself to Portland State. The logs showed that he had

Telnetted from Portland State to the New Jersey Institute of Technology and the University of Texas, and had doctored the log-in program in both. (The Trojan had secret passwords: "bd," meaning "back door," for New Jersey; "fuckme" for Texas.) At Texas he had stored files taken from two machines at Portland State and from three at the Numerical Aerodynamic Simulation facility at NASA's Ames Research Center. Called /etc/fstab, the files listed the outside networks permitted to access Portland State and NASA-Ames machines. (The /etc/fstab files were like .rhosts files, but used for somewhat different purposes.) To judge by the modification times, the intruder had fetched the files two weeks previously, altered them to award himself easy access, and replaced the originals with doctored copies. In addition, he had broken into Harvard University, visited an obscure Internet Relay Chat channel, and gained access to a subsidiary network of Sun Microsystems.

At first, Janaka had been inclined to suspect that this new incident was just Phantom Dialer redux—after all, Phantomd had already demonstrated a penchant for installing defective log-in Trojans. But this round of crackery seemed more purposeful than the earlier intrusions.

The next night the cracker provided further evidence of his intent. Taking advantage of a dormant account, the intruder used Portland State as a base for electronic forays to Oregon State, the University of Texas, the New Jersey Institute of Technology, and two computer-research centers at the National Institutes of Health: the Advanced Laboratory Workstation Project and the Division of Computer Research and Technology.

Cutting-edge computer research at the National Institutes of Health? It amazed Janaka until he recalled that some of society's largest databases are located in big hospitals and medical research centers. If intruders managed to plant back doors in the underlying software, every hospital would be vulnerable to tampering. Already European newspapers had reported that a cracker used a doctor's hospital-network account to alter patients' prescriptions. It would be nice to learn whether this cracker, whoever he was, had something so unpleasant in mind.

Whoever he was? Looking at the logs, Janaka and Paul Mauvais, sysadmin for the central campus network, realized they knew exactly who this was. The transcripts were full of the misspellings and confused commands they were familiar with from the days of the Phantomd attacks. Surely this was the same guy. Except that his mistakes now belonged to a wholly different order of skill. He was, so to speak, failing better—a lot better.

As Janaka and the CAT extracted information from the logs, Paul telephoned the Numerical Aerodynamic Simulation facility at NASA-Ames.* Ames was the kind of site that gave security experts nightmares. Its Connection Machines were used by scientists for simulations of things like air turbulence and laminar flow—and to develop software for the nation's air traffic control system. The phone was answered by a harried woman named Michele Crabb, who told Paul that Ames had been under attack by crackers since at least October. The incident had begun when Crabb, the sysadmin at Numerical Aerodynamic Simulation, learned from a coworker about some funny behavior on one of the machines that loaded the facility's supercomputers. The word "password" in the log-in routine had suddenly acquired a lowercase "p."

Oh, really? Paul said. It was déjà vu time.

CERT doesn't do anything, Crabb complained to Paul. They hire great people like Dan Farmer and then they only collect information. Local cops just throw up their hands. Nor had the FBI been much help. Crabb, who was as organized as Trent, kept track of meetings in a special notebook. The page from her November 12 meeting with the local FBI office was blank—a summary of the substance of the first meeting, Paul gathered. All the computer expertise in the Bureau was tied up in some case in New York City. Before she could get any action from NASA, her own agency, she had to write an extensive report about the problem to the Inspector General's Office, a branch of the agency that handled internal investigations;

---

* He had previously called CERT and reported the problem, an action that was taking on an increasingly ritualistic character.

they would supposedly assess the situation and make a report to the Justice Department. Meanwhile, the report wasn't getting written, because she was so busy fighting off the intrusions and overseeing a huge computer network with more than 250 subnetworks.

Paul knew what she was talking about.

Crabb knew that some of the NASA intrusions had come from pdx.edu, Portland State's Internet address, but there were so many intrusions from so many different places that she hardly knew where to start. It seemed plausible to suppose that NASA was the subject of several groups of crackers; maybe the Portland State cracker was just one in a crowd. Or maybe they were all in it together —it was impossible to tell. In addition to Portland State, Crabb said, the cracker seemed to have visited the University of Hawaii; the Andrew Project, a high-level software development program at Carnegie Mellon University; and an Andrew-related site at Rensselaer Polytechnic Institute, outside Albany, New York.

Most important, he seemed to be going after supercomputers. A sysadmin at a navy lab had discovered the same intruder running a parallelized password-cracking program on their Connection Machine. Rather than taking a brute-force approach, which was difficult even on a supercomputer, the program was based on an enormous dictionary with 2.3 million entries. A souped-up version of ordinary Crack, it was the biggest thing the navy people had ever seen.

The incident was big in another way, too. Paul and Janaka didn't know how Phantomd was slipping into the Portland State network. As a result, they knew it was likely that they were picking up only part of his activity. But even the part they could see was startling. Phantomd was breaking into one system after another. In addition to the government sites, dozens of others were falling before his clumsy but determined assault. He was crunching through the Internet like a one-man ant army.

At the next desk, Janaka had been on the line to the FBI. From the length of the conversation, Paul surmised that the feds were finally paying attention to a call from Portland State University.

Livermore, California
February 1992

Gene Schultz's pager went off—loudly. He could have set it to vibrate silently on his belt, alerting him to incoming messages by feel. But a silent beeper couldn't create a theatrically convincing rationale for ducking out of a meeting, which was what he was doing. As prearranged, he was being paged by one of his staffers, Tom Longstaff. Longstaff had left the meeting five minutes earlier, when *his* pager went off, having been triggered by Ken Pon, who was on Schultz's staff, too. In this way, Schultz regularly managed to smuggle himself and his entire staff out of the contentious meetings into which he was dragged by his nominal superiors at Lawrence Livermore National Laboratory.

A tall, lean man with a neat Vandyke and black hair that swept straight back from a widow's peak, Schultz was the head of the Computer Incident Advisory Capability. CIAC had been created by the Department of Energy to monitor computer attacks on its facilities, which ranged from the giant particle accelerators at Fermilab, in Illinois, to the top-secret O Division at Livermore, which conducted research on the Strategic Defense Initiative. After its creation, its mandate quickly expanded, and by now CIAC was entrusted with computer security for a score of federal agencies, including the National Institutes of Health.

Schultz stopped by Longstaff's office, thanked him, and checked the warboard, a wall-mounted whiteboard showing the status of ongoing cracker investigations. Still at the top was Los Alamos. The attack there wasn't *sophisticated* nasty, as Schultz put it. To the embarrassment of the computer staff at Los Alamos, the cracker—Infomaster, as he called himself—had gained entry by the simplest of methods. No, this attack was just *ugly* nasty. After gaining root, Infomaster had taken the trouble to reformat one of the system's main hard drives, erasing every bit of data it contained. For all practical purposes, he had blown up the system.

Reformatting a drive was a digital version of breaking into someone's home, then writing on the walls and defecating on the floors. As a rule, it didn't inflict much permanent damage, because data generally could be restored from backup tapes, but cleaning up the mess took a long time and wreaked havoc with the user community. Nor did it give anything to the cracker. Unless he wanted to create a diversion while he struck somewhere else, or hide evidence of having stolen information, or set back a project that depended on the computer.

Schultz doubted Infomaster had anything so subtle in mind, though. CIAC had been following his career for several weeks. It was hard to know what to make of him. The scale of the attack was startling—he was taking over network after network in business, government, and academia. Yet he hadn't done much damage, except for trashing Los Alamos, which for all Schultz knew may have been accidental. In fact, Infomaster not only did no damage, he didn't do *anything*. When he broke into a system, he poked around, gained root, then took off for the next system. No apparent pattern, no larger purpose.

Not like the hacker who attacked the human-DNA-mapping project at the University of California at San Francisco some months back. That hacker had jumped into the network, rifled through the project files, then left forever, having stolen or altered whatever data he wanted. Presumably a hacker that skillful wouldn't be caught dead hanging out with Infomaster. Good thing: the thought of combining Infomaster's persistence and another hacker's sophistication was dismaying.

Hear from Dotty yet? Schultz asked Longstaff.

Longstaff said they hadn't heard a word.

Strange—Dotty Alexander, head of security at Los Alamos, usually shared the details of break-ins with CIAC. But she seemed to be avoiding them now. When someone like Dotty stonewalled, it usually meant that sensitive data had been affected.

Los Alamos, as Schultz knew for a fact, persisted in storing sensitive data on computers connected to the Internet, despite CIAC's warnings about this unwise practice. The laboratory was rife with projects for developing instruments of destruction, from good, old-fashioned nuclear bombs to hunter-killer satellites out of a James Bond movie. Schultz didn't like to imagine any of it filtering into the global network.

Schultz, Longstaff, and the five other members of the CIAC team met for a status check. Before closing the door, Schultz stuck his head out to learn whether his boss, Chuck Cole, had again dispatched his secretary to spy on them. She was sitting by the door, pen and pad at the ready. Such petty harassment was standard fare for the superweenies, as Schultz called his superiors at Livermore. They were forever hassling Schultz about how he spent his paltry $1.4 million budget. In a deliberate slight, they had transferred CIAC's clerical assistant elsewhere in the laboratory, leaving Schultz and his cohort to address their own envelopes.

Turning back to the meeting, Schultz asked the question he had been dreading all morning. It concerned Los Alamos. The source of his anxiety was not the prospect of nuclear weapons data spreading on the Internet. Instead, it concerned the dire possibility that CERT might have beaten CIAC to the punch with a response.

Schultz's feelings toward CERT ran the gamut from disdain to detestation. In 1989, when CIAC was founded, the two agencies—CERT, charged with tracking break-ins throughout the Internet; CIAC, with the unique expertise of Energy Department facilities like Los Alamos—were supposed to complement one another. Instead, Schultz believed, CERT treated CIAC as a threat. When CIAC told CERT about break-ins, CERT would rush to release a bulletin about them, giving no credit to CIAC. If CIAC released a bulletin with the smallest inaccuracy, CERT flamed it publicly.

The war had escalated to the point where CERT wouldn't even return calls from CIAC about Infomaster's attacks. Given the scope of the incident, the other agency must have heard about this guy. Why, then, were they publicly silent? Did they want to spring the first bulletin on CIAC, giving it no credit as usual?

Two can play this game, Schultz told his crew. We know how Infomaster operates. We'll get our own bulletin out, and we'll do it now. Officially, CIAC bulletins only went out to Energy Department sites. If CERT's refusal to return phone calls meant that everyone else on the Internet had to wait months for its warning, that was CERT's problem.

---

The Computer Incident Advisory Capability

INFORMATION BULLETIN
New Internet Intrusions Detected

February 19, 1992, 1100 PDT                    Number C-16

---

PROBLEM: A new series of probes and penetrations on systems connected to the Internet has been detected.

PLATFORM: Primarily UNIX systems.

DAMAGE: Trojan Horse programs replacing the su, ftp, and ftpd utilities are common, other Trojan Horse programs detected include telnet and login. Information on penetrated accounts have been posted to public bulletin board systems. . . .

Santa Fe, New Mexico
February 1992

Scott D. Yelich didn't like to cast aspersions, but it was impossible not to notice that the think tank did not look like an institution with a worldwide scientific reputation. Located in a two-story structure with the warm, cheery ambience of a urological center, it was crammed—paper spilling, cables tangling—into cubicles so crowded and poorly furnished that researchers constantly battled over the inadequate supply of chairs. Although much of the work at the think tank involved modeling phenomena on computers, the network was surprisingly small—twelve Sun workstations on the Unix side, together with a pack of Macintoshes. And Yelich's office —he was the sysadmin—was located in a hallway next to the coffee machine, the supply cabinet, and one of the few working printers.

Thin and clean-shaven, Scott had arrived at Santa Fe three months earlier and quickly found himself at odds with the researchers over the think tank's level of security. Exasperating to Scott, many of the scientists refused to learn the first thing about the machines on which they depended. As a result, his e-mail was filled with incoherent questions, many of which he found so incomprehensible that he sometimes responded by firing off a single syllable: "What?"

Truth to tell, he had been lured to the Institute not by the professional challenges but by the chance to live in the Southwest. He picked out an apartment near the foothills. At first it was kind of bare. Later he installed Pythagoras, a six-foot-long python, in a bathtub in one of the two bathrooms. A pool table fit nicely in the living room. He'd scatter his throwing knives across the bezel, make sure the snake was safely wrapped around the shower curtain rod, and drive up the slopes to the think tank.

One of his first concerns was security. The potential for computer mayhem had fascinated him since 1988, when, as a student sysadmin in Old Dominion University, thousands of computers on the Internet were knocked out by a "worm"—a program that hopped from network to network, replicating itself thousands of times. Disappointingly, the worm missed Old Dominion. But the university got into the thick of things in 1990, when its network was broken into by the Masters of Deception. Scott tracked the intruders back to MIT, where they disappeared in the morass of the Free Software Foundation. Fascinated, he subscribed to newsgroups, exchanged e-mail with security experts, and talked to crackers on #hack and the other Internet Relay Chat channels. When he found crackers operating, he followed them to their lairs and dropped a talk.

By diligently cultivating the society of crackers, Yelich acquired considerable expertise in computer security. He also accumulated one of the biggest stashes of cracker tools in existence—a list of the files ran to twenty single-spaced pages. Because the illicit software made him a prime target for crackers, he kept the most important parts of his hoard off the Internet. Moreover, he stored it in encrypted form, scrambling the information with a code to which only he possessed a key. In a joking nod to his own secrecy, he gave his system the Internet name "spy.org."

Scott had run Crack on the think tank network almost as soon as he arrived. The program nabbed dozens of passwords: account names, account names spelled backward, obvious words like "computer" and "hello." Then he stuck Spanish- and German-language dictionaries onto Crack and turned up a few more passwords from visiting foreign researchers who had picked German words. Realizing he had a problem, Scott wrote a little program that notified the users with bad passwords about the intrusions when they logged in and asked them to change their passwords. Perhaps three quarters of them responded. The remaining quarter hardly used the network, and thus either didn't see the notification or insisted on having passwords they couldn't forget on the rare occasions when they did log on. Scott thought about installing a program that would force users to change passwords monthly, but realized balky users would just alternate between two bad passwords, vitiating the exercise. Besides, such a domineering approach was not calculated to make users happy to encounter their sysadmin over a morning cup of coffee.

So many think-tank researchers also worked at the nearby Los Alamos National Laboratory that crackers attracted by its famous name inevitably drifted to Santa Fe. To prevent trouble, he argued for tightening up security—deleting a few .rhosts files, say. That would end up forcing everyone to type their passwords much more often, objected the researchers. If the think tank wanted better security with less hassle, Scott suggested, it could buy a "firewall," a type of computer that acts as a sort of reverse .rhosts file. It screens all attempts to use the network that don't come from a designated list of users and networks. Too expensive, Scott was told. Not as expensive as being wiped out, he said. But no minds were changed. Who would want to break in here? the scientists asked. What do we have that is worth stealing? Walking around the paper-strewn figure eight of the think-tank office corridor, Scott warned everyone that the network was cruising for a bruising.

One crisp morning in mid-February, he drove to his job, walked up the stairs to the second floor, found the researcher who had stolen his office chair, claimed it back, and entered his account name into the think tank network. It responded:

## password:

Ho ho ho, Scott thought. Lowercase "p." We've been Trojaned.

Half a dozen urgent requests for assistance pinged on his screen as he made an emergency backup of the entire system, in case the cracker trashed it. Then, like Janaka before him, he ran Strings on the Trojan, sifting through the program for clues to its operation. In a familiar pattern, the doctored program copied passwords to an obscure file. The file was full of passwords. It had recently been examined, which meant that the cracker had grabbed the passwords. Scott could disable those accounts, which would suddenly deprive his researchers of e-mail. Or he could assume that the cracker had used the passwords to install several back doors, which meant that disabling the accounts was futile. He elected to do the latter; leaving the Trojan in place, he waited for the cracker to return.

For a few days he checked through the logs every morning. It turned out the bad guy had a pattern: he came in around four o'clock in the morning, always from MIT, and clumsily poked around the network at Santa Fe for thirty or forty minutes, looking for .rhosts files, world-writable directories, and people stupid enough to e-mail their passwords. Four o'clock in the morning Southwest time was lunchtime in Europe, which made Scott wonder if the cracker was a hobbyist across the Atlantic.

By now Scott knew the cracker's handle: Infomaster. In his disorganized way, Infomaster had managed to paw through the think tank's network thoroughly. Irritated, Scott, like Janaka, hacked together a program—Sniffnet, he called it—that logged the intruder's keystrokes and dumped them onto a terminal. Sipping tea in the butler's pantry, he watched what the cracker did when he jumped from Santa Fe to other systems. One of these systems was

Los Alamos. How did he break in? Well, a physicist at the think tank had cofounded a private computer company in town and made a lot of money. He also had a five-letter password—short and easy to guess. Infomaster obtained the password at the think tank and Telnetted to the company network, correctly surmising that the researcher/CEO would use the same password for both. Poking around the company system, he learned that the same man also had an account at Los Alamos National Laboratory. That account had the identical password. In a trice the cracker skipped to Los Alamos. Typical, Scott thought. It was always the honchos, the CEOs, who imagined they were too busy to have to follow the rules. Infomaster futzed around Los Alamos, trying to get root. (Scott, of course, did not know that the intruder had already used other holes to get into Los Alamos before.) From there he Telnetted to half a dozen sites, including UCLA, the Oregon Graduate Institute, and MIT, hopscotching senselessly across the country. Crazy—except that he kept getting access and working his way inside. And he sure didn't want to lose access. He would install half a dozen Trojans on a single machine to ensure that he would never be locked out.

Scott's incredulity mounted as he watched the cracker break into system after system.

Bizarrely, Infomaster rarely seemed to *want* anything from the networks he worked so hard to enter. Once inside, he rarely copied or transferred files. The only thing he really chased after, in fact, was Scott's stash of cracker tools. He had discovered Scott's connection to spy.org and spent hours trying to break in. In early March he finally succeeded, copying all the tools and techniques Scott left on-line. They were encrypted, so Infomaster couldn't use them. And Scott had made sure that the most dangerous stuff was on a hard disk that was physically disconnected from any Internet-ready computer. But the whole affair was exasperating. When Scott let Infomaster know that he was being watched, the cracker simply began begging for more tools. Losing his patience, Scott told him in the strongest terms that he was tired of cleaning up his Trojans every morning. Go away, he told the cracker. Now. Do not return. I'm not playing with you. To Scott's pleasure, Infomaster vanished.

Two weeks later, though, he was back.

Scott had never seen anything like this kind of persistence. Irate, he followed the intrusion back to MIT, entering the system there with Infomaster's own back door and observing what he did. The first thing he discovered was that the cracker had thoroughly sliced up the university networks. The second was that the intrusion was not limited to MIT, Santa Fe, and the small group of networks Infomaster had jumped to from Santa Fe. The cracker was breaking into networks all over the place—dozens, scores, maybe even hundreds, of them. And the third thing that Scott learned was that Infomaster entered MIT from some place in Portland, Oregon.

Who is this guy? he wondered. How did he happen to pick on me? And how am I going to get rid of him?

Almost a year earlier, in the spring of 1991, Patrick Humphreys, Steve Singer's high school buddy, had come by with some college friends. Wanting to show off his new access to the Portland State computer system, Patrick had borrowed Matt's computer and logged on remotely. Matt had quietly watched, as he often did. Peering over Patrick's shoulder when he typed his password, Matt memorized the keystrokes. When Steve and his friends left, Matt had logged on himself. Everything afterward stemmed from that single lapse.

The problem was, he had not known enough to take advantage of his opportunities. He learned so slowly! Every triumph was accompanied by a catastrophe. He broke into systems all over the world, but was followed by the sysadmins at Portland State. He got into NASA, but didn't know about parallelization. He got help from Grok, but lost his friendship. He installed accounts at MIT, but couldn't afford to call them. He stole Solaris, but couldn't figure out where to keep it. He war-dialed for calling card numbers, but his brother put on the telephone accountant. He formed a partnership with Jsz, but couldn't keep in contact. He had no choice but to come back to Portland State, but they kept spotting him. By the end of 1991 he was in danger of losing access altogether.

Then had come a lucky break. For the second time, Patrick Humphreys gave him an entree into Portland State.

Bragging about belonging to Janaka's Computer Action Team, Patrick had visited Matt's brother, Steve, at the beginning of the new year. The sysadmins had given CAT members their own Unix boxes to supervise. Meanwhile, Steve couldn't afford community college—that was Matt's view of the proceedings. Showing off, Patrick borrowed Matt's computer and logged on. This time he made sure that Matt couldn't watch him type in the password.

When Patrick and Steve were ready to leave, Matt asked if he could use the Portland State system.

Sure, Patrick said. Loftily self-assured, he had switched to an account with limited access, certain that it provided no opportunities to someone like Matt.

Within fifteen minutes of his departure, Matt had proved him wrong. He broke root and roamed the Portland State network until he found a machine that was used rarely; Trojans were less likely to be noticed there, he knew. Determined not to squander his opportunities, Phantomd installed a Trojan and went on a tear.

All he needed was persistence and a little luck. Matt was nothing if not persistent; every so often he was lucky, too. "Lucky" was the word to describe what happened when he returned to Portland State: he ran straight into the elusive Grok, who, in a good mood, seemed willing to forget his past exasperation. He showed Phantomd his back doors—superb hacks that the Portland State sysadmins would never spot. Which was lucky, because Phantomd had messed up the Trojan again—he'd forgotten to capitalize the "p" in "Password," and the sysadmins quickly noticed it. But the mistake didn't matter, because he was able to use Grok's back doors. Sometimes the Portland State sysadmins could follow him, but they couldn't stop him from getting inside. He was reborn.

Reborn, he needed to be rechristened. He had decided to rename himself Infomaster—Info, for short. A new name for a new hacker.

. . .

*Ever since Matt Singer had moved in with his father, Rose Singer hadn't been sure it was a good idea. On the one hand, he hardly ever came out of his room there; on the other, he didn't seem to be as depressed. He was still trying to make progress; he was still struggling to make his mark.*

*Struggling had been his whole life. As a baby Matt suffered massive asthma attacks, long, seizurelike spells in which his face would turn blue with the strain of breathing. Rose placed the choking, gasping child on her lap, massaging his skin to keep the blood flowing. She could feel his chest barreling out in the shape assumed by asthmatics; losing oxygen at the extremities, his hands and feet gnarled.*

*There was difficulty for Matt in everything he did, though the doctors never agreed on its cause. Mild retardation, emotional disturbance, severe learning disabilities, personality disorder—Rose had heard them all. She herself leaned toward one doctor's guess that it was lack of oxygen to the brain during the asthma attacks. Whatever his defect, it took Matt years to learn to tie his shoes, remember his address and phone number, prepare food for himself. At fifteen he could barely write his name. His eye-hand coordination never went to normal—tightening screws would always be a difficult operation. A driver's license was out of the question.*

*Rose and her husband, a sometime electronics repairman, had split up when Matt was two. For a while the boys went back and forth between Dad in California and Mom in Oregon, but they ended up spending most of the time with Mom. Both had remarried, Rose to a Vietnam veteran who woke up often with screaming nightmares. He couldn't keep a job and the family sank into penury, losing a house, going on welfare, staying in a shelter for a while. Eventually Rose's husband lost the battle against dementia and they moved back to Portland to start over.*

*Rose always said that Matt had taught her patience and good humor in the face of adversity. But even he had had his dark times. Two years ago, he refused to attend his special school—in fact, she'd been almost unable to get him out of the bedroom. The school sent a tutor, but Matt refused to come downstairs. He got angry when his mother tried to get him outdoors in the sunshine. The social workers from the Child Welfare Department said not to let Matt bully her. If he became threatening, she should call the police. One day, she tried to put her foot down about him spending too much time on the computer, and Matt flew at her—scrawny as he was, he was able to knock her off balance, and she fell. She called Child Welfare. To her horror, Matt was committed to the Oregon State Hospital, in McMinnville.*

*The doctors at the OSH mental-health unit promptly unveiled a new diagnosis: Matt was schizophrenic. They engaged him in a war of wills, which was a mistake, because the flip-side of Matt's incredible patience was incredible stubbornness. They wouldn't give him the Doritos and other salty snacks that were major constituents of his diet, so he refused to eat. They put him in solitary confinement. Angrily refusing to speak, he sat for hours in utter silence and immobility. Sometimes she drove down for her weekly visit—that was all they allowed—and she found that he'd been put on restriction and she couldn't see him. Once she got so angry herself that she kicked some of the furniture off the porch on her way out.*

*After a year, he was released to a United Way halfway house called the Janus Project near all the hospitals in northwest Portland. The Janus Project had a three-story house with gingerbready trim on the outside and posters of the Earth on the inside. Games of Monopoly at night, jobs at the Goodwill and the Veterans Administration by day. They had him making little things, which his poor eye-hand coordination turned into a species of torture.*

*When he was finally allowed to go back home, Matt couldn't hold a job; he was deemed sufficiently disabled by the government to receive Social Security payments. But at least he was out, thought Rose. Maybe moving to his father's house would herald a new beginning. She hoped he wasn't spending all his time on the computer in his room.*

# 9

## THE DOT ZONE

Basically, once you're in a network, you're in. It only takes one mistake, and then you've let them in, and then you're more or less dead, because if they know what they're doing you'll never get them out.

**—GENE SPAFFORD, DIRECTOR, COMPUTER OPERATIONS, AUDIT, AND SECURITY TECHNOLOGY (COAST) PROJECT, PURDUE UNIVERSITY**

Portland
Winter 1992

In mid-January Special Agent E. Brent Rasmussen of the Portland branch office was telephoned by a gentleman with an Indian name who claimed that someone was breaking into government computers—NASA, NIH, Los Alamos. I've called you guys on this more than once before, the man said. And you didn't do anything, and now the problem's much worse.

Rasmussen wasn't surprised by the man's charges. During his twenty years in the FBI, he had received hundreds of such calls. Although the tips came from honest taxpayers who sincerely believed in the value of their information, most of the reports concerned crimes that were not under FBI jurisdiction, or crimes that had not actually happened, or crimes that were not crimes even if they had happened. When the phone rang, agents picked up the receiver with the expectation, almost always borne out, of wasting time. Not being endowed with second sight, they sometimes guessed wrong.

In any case, this time Rasmussen found the story disturbing enough to think of beginning an investigation. He approached Gary Gipson, who supervised white-collar crime for the Portland office. What do you think about going after a hacker? Rasmussen asked.

Say what? Gipson asked. He was a burly, outgoing man with a walrus mustache.

We got a hacker. He's apparently inside several government systems.

What do I know about hackers? Gipson said. Call the U.S. attorney.

This response was predictable; Gipson, who respected Rasmussen's experience, rarely interfered. The U.S. attorney was another matter. Opening an investigation without first determining whether the local U.S. attorney would prosecute the responsible party was like buying a car without first getting a driver's license. High caseloads, legal technicalities, policy decisions, fear of losing —prosecutors had many reasons for declining a case. Getting a refusal, most FBI agents simply moved on to the next investigation.

When Rasmussen called the U.S. attorney's office in Portland, he was put through to Charles Stucky, the assistant U.S. attorney who was on point that day. After Rasmussen ran through the basic details, Stucky told Rasmussen that he needed a second opinion. A few minutes later he called back and said that they would give this one a pass.

Rasmussen was not disposed to listen. In the 1980s, he had ignored the demurrals of local U.S. attorneys and initiated a five-year investigation in Alaska that led to sixteen convictions against the most powerful political figures in the state. It was one of the biggest corruption cases in the annals of the Federal Bureau of Investigation. Given this track record, Rasmussen had no intention of letting himself be stopped by what he viewed as prosecutorial laziness. He told Stucky that the case sounded worthwhile.

Aren't these hackers mostly kids having fun? Stucky asked. What damage did this guy do, exactly?

What if he's a spy? asked Rasmussen.

Stucky thought this was amusing. A *spy*?

Rasmussen waited.

If you really want to discuss this, fine, but I don't think . . .

I'll be right over, Rasmussen said.

When Rasmussen told Gipson he was heading over to the U.S. attorney's office to twist some arms, Gipson said he'd tag along. Rasmussen was a good man, a real pro, but he could also be short on patience.

They decided to walk the twelve blocks to the U.S. attorney's office. Typical for Portland, the air was full of heavy mist. The streets were narrow and in this part of town lined with glassy new construction and bright storefronts with goods for the tourist trade. Some of the buildings had transparent tubes encasing walkways that crossed the street thirty feet above the ground. To Rasmussen, a newcomer to the city, Portland seemed torn between wanting to be part of the outdoors and wanting to be sheltered from it.

The U.S. attorney's office was located—appropriately, as far as Rasmussen was concerned—at the edge of a yuppie indoor mall. The stately offices upstairs could have belonged to any high-priced law firm, except that the heavy hardwood doors bore keypad-coded entry locks and small, tastefully engraved plates that read "Restricted Access."

Rasmussen and Gipson met in a conference room with Assistant U.S. Attorney Stucky and another AUSA, Barry Schaldall. Stucky and Schaldall took turns asking questions: Had the hacker stolen anything? Did he transfer any money to himself? Did he get hold of classified information? Did he do any permanent damage to a computer system? Did he threaten anyone?

No, Rasmussen said. The salient points, to his mind, were: 1) the hacker had broken federal law; 2) he had entered systems that contained scientific research, government databases, and maybe military information; and 3) he was troubling people across the nation. Most important, by spending twelve hours a day on the machine he acted like someone looking for something—maybe something to sell to enemies of the United States.

The AUSAs held their ground. In the absence of tangible theft, the office couldn't spend time on the case. They had too many real criminals to prosecute.

On the way back, Gipson offered to take the case all the way to the U.S. attorney, Charles Turner. But Gipson and Rasmussen both knew that Turner wasn't likely to countermand his AUSAs. Rasmussen went back to his desk to mull it all over. He hadn't been enthusiastic about taking on a hacker case—the crime was as incomprehensible as the technology used to commit it. Nor did he want to tell Portland State that, once again, the FBI would sit on its hands.

Afterward, Gipson dropped a sheet of paper on Rasmussen's desk: a routine message from headquarters. One item, circled in pen, described the new National Computer Crime Squad, which was ready to support field offices dealing with hacker cases. The Justice Department had set up a computer-crime office, too.

Thought you might find this interesting, was Gipson's comment.

## Tysons Corner, Virginia

The nearest Jim Settle had ever come to taking a bullet was when he and his partner had knocked politely at the door of a house belonging to a deserter's father. The knock was answered by Daddy himself, who charged out of the house with a deranged look in his eye and an automatic in his hand. Without waiting to think, Settle's partner reached out and plucked the gun from the man's fingers; if he hadn't, there might have been blood all over the stoop.

That was one reason Settle was careful about choosing the people with whom he worked.

By Bureau standards, the National Computer Crime Squad was like the FBI's Dirty Dozen: women like Barnett, African-Americans like Burns, and eccentrics like Kolouch and Kintigh. But

Settle was proud of the group, which he had installed on a floor of the Washington Metro field office in Tysons Corner, Virginia.

Settle and his boss, Bill Esposito, had convinced the top brass to give them the go-ahead the previous September. Even as Barnett, Kolouch, and Burns slogged through the unwieldy Masters of Deception wiretap in New York City, Settle was planning to make them the nucleus of a computer-crime team. Because FBI headquarters, in a decades-old tradition, rarely handled individual cases, the squad had to be based in Washington Metro. Unfortunately, Bob Bryant, Washington Metro's special agent in charge, opposed the plan.

In an agency that esteemed the men of action who fought criminals in the street, SACs were given leave to run their branch offices like fiefdoms. Esposito negotiated with Bryant for months. Only in February of 1992 did Esposito summon Settle to his office. You've got the squad, he said. But it's on a ninety-day trial basis. At the end of the trial, Bryant can throw the squad out if he wants.

Remembering how difficult it had been to pull together the telephone outage task force, Settle asked how long he had to prepare the squad.

It starts Monday, Esposito said.

There was no shortage of business. Across the nation, Settle learned, sysadmins had been begging the FBI to do something about electronic crime. As calls came in, squad members took turns answering the phones. In theory, the computer team was a supporting player; each investigation was supposed to be directed by the field office nearest the hackers, if their location was known. In practice, Settle's group ran the cases. The field offices avoided hackers—assuming, with justification, that chasing them was injurious to agents' careers. Indeed, when the special agent in charge of a big eastern office visited the squad office, he proclaimed his disgust at the sight of FBI agents pounding on keyboards. Boy, he said loudly, if there's anything I hate, it's seeing a bunch of agents at their desks.

Most of the calls came from sysadmins who had observed hackers knocking on their doors—that is, trying unsuccessfully to break in. Successful penetrations were rarely observed. When they were, the squad encouraged victims not to close the hole through which the hacker entered. As Settle explained it, any hackers clever enough to crawl into a system one way can find nine other entrances if they need to. Closing the door wipes out a chance to monitor them long enough to see whether they are dangerous.

But the sysadmins didn't want to wait. They wanted the FBI to step in instantly, wiretap the hackers, and summarily arrest them. The funny thing was that half the time this group of Internet denizens wanted government out of everything, because Uncle Sam would supposedly trample their civil liberties. But when they were hit by hackers, they wanted instant action, no matter how unconstitutional.

Frustratingly, Settle knew that he wasn't hearing about the worst incidents, because companies and organizations didn't want to admit their vulnerability. The victims called CERT for help, but the agency's charter forbade it from passing on information to anyone, including the FBI. Settle asked CERT to push the victims to contact the FBI, but the offer was never taken up. Even federal agencies reported problems to CERT that they hid from the FBI. The irascible Kolouch once lost his temper with CERT chief Edward DeHart: We *own* those guys, he growled. They're part of the government! They have an obligation to report to us. DeHart didn't argue. But he didn't pass on information, either.

Mindful of the ninety-day trial status of the squad, Settle decided to purchase some insurance: good PR. The day he was installed in the Washington Metro office, he began getting the word out about the National Computer Crime Squad. He called FBI field offices, telephone companies, computer-security agencies, and sysadmins at government and university networks. He followed up with written bulletins, and offered himself as a speaker at computer conferences. Most important, he let in the press.

When CNN asked to send a camera crew, Settle set up an interview. This was a departure—FBI agents are known for loathing journalists. Indeed, no media had come into the Metro field office for more than twenty years. Settle told team members to look smart, to think of their answers beforehand, and to get across the dual message that hackers were a serious threat and that the FBI was now on the case. When Public Affairs announced that CNN was in the lobby, Settle emerged from his office to give his group the heads-up. The area was strangely quiet. No one was at the coffee counter; no one was talking in the hall. One after another, Settle opened the door to every office. All were vacant. The entire squad had fled. Fearing that the exposure would ruin future undercover operations, Kolouch had stampeded them. Settle ran cursing into the main offices and ordered a group of young agents to pose as members of the computer-crime squad for the cameras; instead of talking with reporters, they were to refer all questions to him. The encounter, mercifully, passed without incident.

The squad made up for it when Settle learned that something solid had popped out of the haze of hacker incidents. A single individual—apparently a single individual, although he or she worked with others—had been running through networks across the nation. Kintigh had received extensive reports from the field office in Portland, where the incident seemed to be centered; NASA and NIH were involved. Most worrisome, the hacker was into Lawrence Livermore and Los Alamos. He or she seemed to have a special affinity for supercomputers, said Kintigh, who had taken the case.

Settle asked if anyone knew what the hacker wanted.

Nobody knows, Kintigh said. Apparently these people in Portland had records of the hacker that went back a year. He simply steamrollered through networks, grabbing root on one box after another, then taking over the next one. Sometimes he went at it for twenty hours straight.

The description corresponded to one of Settle's fears. Criminals could spend months or years trolling through the global network for systems worth breaking into. After accumulating a list of targets, the hackers would commit a rash of crimes in two minutes and leave the country. If they were thieves, they would electronically funnel the stolen money overseas; if they were terrorists, they would be content to watch the chaos and destruction on CNN from their hotel room abroad.

Of course, this intruder might simply be a thrill-seeking adolescent with a modem. But that was one of the curses of the Net—you never knew who was at the keyboard. Law enforcement had to assume the worst, because the consequences of ignoring a criminal could be awful. Even if the hacking were being committed by a teenager, the teenager could be helping criminals. Without understanding what he was doing, he could be amassing sites for them to hit. It would be far from the first time that adolescents had gotten themselves into deep water.

The whole business might be simpler than that, Kintigh said. He fixed Settle with a rare smile. At the rate this guy is accumulating sites, he could be trying to take over the entire Internet.

Washington, D.C.
March 1992

All through law school at the University of Chicago, Joshua Silverman had envisioned himself facing down rapists and murderers in the wood-paneled courtrooms of the federal justice system. But such jobs were hard to find, thanks to the increasing conservatism of his generation, which had made prosecution fashionable, and the burgeoning deficit, which had made government hiring freezes equally fashionable. But after graduation Silverman had been accepted into an honors program that installed him for three years in Washington in the General Litigation and Legal Advice Section of the Department of Justice's Criminal Division. Despite the section's name, it took on little litigation. Mostly it set policy and provided legal expertise for U.S. attorneys around the country, whose offices performed the actual prosecutions. To Silverman, the chief attraction of the program was that afterward he had a good shot at a post outside the Beltway as an assistant U.S. attorney. In addition, the second six months of the program entailed a tour of duty as a sort of apprentice AUSA at a U.S. attorney's office nearby.

Silverman's six-month tour took him to the misdemeanor court in Washington, D.C. (Like all other crimes in the nation's capital, misdemeanors were federal business.) It had been the most grueling work of his life. He carried an average load of 225 cases, and rarely had time to do more than get dressed, run to court, flip through the documents pertaining to the next hearing or trial, stumble through the court proceedings, repeat the last two steps another dozen times, hole up in his office for the evening trying to crank through some small percentage of the next day's paperwork, stagger home, and pass out.

He had hung his first case, a young thug picked up on a firearm rap. His second was a "dropsy"—the suspect spotted a cop and ran, leaving crack tubes in his wake. He'd won that case. After that was a long, blurred parade of prostitutes, junkies, thieves, hustlers, gang-bangers, and barroom brawlers—every form of wreckage that walked on two feet. He loved every minute of it. The long hours, the petty annoyances, the nasty people—he had discovered his life's work.

Returning to the General Litigation Section was a letdown. The sole possibility for further courtroom experience emanated from one Scott Charney, a Justice Department honcho who had taken to Silverman. They were opposites: Silverman was a bachelor, whereas Charney was a married man with children. Silverman was a bit of a young blade, handsome and muscular in the aerobicized '90s way. By contrast, Charney had thinning hair, a scrawny build, and eyeglasses so thick that an image of his entire head was visible through the lenses. Nonetheless, he projected an almost visible aura of toughness; having spent seven years as a prosecutor in the Bronx, he could readily produce war stories of surpassing ghastliness. Despite their personal disparity, the two men had immediately sensed each other's outsized ambition and love of litigation. They also shared the burden of being geeks, at least by law-enforcement standards. Silverman had taken programming in college and been a teaching assistant in a computer lab. Charney's boss had observed him making new directories on his personal computer soon after his arrival in the Criminal Division. Although creating directories—that is, creating repositories for computer files—is a basic housekeeping task on a PC, it nonetheless convinced the section head, a computer neophyte, that Charney was an electronics wizard.

Charney had already taken advantage of Silverman's technical expertise—he was always on the lookout for bright people who might be able to assist him on the increasingly complex cases he was handling. When Silverman came back from his stint in misdemeanor court, the other man welcomed him back with lunch at the new, Deco-ish headquarters of the Justice Department's Criminal Division.

A year before, Assistant Attorney General Robert Mueller had created a computer-crime unit within the Justice Department and put Charney in charge. It was a counterpart to Settle's operation at the FBI. Officially, Charney explained, the Justice Department unit was intended to set policy, direct legislation, and give advice. But most U.S. attorneys' offices were unprepared to prosecute hackers; more than likely, they would be happy to turn cases over to the computer-crime unit. And that would mean actual trials. Some of those cases were bound to be big cases, career-making cases.

So what do you want to do for the next two years? asked Charney. Push papers and read about law or try cases and *make* law?

Silverman had no problem coming up with the right answer. Which, from Charney's point of view, was good. The reason was that he intended to do more with his new unit than put away bad guys, desirable though that was. Because computer-crime statutes were untested in court, prosecutors were ducking hacker cases. The Justice Department wanted to go all the way with an especially glaring incident. Stringing up a big-time hacker would not only warn a generation of digital vandals that the cops were on the beat, it would create a body of case law that would guide prosecutors for years to come.

There was a case percolating in Oregon that had definite potential. It had made its way into the FBI. Best of all, the local U.S. attorney didn't want to prosecute it, so the job would fall to some young, ambitious person in Washington, D.C.

Grok soon disappeared, maybe because he'd found out that Info had botched the Trojan. Then, suddenly, he showed up again. Info dropped him a talk and they exchanged messages. Something was off, though. Puzzled, Info realized that Grok wasn't Grok, but someone else using his account. When the imposter asked him if he had any new techniques, he recognized who it was: Scott. Scott—Info didn't know his last name—was a recognizable character on #hack, always joining the discussion from Santa Fe. Like Info himself, he had come to Portland State looking for Grok.

If Scott was trying to fool Info into thinking he was someone else, Info would play a trick on him. The next day he followed Scott back to the think tank in Santa Fe.

The visit was fruitful.

It was surprisingly easy to gain admission. Nice.

Some Santa Fe researchers used the same passwords for their accounts at Los Alamos and Lawrence Livermore. Nice.

Another researcher had a friend who had e-mailed his password at NASA to Santa Fe, asking the researcher to check his electronic mailbox while he was on vacation. Nice again.

Scott turned out to have two hundred megabytes or so of cracker tools. Very nice.

Frustratingly, the tools were encrypted, but Info figured that if he came back often enough, the opportunity for decoding them would come along. All he had to do was be patient. Not that he was devoting much time to the quest—he had too many other things going. Finally equipped with good Internet access through Portland State, he stayed on-line ten, twelve, fourteen hours a day, grabbing root on one system after another.

## Santa Fe

No matter how many times Scott Yelich warned that he was watching Infomaster's every move, the cracker kept returning. As a practical matter, it was impossible to keep him out, because the researchers would have rebelled at the measures required to tighten security. Even if they would have accepted them, the Institute did not have the money for, say, a firewall. On the other hand, the cracker seemed not to have malign intentions. He simply kept knocking until he got in, an unstoppable visitor from the dot zone on the other side of the cathode-ray screen, and then he checked Scott's archive for new cracker tools.

To amuse himself, Scott played with Infomaster's head. Sometimes he broke into Infomaster's sessions and corrected his spelling errors. At another point, he copied some of his tools into a new directory, renamed all the files, and reencrypted them. Then he sat back and watched Infomaster excitedly copy the "new" programs. Then he did it again. And again. After a few weeks of intermittent effort, Scott had given him four or five copies of the same things. Infomaster never caught on.

What an idiot, Scott thought.

On the other hand, being an idiot evidently wasn't a handicap when it came to breaking into systems. Security at most sites was so bad that Infomaster always got in, despite his lame skills. With blind tenacity, he had taken over an amazing number of systems. The situation teetered between the ridiculous and the alarming. Reluctantly Scott found himself impelled to action. He notified CERT about the problem, although he was sure nothing would come of it. He looked up the affected networks in a special Internet database called "Whois"—maintained by the military as a legacy of the ARPANET, it identified networks from their Internet addresses and provided a contact name and telephone number. He called sysadmins at Purdue, Reed, Rutgers, Stanford, the University of Hawaii, and the University of Texas and told them to check for Trojaned log-ins. To his annoyance, the sysadmins kept asking him who he was and how he knew. Obviously they believed he himself was the cracker. How else would he know about an attack on their networks that the sysadmins didn't know about?

Much of the time the sysadmins did nothing, and sometimes less than nothing. After Scott warned Hawaii about the break-in, he was exasperated to find that Info not only remained able to roam the network, but the sysadmins' e-mail—which Info was reading—was full of dark speculation about the identity of the mysterious "Scott." When the Whois contact at the University of Texas—a network that Infomaster was breaking into in a particularly egregious fashion—proved to be a receptionist who hadn't heard of the word "Internet," Scott used the cracker's back door, shut down the box, and left an electronic message on its drive explaining who he was and why he'd performed this drastic action. He called MIT late one Sunday night and informed a sysadmin there that they had cracker problems. When the sysadmin—a student, perhaps—couldn't find Infomaster's traces, the exasperated Scott assured him that the intrusion was real. You have Trojans all over your network, he said. Indeed, he had collected the cracker's log-in Trojans, eight or nine of them, each for a different flavor of Unix.

Sometimes he slipped through one of the cracker's back doors into his lair in Portland State. On an early visit, he found Infomaster on their machines talking to Grok, whom Scott had recently encountered on places like #hack. In Scott's estimation, Grok was one of the few crackers who truly understood the Internet. They'd hit it off, and Scott had even chased after him into half a dozen places he could no longer remember. Now here he was talking to Infomaster— an unlikely pairing in an unlikely place. When Scott showed up, Grok told Infomaster to stay away from Santa Fe. It did no good. The cracker kept using Scott's network as a basis for forays against Los Alamos, Lawrence Livermore, and NASA. Scott returned to Portland State, impersonating Grok, and harassed Info. That, too, did no good. Hoping to eject the cracker from the Internet altogether, Scott called the sysadmins at Portland State—yes, they, too, were watching him. No, they couldn't get rid of him, either.

Like most hackers, Scott was dismissive of government. But he was distressed by his inability to stop the attack and worried about what kind of mischief Infomaster would get into. For the first time in his life, he called the police—or, rather, the Albuquerque office of the FBI. The conversation exceeded his expectations. Internet? The FBI agent was clearly baffled. You say he comes in over the telephone? Over the telephone wires? No, through the Internet —through the computer. So how does he contact you through the computer? He logs in. Does he log in on the phone? No, he does it from his home base in Oregon. So you think he's coming in from a different state? It's a long-distance call? Later he was visited by a

AT LARGE

bewildered FBI agent who sat in Scott's office, blinking at the machinery and dutifully taking notes.

When Scott called the FBI office later to see what the Bureau was doing, he received the distinct impression that nothing was happening whatsoever. Scott had seen the CIAC warning, but afterward the agency subsided into its habitual silence. Nor did he spot any signs of life from CERT. As Info continued his absurd, dangerous, monomaniacal course, the entire federal government seemed to be sitting on its collective thumbs.

San Francisco, California
Spring 1992

Early in Dan Farmer's tenure at CERT, he learned that crackers had attacked an army network. After being shunted from one uncomprehending receptionist to another, he finally reached the sergeant who functioned as the sysadmin. Dan unspooled his preset speech: I'm from CERT, the coordinating center for Internet security problems, and we have information that your network has been compromised.

The sergeant said: I appreciate the call but I really don't want to know about it.

It's your network and you can do whatever you want, Dan replied in his soft, courteous tenor. But I'm curious—why don't you want to know?

In my job, the sergeant explained, if I know about a problem, I have to fix it. I'm already swamped and I just don't want to deal with this right now. And then he hung up the phone.

Dan never spoke to the man again.

Although such flat rejections were uncommon, it was an endless battle to convince sysadmins that security was important. ("What do you mean, have I checked for .rhosts files? What's a .rhosts file?") Worse, the good guys silently locked themselves inside CERT's lushly carpeted headquarters, while the bad guys spent all day talking to each other. Because the agency's charter prevented it from revealing information about break-ins, Dan was constantly playing Black Hole—sucking in information and emitting nothing in return. When sysadmins reported problems, he listened sympathetically, wrote a description of the problem, and notified the manufacturer of the computer involved (if it had security staff—some vendors didn't). Then he twiddled his fingers until the manufacturer announced it had fixed the bug (if it did—even with security staff, some vendors ignored the problems). When the patch was ready, CERT issued a bulletin that said certain products had experienced security difficulties, but all was well now, would all the sysadmins who used this particular product please obtain a copy of the revised program? Meanwhile, months would have gone by, during which the crackers would have passed the technique around and happily broken into networks whose sysadmins had never been informed of the problem.

Incredibly, the CERT bulletin often did not end the matter. Although vendors sold many flavors of Unix, the operating system came in two fundamental variants: AT&T Unix, based primarily on the original source code from Bell Labs, and Berkeley Unix, adapted from the revised source code produced at Berkeley. SunOS and Solaris, for instance, were offshoots of Berkeley Unix. The various Berkeley- and AT&T-style operating systems had similar underlying code—sufficiently similar that security flaws in, say, SunOS might easily be relevant to the Berkeley-style Unixes sold by Digital and Hewlett-Packard. Yet when CERT discovered a problem with SunOS, its nondisclosure policy prevented it from talking to other manufacturers. Crackers could thus read the CERT bulletins for problems with one company's software and use them as guides to possible lapses in other companies' software. Maddening!

All in all, Dan had been glad when Sun offered him a job in computer security research.

By the spring of 1992, he had transferred operations to the archipelago of stucco-colored boxes that made up the Sun campus in Mountain View, California. Home base was a one-bedroom apartment in the Haight-Ashbury district of San Francisco that Dan maintained, hacker style, in a state of breathtaking confusion— computer equipment piled in a jumble, boxes spilling their contents thisaway and thataway, louche friends snoozing on the furniture. Finally able to speak with complete freedom, he was involved in busy e-mail discussions of potential security problems with his friends and coworkers.

One of the topics was Sendmail, the ubiquitous program for sending and receiving electronic mail. Sendmail was written by a Berkeley grad student/sysadmin named Eric Allman in the Unix ferment of the late 1970s and given away in good free-software fashion. Having created Sendmail in the days when the Internet was the playground of a few thousand computer scientists and military personnel, Allman paid little attention to security. Unfortunately, the program became Cracker Cornucopia—an endless supply of new holes. Indeed, so many Sendmail holes were known of that hackers joked about setting up a "bug-of-the-month" club for the program.

The circle of security experts Dan knew was especially troubled by a new Sendmail bug. To take advantage of the bug, crackers would send an e-mail message—it didn't matter to whom, as long as they maintained the connection after the message was sent. If they stayed on-line, the crackers would have gained their goal, because—in a programming lapse—Sendmail performed security checks only on a user's *first* message. The program was like a customs inspector who believes that if a traveler's first suitcase contains no drugs or contraband, the traveler can not possibly be a smuggler. As a result, the program would execute no security checks when the crackers transmitted a *second* message—a message that those checks would usually reject.

Instead of being sent to a person, the second message would be sent to an address consisting of a pipe symbol (|), the mysterious vertical character on every computer keyboard. Invented for Unix, the pipe is also used in MS-DOS; in both it has the same function. If a user types "program A | program B," for example, it means "execute program A, then direct its output to program B, which will use it as input." Placed in a Sendmail address, the pipe—in a second programming lapse—instructed the program to use the e-mail message as input.

The body of the cracker's second message would consist of a sequence of Unix commands that instructed the computer to install a passwordless root account. Ordinarily, writing such commands in e-mail has no effect, just as writing the instructions for making a model airplane doesn't cause the model to be constructed. But when the pipe directed Sendmail to send the commands as input to the computer, the computer docilely executed them, installing the account. Then the intruders were able to log on freely.*

Because sending and receiving electronic mail is a basic network service, Sendmail runs on almost every system on the Internet. Even networks with firewalls—the special filtering computers that Scott Yelich wanted for his Institute—let through electronic mail. As a consequence, security problems in Sendmail compromise the entire Internet.

Worse, the hole was incredibly easy to exploit—type a pipe and some commands, and Sendmail would be forced to execute those commands. This exposed networks to a huge range of potential threats, for Sendmail, in the automatic fashion of computers, would execute any commands it was given. And the flaw was hard to fix, because the program needed to be able to execute commands.† Working around the bug would require Allman—and manufacturers who had adopted versions of his program—to rewrite Sendmail completely.

Meanwhile, security experts who knew about the problem faced a difficult choice. Crackers apparently had not discovered the bug. If the white hats publicized its existence, they would alert the black hats to a powerful security problem with no remedy. But if

---

* Actually, it was a touch more complicated than that. From Sendmail, the message went to a little program that stripped off the e-mail "headers"—the address and other routing information—and then piped the results to a "shell" program, which executed the commands. Despite these complexities, though, the point is simple: crackers could e-mail themselves root access.

† Later, when the bug was widely publicized, some sysadmins suggested having Sendmail simply reject addresses with the pipe. Unfortunately, many non-English-speaking users have e-mail addresses with a "|," which represents non-English characters like "ä." As a result, rejecting all pipes would end up bouncing legitimate e-mail.

they did not ring the alarm bell, the good guys would be helpless when the bad guys discovered the bug, which they inevitably would. Massive attacks would come out of the blue, and the sysadmins would once again be furious that they had been left out of the loop.

Hesitantly—this being discussed, of course, via e-mail—Dan and his friends decided to say nothing about the problem until it was fixed. Of course, that presumed that the security experts could keep it secret, which was much less likely than they hoped. Since Dan had come to Sun, for example, his e-mail at corp.sun.com had been inspected by the cracker Jsz.

Jsz had been invited into Sun by Phantomd and never left. Phantomd himself hadn't stuck around, because he was more interested in conquering new places than exploiting old victims. But Jsz found Sun e-mail fascinating. Not that he could encompass it all— Dan Farmer alone received more e-mail than either he or Jsz could handle. He sent Dan's e-mail to Phantomd, but he, too, was too busy to read it. Phantomd planned to go through it later, when he had time.

As it happened, some of the e-mail Phantomd and Jsz weren't reading came from Tsutomu Shimomura, a security expert at the San Diego Supercomputer Center and one of Dan's closest friends. In several messages about the Sendmail hole Shimomura gave what amounted to detailed cookbook instructions for grabbing root at almost every system on the Internet. Throughout the spring and summer of 1992, these messages sat on a hard disk, waiting for Phantomd to get around to them.

# 10

# @ LARGE

Despite a plethora of fine books on the subject, Unix security remains an elusive goal at best.

**—SIMSON GARFINKEL, DANIEL WEISE, AND STEVEN STRASSMANN,**
**PREFACE TO *THE UNIX-HATERS' HANDBOOK***

Unix and C [the language Unix is written in] are the ultimate computer viruses.

**—RICHARD P. GABRIEL, CONSULTING PROFESSOR OF COMPUTER SCIENCE,**
**STANFORD UNIVERSITY, *AI EXPERT*, JUNE 1991**

Cambridge
March 1992

Hey, Nick? This is Jeanne Darling. Can you come up here? The machine's not working. I log in and nothing happens.

Nick Papadakis, one of the two sysadmins at the MIT Laboratory for Computer Science, received such requests for aid every day. Because lab staffers understood computers, the requests were rarely foolish. In full confidence that an actual problem had surfaced, Nick padded in his sandals to Jeanne's fourth-floor office. It was 9:30, maybe 10:00, in the morning, early by his standards; yawn-suppressing time.

Jeanne was the assistant for Professor William Gifford. Nick materialized in her doorway, a tall, twenty-nine-year-old Skinny with a loose T-shirt, a ponytail that dangled to his scapulae, and the sort of beard that outside academia would be described as "scraggly." Producing an amiable greeting, Nick took a seat and began working on her machine. Or, rather, *only* on her machine. It couldn't reach the rest of the network.

The box on Jeanne's desk was not communicating with the other boxes because it was not getting Kerberos tickets. Kerberos was an MIT security tool that awarded users a "ticket"—a special, onetime authentication that simultaneously identifies the user to the computer and encrypts their account name and password. When Jeanne logged into her computer, it encrypted her password and sent it to a special Kerberos server that decoded the password, verified it, and then issued a ticket that other machines could use to check the user's identity. Here, though, the system had broken down. Jeanne's machine was not getting its tickets, which meant that it couldn't contact any other machine.

Is the log-in program broken? Jeanne asked.

Broken is not the word for it, he told Jeanne. The log-in program has been replaced.

Crackers again. Annoying. MIT sometimes seemed to be Cracker Nirvana, the destination that all aspired to reach. Three or four of them tried to get into Nick's machine every night—who knew why, because nothing on it was worth stealing. If they read his e-mail, for instance, they would have learned much more than they wanted to learn about juggling. Nick devoted much of his spare time to juggling and in his office kept several torches of the kind usually tossed about while afire.

After reloading the log-in program, Nick returned to his office, sat before his monitor, and contemplated his options. He didn't want to waste mental energy thinking about this cracker for another second. But this guy wouldn't have put in his Trojan unless he intended to return. In addition, if he had installed Trojans on one box, he had probably done other things to other boxes, suggesting that

Nick would have further problems. There was no help for it, he concluded. He would have to paddle through the university's networks, looking for the intruder's spoor.

At first glance, the quest was hopeless: MIT was the original electronic megalopolis. The Laboratory for Computer Science alone had three hundred machines—more than two per staff member—and that figure did not include the Artificial Intelligence Laboratory upstairs. Thousands more stippled the offices, hallways, and laboratories of the main campus, home of such computer-intensive neighborhoods as the renowned Media Lab, with its Things That Think, Holography Laboratory, and Opera of the Future projects. Hunting for individual footprints on the floor of this digital Grand Central Terminal was not a task Nick relished.

Happily, by choosing Jeanne's machine the intruder had somewhat lightened the load. As a rule, she connected at regular times to a small number of other computers. Her logs could be searched without undue effort for unusual activity. Indeed, Nick soon discovered a series of hookups between Jeanne's machine and Terminus, a dial-up server on the second floor. The intruder had jumped to Jeanne's computer from Terminus.

Nick was not surprised to see Terminus. In a nod to the old MIT hacker tradition of free access, Terminus was open to the world. Anyone could dial into it from his home and launch himself on the Internet—something that had cost Nick and his fellow sysadmin, Mike Patton, many hit points over the past.* Other sysadmins constantly complained about crackers' taking advantage of the open access at Terminus. To Nick, the problem wasn't Terminus, the problem was the lack of security in the targeted machines. Besides, if MIT dumped the crackers off Terminus, they'd just go somewhere else. At least this way you knew where they were.

Unlike Jeanne's machine, Terminus was used by many people

---

* "Hit points" is terminology from the fantasy adventure games popular among hackers. Characters in these games typically can absorb a given number of hit points before dying.

to contact many computers—so many that Nick shrank from the prospect of trudging through its logs. Instead, he decided to wait for the cracker's return. Returning to his regular work, he instructed his computer to run Finger on Terminus periodically. Finger, a basic element in the Unix tool kit, reports who is connected to a particular computer. Nick asked Finger to identify every account going from Terminus to other machines at MIT.

The approach was still indirect, but after a while it produced results: someone on Terminus was connecting repeatedly to a box with the Internet address of mit2e.mit.edu. The address identified a SPARCstation—a common Sun machine—on the main campus that belonged to a professor of electrical engineering named Stuart Madnick. An unassuming hacker with glasses of the classic Coke-bottle variety, Madnick had literally written the book on Unix, a hefty volume that was the bible for a generation of Unix fanatics.

Not wanting to invade Madnick's private machine, Nick called the assistant sysadmin responsible for mit2e.mit.edu. The sysadmin reported that Madnick almost never used the workstation, which was too small for his research. It was simply taking up space in his office. Indeed, he used it so rarely that, evidently afraid of forgetting his password, he had chosen as his username Smadnick. Nick asked the sysadmin to inspect the machine's hard drive for evidence of malfeasance.

The evidence wasn't hard to find. On the drive was a directory called "tools" with hundreds of files, many of them encrypted. It was a storehouse of cracker tools, from common programs like Crack to routines that Nick had never seen before. Another directory contained a dozen password files, including one called think.com.pas. Think.com was the electronic address for Thinking Machines, the supercomputer company down the street from the Laboratory for Computer Science. The logs for mit2e.mit.edu showed dozens of connections to a machine named ernie.think.com.

Nick telephoned a sysadmin at think.com and asked if, by any chance, the company owned a box named Ernie. Yes, was the reply. The company SPARCstations were named after *Sesame Street* characters. Why do you want to know? Nick asked whether Ernie had a directory full of password files. Why, yes, was the surprised reply. A minute later, the sysadmin reported that someone had been running Crack on Ernie for months. Not only that, the box had a lot of Solaris source code—a hundred megabytes or more.

Nick was rapidly revising his picture of the incident, which was bigger than he had imagined. The question was whether it was serious.

The answer depended on what one thought about Internet security. On the whole, Nick believed that "Internet security" was an oxymoron. The Internet was based on Unix, and Unix, in Nick's humble opinion, was a crock, a kludge, a huge cluster of misfeatures, a blight upon the digisphere. To be sure, the operating system had been a major accomplishment when it was invented, but that was back in 1969, and we don't drive our 1969 Ford Falcons anymore, now do we? So why did the global computer infrastructure rest on software thrown together at Bell Labs when the Beatles were still together? The idea of an operating system as a collection of single-purpose tools had been clever back then, but people had been adding tools for a quarter of a century, and Unix had turned into a morass of illogically interwoven software that nobody understood. It had become this hideous irreparable glob of bugs, a veritable Swamp Thing of fused-together digital crud, that was just flat-out impossible to keep secure, and would never be secure— never!—no matter what the Unixoids said. As long as Unix reigned, the only way to keep a network safe was to avoid the Internet entirely.

One answer to the question of how to treat incidents like this one was to ignore them as the utterly predictable consequences of living with Unix. On the other hand, he was supposed to maintain the network even though it was based on this idiotic operating system. Like a cardiologist faced with patients who smoked and gobbled steaks, he couldn't ignore the resultant ailments. Instead, he decided to consult the rest of the administrative team at the Laboratory for Computer Science.

Nick's office adjoined that of Mike Patton, a long-haired Bulky who was the network manager. All along, Nick had kept him informed of his progress. Now others came into the picture, including Jeremy Brown, a student sysadmin, and a hanger-on universally known by his log-in of Mycroft, which derived from the name of a helpful computer in the science-fiction novel *The Moon Is a Harsh Mistress*. Although Mike and Jeremy were soft-spoken, they were exuberantly extroverted compared to the pale, almost violently shy Mycroft, whose aversion to social situations was remarkable even by the lofty standards of computer hackers.

Headquarters for what Jeremy called the Cracker-Bashing Squad was a set of carrels, each with a workstation, lined up in the hallway across from Nick's office. Beyond the carrels was a glass wall that provided a view of the brightly lighted, air-conditioned space in which the lab kept its bigger machines. Twenty-four hours a day the disk drives and fans hummed away, which meant that the second-floor hallway with its inviting carrels was the scene of a constant floating conversation among the sysadmins, their under-graduate assistants, and the inevitable hackish fellow travelers, who had tumbled into the gravitational well created by massive computing power.

Examining his own logs, Mike Patton ascertained that the in-truder had jumped from mit2e.mit.edu to the machine that hosted the building's e-mail, logging on as one of Nick's friends. Indeed, he had also logged on as Nick—and as Mike and Jeremy, too. Mycroft's account alone had not been compromised. If the sysadmins' ac-counts were broken, they couldn't discuss the intrusion by e-mail, the hacker's natural means of expression. They had recourse to an old-fashioned whiteboard, which was soon filled with the names of stolen accounts and busted machines.

Examining Terminus, they tried to find the cracker in the tan-gle of incoming and outgoing connections on this extraordinarily active machine. It was Mycroft, long hair tumbling over his moonlike face, who announced in his inaudible way that it was hard to pick out the cracker because he was on *all the time*. Eight hours a day, seven days a week, the cracker was using Terminus. Mycroft, who had fingered the connection, had a question. Anyone ever hear of pdx.edu? Some place called Portland State University?

By March 26, a few days into the search, they had enough data to write up a summary. The memo was signed by everyone except Mycroft, who was leery of setting his name to paper:

Methods Used by Crackers on LCS Machines
The Cracker-Bashing Squad:
Mike Patton, Nick Papadakis, Greg Troxel,
Tim Shepard, Steve Wadlow, Mike Bauer

If you know of any cracking-related items not on this list, please report them to Mike Bauer, Nick Papadakis, or Mike Patton, and they'll be added.

- Password cracking. Multiple accounts are known to have been broken; see next column for a list . . .
- Versions of Telnet that log all keystrokes. /usr/lib/adb/.ctl-A or /usr/lib/lint/.ctl-E are common directories for these logs . . .
- Accounts added to /etc/passwd [the password file] . . .
- Changes to /bin/login [the log-in program] which allow any username not in /etc/passwd [the password file] to log on as root with no password.
- /bin/login -p allowing root access . . .
- [Creating] .rhosts files and logging in.
- Breaking in via existing .rhosts files.
- Hard-wiring a password into su (visible using strings) to give root access.
- Leaving [programs that grab root] in obscure places. A common one is "/usr/lib/lint/. . .". (Yes, there's a SPC [space] after those three dots.)

Known sources of crackers:
- cs.pdx.edu (Portland [OR] State University)
- uiuc.edu (University of Illinois at Urbana-Champaign)
- terminus
- gnu.ai.mit.edu

The Cracker-Bashing Squad dropped a talk to the culprit. Because they hoped to persuade him to stop, the note was polite. He promptly disconnected. But he hadn't been scared away, because he returned half an hour later. Another attempt at communication. Another disconnection. Annoyed, Nick and Mike pulled the plug on him the next time he appeared. A few minutes later, he returned. They disconnected him again. He showed up again. The man did not take hints, Nick concluded.

Meanwhile, Jeremy and Nick had cobbled together a program that recorded keystrokes. Much like the code written earlier by Janaka Jayawardene in Portland and Scott Yelich in Santa Fe, it displayed keystrokes on the screen, allowing the sysadmins to observe the cracker's behavior in real time. Jeremy, Mike, Mycroft, and Nick attached a SPARCstation called Snark to Terminus, waited for Portland to connect, and sat down for a night of Cracker TV. The output was hard to read, because the program had trouble interpreting backspaces, deletions, and control codes; worse, the cracker was such an awful typist that much of the show consisted of computers rejecting his misspelled commands.

After a night trying to decipher the garbled letters marching across Snark, Mycroft decided to improve the cracker-hunting ambience. An expert programmer, he wrote a snooper that delivered much cleaner text. The next sessions were easier to follow. What Nick saw forced him to revise his picture of the incursion once again. He had known that the intruder was using MIT as a springboard to attack other sites. But he hadn't understood that he was going from those networks to other networks, and from those to still others. He had taken over hundreds of sites, if not thousands—crackery on a scale Nick had never imagined possible.

The MIT group watched in appalled fascination as the intruder knocked on one door after another, trying the same tricks time after time, always in the same order, seizing root on one machine and moving on to the next. Sometimes the chain stretched so far that he lost track of his location, and had to ask the current machine where he was. At other times the signals from his home base to his target bounced through so many stations along the way that the connection was agonizingly slow. But he kept moving, rolling through networks eight hours a day like a drunken steamroller.

The doggedness of the enterprise was like nothing Nick had

ever seen. He found himself momentarily possessed by the mad suspicion that he was tracking not a human being but a robot—a computer that crawled through the global matrix, taking over all it encountered. Then, of course, he realized that this notion was impossible. No computer would misspell so many words.

On the other hand, the sessions were so long that Nick and Mike wondered whether the perpetrator, though not a robot, might be cracking networks as a job. Where would the cracker have to be located if he worked from nine to five, but the results appeared at MIT from one to nine in the morning? The answer was Singapore. Visions of exotic Asian gangs danced in Mike's head. Had he stumbled across crackers from a Chinese triad? Maybe crackers there worked so cheaply they could spend hours randomly breaking and entering on the Net. . . .

Ridiculous, of course. But it was at about this time that Nick and Mike decided to take an unprecedented step: tracing the calls *into* Terminus. That is, rather than tracking what the cracker did while going from Terminus to other computers at MIT, they would try to learn how he got to Terminus in the first place. The decision was not made lightly. Having been a teenager enthralled by computers, Nick was reluctant to call in the heat on someone who might be a distorted younger version of himself. But even if the culprit was an adolescent in his off-line life, in his on-line life he was acting in a way Nick found odd and unsettling.

As a first step, the two men met with Jeff Schiller, the sysadmin for the wider campus network and a familiar figure on campus. A fair-skinned Bulky with a long, thin mustache that he had waxed into twin dental-floss-like coils, Schiller and five assistants maintained network resources for the entire campus—a miracle of sysadmin efficiency, to Nick's way of thinking. He was also a recognized security expert. Schiller operated out of a catastrophic office that was guarded by a five-foot iguana named Iggy. Attached to Iggy's cage was a graph of Iggy's "life states." Enumerated in binary code, the life states went from 0000 (sleep) to 1111 (defecation). Stepping around the knee-high heaps of paper on the floor, Nick and Mike explained their problem.

You guys, Schiller said, are in luck.

MIT, like many large institutions, operated its own telephone company—telco, in the palaver. Terminus had twenty-four incoming lines, all of which could be traced by the campus telco. If Nick and Mike ascertained when the cracker began and ended a session, the telco could identify the long-distance company that had carried it to MIT. Then the MIT telco could contact the long-distance company and ask it to check the incoming trunk lines for the same call. And that, presumably, would lead them one step closer to the cracker.

After a few initial glitches caused by the telco's lack of experience with this complex technical process, the trace worked. It appeared that the cracker always used the same long-distance carrier, which the campus telco asked to continue the trace. After doing so, the phone company revealed that the calls came from a single geographic location. It could be more specific, but only to the constabulary. MIT had its own officers, who were affiliated with the Massachusetts state patrol. The MIT police called the telcos, which revealed that the calls originated in the state of Oregon. The Massachusetts police could do nothing on the West Coast. Amazed at their own actions, Nick Papadakis and Mike Patton contacted the FBI.

Portland
April 1992

It was about one o'clock in the morning, a spring night with exam time nearing. At the Portland Center for Advanced Technology, students were running last-minute design projects on Jove, the big Sun server at the center of the computer-science department network. In the room taken over by the CAT, Patrick Humphreys and the other team members were getting ready to play X-Tank. And Mike Wilson was stalking about, muttering to himself as he tried to put together a paper.

Mike was the burly student sysadmin who had read Patrick Humphreys the riot act last summer. Despite his passion for computers, he was a history major. For several months he had been

Trent Fisher's principal assistant, which in Mike's opinion said much about Trent's broadmindedness—the two men were personal and political opposites. The quiet Trent loathed confrontation, whereas the intense Mike liked to settle conflicts directly. During the Gulf War, Trent attended protests downtown; Mike, by contrast, was an ROTC student who supported the Strategic Defense Initiative. Trent had been upset when Janaka and Paul called the FBI; Mike welcomed the move. But Trent fully trusted Mike to run the computer-science network when he wasn't there.

Suddenly Mike heard shouting. Yanking himself out of the eighteenth century, he raced to the terminal room to discover that Jove had crashed, that the design students were flipping out because of the crash, that it would take hours to reinstall the operating system, that Mike would have to stop working on his paper to help, and that the crash had occurred because an intruder had been running some wacko version of Crack on the damn box.

Later Mike discovered that the program wasn't Crack per se, but an attempt to create a new password program that was unkillable, a program that literally could not be stopped unless the owner typed the magic command. Unfortunately, it sucked up so much processing power that Jove went on tilt. An interesting hack, perhaps, but at the moment all that Mike saw was Jove in casters-up mode, and some cracker had just ruined his evening. *Some* cracker? Everyone knew who it was. Infuriated, he asked Patrick for Matt Singer's telephone number.

The phone was answered by an odd, phlegmy voice that said Matt wasn't around.

Says he's not here, Mike told the room. Would somebody double-check this?

He handed the receiver to Adam Harrison, a friend of Patrick's who knew the Singers. Adam put the receiver to his ear for a moment.

It's him, Adam told the room.

Mike took the phone. You're coming down here tomorrow, he said. And if you don't, I'm going to kick your sorry ass.

Hearing the next morning about Mike's impulsive move, Ja-

naka was annoyed. He had been asked by the FBI not to disturb
this Singer. But he couldn't do anything about the meeting now.
And, of course, he and everyone else wanted a little face time with
this peculiar figure in their lives.


It took all of Steve Singer's will to get his brother to the meeting.
They'd been arguing about Matt's behavior for months, but Matt
had this way of intransigently refusing to hear. They've caught you,
Steve said. They know who you are. They've called the FBI. Or, on a
more personal level: Matt, some of these people know me, and they
know you, and they are angry at you. Not some mysterious cracker
—you. You, Phantom Dialer, Matt Singer.

Sometimes Matt said he was going through so many hops that
they could not possibly have caught him. Or he hinted that he was
doing things Steve would never know about. Most of the time,
though, he responded only with the shrunken impenetrability that
was the tragedy of his life. It was as if his fluid on-line existence as
Phantom Dialer and Infomaster was so separate in his mind from
his closed-in days in the 3-D world that he couldn't grasp that the
one could have consequences for the other. Maybe he regarded
Phantomd as the better of the two, and was prepared to sacrifice his
existence in the mundane world.

Riding the bus to campus, Steve was almost as nervous as his
brother. The affair had already cost him friends. He tended to blame
Patrick for the hostility, feeling that Patrick hadn't stepped up to
defend him. Here Steve had tried to help—had turned in his brother
to the FBI, for God's sake—and he was being treated like a pariah.

The kind of training Janaka gave the CAT was a ticket to a
good job in the computer business. If not for Matt, Steve would have
been allowed on the CAT even though he was a nonstudent.

Once again, Matt was ruining things for Steve. That was the
way it had been all his life.

Outside they passed by the flimsy wooden houses that filled
the east part of town. Socked into the Willamette Valley, Portland

hadn't fully emerged into spring. All the yards were dark and wet and the outside seats in the cafes on Hawthorne were still empty. The bus shuddered over the river and then toward the gray and beige slab buildings at the edge of campus.

They walked into the Portland Center for Advanced Technology, Steve in his anger pulling Matt up the cement steps and through the double doors. He was ready to curse him out right there.

In the hallway was the wanted poster of Matt. Steve had let Patrick photocopy Matt's photograph, the face turned from the lens as it always was. Stood over the glowing machine while Patrick repeatedly enlarged the picture until it was big enough for a poster, WANTED right on top in red letters. Steve had uneasily acquiesced—better they hang a poster than hang Matt, right?

Little pinprick holes were scattered across Matt's picture.

Darts, Steve realized. His brother's face was on a dartboard!

Janaka, Paul, and Mike were waiting in the conference room off the departmental secretary's office. The room fell silent when Matt and Steve entered.

A curious feature of the Information Age was its propensity to let people interact without ever meeting physically. When they met, they were abashed by the simple fact of their physical presence.

Matt sat in the furthest chair, crumpled and withdrawn, concealing his lower face with the hand that nervously plucked at his beard. He would have hidden behind a curtain if he could. Steve took a seat a few chairs away, still shaken by the dart holes in his brother's picture. His brother had no right to break into systems but they had no right to demean him, either.

Matt was his best friend. Steve had always taken care of him, despite—because of?—never knowing exactly what Matt was getting into.

Curiosity made Janaka lean forward, thrusting his big bearded head at Matt, eyebrows raised interrogatively—almost a friendly expression. By contrast, Mike had his arms folded and a scowl wrapped around his blond head.

Matt said nothing.

Janaka described the trouble that Mike had gone through to restore Jove the previous night.

No response from Matt. Not a word.

Why do you do this? Janaka asked. He had small, almost pearly teeth. Why are you breaking into all these systems? What do you *want*?

Access, Matt said suddenly in his distinctively scratchy voice. I want access.

Janaka said, If we give you an account here so that you can have free access to the Internet, will you stop breaking into systems?

Matt looked at the other people in the room for the first time.

I'll stop breaking into *your* system, he said.

That's not good enough.

No response.

If we give you an account for free, Janaka said, an account with total Internet access, will you stop cracking?

Matt turned his face to the wall.

No, he said.


## Cambridge

Chasing the cracker was less tedious than Nick Papadakis had feared. The cracker himself, though odd, wasn't technically interesting—his techniques were too simple. What Nick liked was the code that Mycroft had written to monitor him. The program ran in the background, unobtrusively monitoring traffic. More exactly, it inspected all the packets—the chunks of information shuttled around the Internet by the TCP/IP method—passing through the computer. Mycroft's program was different from the previous monitoring program, because rather than scanning a single service—Telnet, for example—it examined the entire flow of data.

Later, such programs, known as "sniffers," would become common. At the time, though, they seemed like magic. You turned on the program, went to get a cup of coffee, and came back to find a copy of every packet sent via Telnet, or every packet with an address of pdx.edu, or every packet that contained the word "password." Intrigued, Nick and Mycroft spent several days learning how to run the sniffer, passing the code back and forth and improving it in the old hacker style.

Because the sniffer was a computer program, it exercised no judgment; if not set up properly at the beginning, its efforts would misfire. If, for instance, Nick and Mycroft simply configured the sniffer to capture all packets from pdx.edu, they would not see the cracker if he Telenetted from other locations. On the other hand, if they snatched all Telnet packets, they would end up with a mess, because the cracker was only one of many users leaving Terminus via Telnet. Worse, grabbing all users' Telnet packets would constitute a big invasion of privacy.

In the electronic era, it seemed, ordinary sysadmins had eavesdropping powers that federal agencies could obtain only after following rigorous legal procedures. Compared to Nick, an agency like the FBI was badly handicapped.

To avoid violating privacy, he decided to construct an electronic profile of the intruder. A cracker metric, as it were. He set up the sniffer with trip wires set to the cracker's absurdly regular habits. The program scanned for his known account names, for instance. When it came across those names logging on, the program would follow the rest of that connection. Nick added similar trip wires for the cracker's favorite Trojan horses. By trial and error, he molded the sniffer into an ever-more specific tool. It reached final form on April 11, when he began recording the sniffing sessions.

In the next few days MIT learned that the intruder called himself by a plethora of different account names, depending on the system he was in, but that on Internet Relay Chat channels such as #hack he preferred Infomaster or Info. Nick also discovered that other sites were after the guy. Someone in Santa Fe was warning Infomaster to go away; Reed College had it in for him as well; a sysadmin at a company in Colorado was concerned. The hostility seemed strongest at Portland State—Nick had called them, and was surprised to hear that they had complained for a year about this cracker and he was still on the loose.

By chance, the cracker had broken into the network at Berkeley used by Eric Allman, the author of Sendmail. Indeed, he had taken over Allman's own account and was reading his e-mail, much of which was about the incursion, which Allman had discovered on April 4. Reading, so to speak, over the cracker's shoulder, Nick watched Allman discuss the attack with his friends:

> Someone tried to break into antipodes (one of the instructional machines in Cory [Hall]) as system user 'bin.' A .rhosts file had been inserted (and since removed) that allowed login from anywhere without a password. But notice where the attack came from--Thinking Machines Corporation!

Allman was reluctant to inform the administration that the university had been compromised.

> It would tend to clue them in that we are having [security] problems. On the other hand, CERT probably needs to be informed, so it will get back to them anyway. I'm in quite a quandary.

Until the end of April Nick noted down the machines the cracker had taken over. Worn out by the cracker's preternatural vigor, he flagged when the list grew into the hundreds. Each night the sniffer generated about sixty megabytes of logs, streams of connections and commands that took Nick hours to sort and edit to a more manageable three or four megabytes. Nick's other work piled up as he followed the cracker's path.

The cracker seemed to be working from lists of Internet addresses, for he tried one machine after another on the same network. On each he searched for the same eight or ten security lapses, hitting box after box like a one-man incarnation of the proverbial million monkeys. The process was, to Nick, eye-glazingly mechanical. He couldn't imagine doing it for fifteen minutes, let alone fifteen hours. Still, it had to be said: sooner or later the cracker almost invariably succeeded.

From a security standpoint, the implications were discouraging. All of the cracker's tricks were well known. They had appeared in CERT and CIAC bulletins and been warned against in security books. But Unix was such a mess that it was next to impossible for even the most competent sysadmin to close down every hole on every machine. And most sysadmins weren't competent. As more and more businesses went on-line, the Internet was growing so fast that the supply of expert administrators was not equal to the demand. In the past, sysadmins were always hackers with years of Unix experience; today they were ever more likely to be personal-computer jockeys who could operate what true hackers scornfully called Microsloth Windoze but were clueless about real operating systems, which Unix was, for all its faults. As a result, the average level of expertise on the Internet was declining in inverse proportion to its expansion, and the crackers were having an ever easier time of it.

The problem was getting so bad, Nick discovered, that even the FBI had set up a computer-crime squad. He learned this from James Hegarty, the agent who returned Mike Patton's call. Hegarty was intrigued by the case—and especially by the sniffer, a tool with obvious law-enforcement implications.

On May 5, Nick and Mike prepared a memo for a meeting with the FBI three days later at campus police headquarters. Sitting in a conference room, the two sysadmins met with Agent Hegarty, Jeff Schiller and one of his aides, and Lieutenant McCoy of the MIT police and one of *his* aides. Hegarty proved to be a squared-off fellow whose hair was about two feet shorter than Nick's. After the sysadmins presented their information, he read their memo, which was accompanied by a list of networks victimized by the cracker.

Since early April, LCS [Laboratory for Computer Science] has been following the activities of someone who has been using our dialup server, TERMINUS, to break into many (>50) other machines on the network, including machines at MIT, government machines (eg. NIH), some commercial sites (eg. Thinking Machines), Rutgers, UC Berkeley, PSU, and elsewhere.

This individual works an average of 6–8 hours a night, using a "cookbook" of several well-known, not very subtle, but nonetheless extremely effective techniques for gaining illegal access. The typical strategy used is to exploit a weakness . . . that allows him to write a file (.rhosts) into a user's directory, giving that user unrestricted access from his base machine. He then "becomes" that user on the base machine and gains access to the target. Once there, he exploits a variety of other weaknesses . . . and gains privileged access (super-user or root).

This privileged access allows him to replace a crucial piece of system software (/bin/login [the log-in program]) with his own version that logs every password typed, as well as providing him with a "back-door" that gives him privileged access quickly, without him showing up in a list of logged-in users. . . . He then uses the passwords gleaned to gain access to still more machines (since people frequently use the same passwords on all the machines where they have accounts).

Another technique involves getting a copy of the password file from a target machine; the Unix operating system stores passwords encrypted, so normally this is not very useful. Recently, however, software has become available that encrypts every word in a dictionary, and then compares the entries in the encrypted dictionary with those in the password file. Typically, this approach finds 20–30% of the passwords on any given machine. We have seen him running such software on a machine at TMC (Thinking Machines Corporation), a manufacturer of supercomputers, where he also has been storing a copy of some SUN Microsystems proprietary source code.

We have not been able to discern any pattern in the machines that he breaks into (except that he seems interested in supercomputers); it doesn't seem that he is looking for anything specific. His goal appears to be to gain privileged access on as many machines as possible. . . .

What this individual has been doing for the past month or more is the rough equivalent of breaking into houses all around town, and then rigging the locks so that he (and anyone else) can get back in easily, although the locks don't appear to have been tampered with. . . . Particularly given that he seems to be doing this as a full-time job, we believe that prosecution in this case is quite warranted.

Nick Papadakis
System Manager

Michael Patton
Network Manager

Hegarty explained that the Bureau had to ensure that its agents didn't pursue small-scale crimes. Could you guys, he asked, describe the fiscal impact here?

Nick had been expecting this question, which was not to say that he welcomed it. He was often confused by the extent to which ordinary people set stock in money. That the FBI would be so financially oriented was no less confusing, though hardly surprising. The fact was, though, that the impact of this kind of crime could not be measured in monetary terms with any satisfaction.

Look, Nick said, this incident is different from any other cracking I have ever seen in terms of the scope of what's going on. It's not that he's stealing something. This guy is controlling thousands of machines. He's inconveniencing an entire hemisphere.

Is he looking for anything in particular? Does he seem to be singling out government computers?

No, Nick admitted. I wish I could say he had a target, but I can't see one.

But aren't there any measurable costs?

The real response was, How much would you pay to stop someone from reading your mail? To keep your credit history inaccessible? How much was it worth to a business to ensure that its research was not pirated? How much did the government want to keep its own information secret?

But that wasn't the kind of response Hegarty needed, so Nick and Mike took a stab at estimating the salaries of all the sysadmins involved, and the number of hours they would have to devote to rejigging their systems after the break-ins, and came up with a figure of $100,000 or so, which Hegarty said was high enough.

What's important, Nick emphasized, is that this guy is acting like cracking is a job. Six to eight hours a day, sometimes more he's out there accumulating control. Eventually, it's going to add up to something big.

Hegarty's face lighted up, and Nick realized that he might have inadvertently hit upon the correct formulation. The way to describe the cracker was not as a thief, but as a spy. And just as the Bureau appreciated that the impact of spying was not purely economic, cracking might be regarded as important even if it did not have dire financial consequences.

That Friday the sysadmins ceremoniously presented Agent Hegarty with the logs in the office of Jim Bruce, the MIT vice-president who was Jeff Schiller's boss. Afterward, Hegarty asked for a tour of the Laboratory for Computer Science, which Mike and Nick were delighted to provide. During the tour, Hegarty unhappily fingered the floppy disk on which the sysadmins had stored the sniffer logs. If the Bureau was going to nail this hacker, he explained, it probably would be necessary to wiretap his computer, because that was the only way to establish the source of the attacks with certainty. More than likely the request for permission would be based on the MIT logs. Unfortunately, they would have to submit the documentation to a judge in printed form. He was therefore going to the office to print it up.

Nick had compressed many megabytes of data on the floppy disk; he couldn't guess how many hundreds of pages it represented. And this was just the first batch of logs. Yes, Hegarty said, he had figured out that it was going to take all weekend. Nick was appalled. The thought of turning the small, electronically searchable chunk of data in Hegarty's hand into an unmanageable three-foot stack of paper was like fingernails scratching across the blackboard of his tidy soul.

Afterward, Nick and Hegarty ate at an Indian restaurant down the street from the Laboratory for Computer Science. Cop and hacker faced each other in dim light across a small, sticky wooden table. Hegarty was wearing a dark blue suit—surely the only one for blocks around. To Nick's embarrassment, his own attire was singularly inappropriate. He was wearing a T-shirt. Bought as a hack, the shirt bore two lines of lettering across the chest:

### LEGION OF DOOM
### World Hacking Tour 1990

Nick, a vegetarian, ordered a meatless meal. Meanwhile Hegarty quizzed him about TCP/IP, Unix, and a host of other topics. But every time Nick got halfway through an explanation, Hegarty waved a hand and asked him to stop. He was having a hard time understanding this stuff, he said. He knew it was terribly important, but it made his eyes glaze over.

Nick experienced a moment of sympathy. The world had gone funny on guys like Hegarty. They were trained to run, guns drawn, into the heart of Mafia shootouts. It took a special type of person to survive in that violent, difficult world. And now they had to function in a totally different environment, in which crimes were committed coolly, by remote control, with the criminals thousands of miles away from the crime.

Not until later did Nick consider that Hegarty might have been feeling the same pity for the poor sysadmin who had to spend twelve hours a day with these horrid machines, slaving at a keyboard while streams of gibberish came from his fingers. From Hegarty's point of view, perhaps, Nick's life looked like pure hell.

# 11

# INTEL INSIDE

*Security through obscurity:* A term applied by hackers to most [operating-system] vendors' favorite way of coping with security holes—namely, ignoring them, documenting neither any known holes nor the underlying security algorithms, trusting that nobody will find out about them and that people who do find out about them won't exploit them. . . . After all, actually fixing the bugs would siphon off the resources needed to implement the next user-interface frill on marketing's wish list—and besides, if they started fixing security bugs customers might begin to *expect* it and imagine that their warranties of merchantability gave them some sort of *right* to a system with fewer holes in it than a shotgunned Swiss cheese, and *then* where would we be?

—**THE ON-LINE HACKER JARGON FILE, VERSION 3.3.1, JANUARY 25, 1996**

Oroville, California
Spring 1992

Lake Oroville shimmers like an oasis in the dry hills north of California's Central Valley. More than seven hundred feet deep and one hundred fifty miles around, the lake was created when Uncle Sam blocked the Feather River with eighty million cubic yards of concrete, clay, and rock. Now owned by the state of California, the Oroville Dam provides boating and swimming, controls flooding in the farmland below, supplies water to the Central Valley, and generates hydroelectric power for all of California.

To accomplish these multiple ends, the engineers who operate the dam must regulate its outflow. This usually involves opening and closing the valves on two pipes, each twenty-two feet in diameter, which run from the reservoir into an underground power plant. As much as eighteen thousand cubic feet of water per second courses through these pipes into the blades of six turbines, thereby generating up to 678 megawatts of electrical power.

During spring thaws, the engineers discharge excess water through eight gates in the middle of the dam. Each gate is thirty-three feet high and seventeen feet wide. When fully opened, the eight gates can release one hundred fifty thousand cubic feet of water per second. Gushing from the face of the dam, this cataract is a river in its own right, with twenty-five times the average natural flow of the undammed Feather River.

Opening these gates while the river is at high water would create catastrophic floods. More than likely, many people would be killed. Thousands of acres in the nation's agricultural heartland would be lost; the economic loss could be as high as a billion dollars. Naturally, Oroville incorporates many safeguards against this possibility. In a facility a mile downstream, dam operators use computers to monitor water flows. The valves in the power plant pipes and the heavy steel gates are also controlled by these computers. Dedicated phone lines tie the dam's computer system to a server in Sacramento, the capital, allowing the state water bureau to order releases of water electronically. Dozens of dams and sluices are connected by the state network, allowing Sacramento to oversee water flow throughout the state.

Because water management is vital to the entire southwestern quarter of the nation, the California computer system is in turn networked to related agencies, including the Bureau of Land Management, which supervises federal land. The BLM network stretches across the West and includes machines in its office in Portland, Oregon.

In the spring of 1992, this situation came to the attention of

Special Agent E. Brent Rasmussen, who had asked FBI field offices in northern California for help in obtaining information from CIAC, Lawrence Livermore, the University of California at Berkeley, and other sites penetrated by Infomaster. To his shock, he was informed that the cracker had penetrated the BLM network in Portland, roamed the agency's national network, and skipped to Sacramento, where he had easily obtained root access on the computers that controlled every dam in the northern part of the state. With a few keystrokes, he could bury some of the world's richest agricultural land beneath a tidal wave, killing hundreds of people, destroying thousands of homes, and throwing the futures markets into chaos. It was like the plot of an Arnold Schwarzenegger movie: computer hacker floods farmland to make billions on the commodities exchange.

In speaking to Rasmussen, the sysadmins at Portland State and MIT always described Infomaster's attacks by words like "rudimentary." Indeed, the hacker frequently made what the computer guys regarded as rank errors. He kept typing the wrong commands and crashing his victims' networks. This news was supposed to be comforting—Infomaster was no wizard, from their point of view. But Rasmussen saw only that the Internet was so insecure that it could be victimized by almost anyone. The Internet was so insecure that some amateur could create one of the biggest calamities in American history by mistake.

Portland
Spring 1992

Rasmussen visited Portland State University for the first time to pick up the sysadmins' logs. He met with Janaka Jayawardene, who proved to be a cheerful man who wanted to help. Nonetheless, the visit had not gone well. The problem was the language gap. It was not Janaka's Sri Lankan accent, which was barely noticeable. The problem was that he answered Rasmussen's questions in a language that resembled English, but in which most of the familiar words had been replaced by terms that meant nothing to Rasmussen. He didn't even call the criminal a "hacker." For some reason, the guy was a "cracker." It was as if Janaka and his colleagues employed an entirely alien vocabulary when it came to talking about computers.

After a while, Janaka seemed to realize that Rasmussen was holding his pen but not writing anything. Patiently, the sysadmin tried again, in what Rasmussen guessed were supposed to be simpler terms. It didn't help. After half an hour of fruitless dialogue, Janaka gave Rasmussen a tour of the lab. It was a strange experience—all this superadvanced equipment, and in the middle of it this assortment of oddballs. One hid in his office the entire time; another rocked on the balls of his feet as though he were about to fall over; a third had been out of the sunlight so long that his skin looked green. They worked in a big room that was almost completely dark except for the glow of computer monitors. It was like visiting a twenty-first-century version of *The Addams Family*.

Rasmussen took the logs and said he'd be in touch.

For the next visit, Rasmussen brought along Mike West, the office computer clerk. With West acting as translator, the conversation was more edifying. The clerk seemed to know enough about computers to understand Janaka, and he had spent enough time around FBI agents to know what Rasmussen needed to get out of Janaka's responses. In any case, Rasmussen was beginning to gather how wide-ranging and effective Infomaster's penetrations were.

He had already telephoned the Bureau offices near Infomaster's more conspicuous victims. Some had already fielded reports from the penetrated parties, and several had even made stabs at investigation. There was an Agent Hegarty in Boston; a Williams in San Jose; a Heuston in Palo Alto; a Doyle in Oakland; a Mazza in Santa Fe; and others. All had caught sight of what was rapidly developing into the biggest hacker incident in history.

But Portland U.S. attorney Charles Turner wouldn't prosecute.

Rasmussen was pleased when Scott Charney flew to the Northwest to resolve the matter. At the same time, he had a field agent's natural suspicion of Justice Department staff attorneys like Charney. Agents want to put bad guys in jail, whereas staff attorneys can fulfill their duties as advisers even if an investigation never reaches a judge. Friction is inevitable. Charney turned out to be a small, wiry man with a knack for conversational openers of the sort calculated to put FBI agents at ease—telling a story about how as a prosecutor in the Bronx he had convicted a man of murder by the bite marks left on the victim's body, for example. Not to mention the man he put away who had sodomized nineteen children. This is no mere desk jockey, the stories said.

In just a few years, Charney told Rasmussen, the Internet was going to explode, and half the nation would be on-line. Hackers would have a field day. By sending a few to prison now, the Justice Department might save itself and the nation a lot of trouble later. If Rasmussen turned up the goods, Charney would ensure prosecution.

Charney told Rasmussen not to be concerned about Turner's attitude. In Washington, he had telephoned Turner, The prosecutor had made it clear that he didn't grasp what the concern was about. After all, he told Charney, the hacker hadn't stolen anything valuable. Charney was not reassured—he had a story about hackers who had taken no items of value. In 1989 an astronomer from Berkeley named Clifford Stoll had alerted the FBI about a hacker. When agents asked what he had stolen, Stoll had only been able to point to 75 cents' worth of computer time. Bureau headquarters had laughed in his face—only to learn that the hacker had gone on from swiping computer time to selling military secrets to East Germany. Never again, Charney vowed, would Washington make the mistake of judging the hacker threat in terms of dollars and cents. With Turner making clear his lack of interest, Charney had come to Portland to negotiate the terms under which his computer-crime unit would take over the prosecution.

After he met with Turner, the U.S. attorney agreed to make room for one of Charney's staffers in his office, and to provide that person with the necessary support. Charney doubted that such local support would be forthcoming, but he didn't think that Josh

Silverman would need it. This looked to be a big case—the biggest Charney had come across—and Silverman was smart and ambitious enough to give it the push it needed.

A few days later Josh Silverman appeared in Portland. Although he bore all the signs of yuppiedom, he also appeared eager and aggressive. On one point he was adamant: to establish guilt, the Bureau would have to install a device to record the hacker's computer sessions—a datatap. Because Dennis Kintigh had told him the same thing, Rasmussen had been expecting as much. Nonetheless, the news was unwelcome. Paperwork, unrelenting tedium, and stale, lukewarm coffee, here I come.

After carving out a sliver of space from the offices of the U.S. attorney in Portland, Silverman began the T-3 affidavit necessary to obtain permission for the datatap. He set about gathering every detail that could possibly be put to use to convince a judge that crimes were being committed, that Singer was the likely candidate, and that electronic eavesdropping was the only way to prove it. Inevitably, much of the affidavit recounted the circumstances of past T-3 cases, because judges felt comfortable granting permission to wiretap only after another judge had granted it in similar situations. In this case, the sole precedent was the Masters of Deception datatap in New York City; in the affidavit, Silverman diligently cited the details of that case. He also kept Rasmussen busy with requests for information from Janaka—Rasmussen and Mike West shuttled back and forth to Portland State half a dozen times that May.

Taking a suggestion from Kintigh, Silverman was going to ask the judge for something unusual—an exemption from the standard requirement that the prosecutor report every ten days to justify continuing the wiretap. As a rule, judges granted permission to wiretap in ten-day increments, forcing prosecutors and police to reauthorize the bug by proving to the judges that they were intercepting important material. Because the datatap on the Masters of Deception had inundated the watching agents with information, Kintigh had recommended that Silverman ask for twenty days between reauthorizations to allow Washington to pore through the intercepts.

After two weeks of work, Silverman had produced an impres-

sive document: more than a hundred pages of double-spaced manuscript. Annoyingly, the Portland AUSAs insisted on their right of
approval. Indeed, they wanted to see every scrap of paper generated
by Silverman. While Portland pawed through the T-3, Silverman
left for Washington.

There was nothing for Rasmussen to do but wait and gather
more data. He had a dozen other cases pending, though with a
wiretap hanging over his head he knew he had to start phasing out
as many as possible. Hegarty telephoned regularly, passing on MIT's
impatience. Meanwhile, Rasmussen was hearing about it directly
from one Nick Papadakis, Janaka's counterpart at MIT. Papadakis
was chafing at the slowness of the legal process. Rasmussen sympa-
thized. He, too, was impatient. But that was what happened when
you had a Constitution to uphold.

Eventually Portland approved Silverman's work, and Rasmussen sent the T-3 to Washington, where it faced a second, larger
round of bureaucracy. Kintigh and Settle would push it through the
hierarchies, first at the FBI and then at the Justice Department,
giving everybody in a position of authority in either agency a chance
to kill the request before it was sent to the final authority, a judge in
Portland. But even as the affidavit crawled slowly but surely
through the bureaucracy, Kintigh announced that he was leaving
the computer-crime squad. The case was being handed over to a
woman named Beth Barnett, who would be calling him soon. Then
Kintigh said so long and good luck.

Rasmussen squinted at the dead receiver. Was the case being
dumped? Hard to know what to make of this sudden change.

Santa Fe
May 1992

Late at night, when he had time, Scott Yelich continued to
follow Infomaster on his antic sojourns through the Internet. His
sysadmin work filled one window in his monitor; another was devoted to #hack or another Internet Relay Chat channel; a third monitored the cracker's progress, logging his every step. Scott had

acquired the ability, unique to the contemporary era, of simultaneously talking on the phone, typing remarks into #hack, cutting and pasting text in the Institute window, and keeping an eye on Infomaster.

If the cracker seemed on the verge of breaking into something valuable, Scott cut his connection or erased his Trojan or deleted his .rhosts file. Or he unexpectedly sent huge files to Infomaster, swamping his modem for so long that he had to go off-line. Mostly, though, Scott did nothing about the cracker's depredations. He watched Info get the # sign of the root prompt and, amused, thought, Well, too bad for *those* guys.

But early in the morning of May 21, 1992, Scott reexamined his views on noninterference. Info had been performing his usual boring practice of examining every single file in every single directory on a computer, in this case some box at Portland State. Then, suddenly, he Telnetted to ssd.intel.com, the supercomputer division at Intel, the microchip firm. Evidently some students worked at the company and used the same passwords at Intel and the university. Intel had firewalls—the special computers that screen Internet connections. When people Telnetted to the corporate network, they were, of course, asked for a password. If, like Infomaster, they then tried to Telnet into the subsidiary network of the supercomputer division, they encountered a firewall, which demanded a second, presumably more secret, password. Info tried the same passwords as before and the firewall kicked him out of the system. He Telnetted back several times, always with the same result. Then he tried entering with File Transfer Protocol. FTP, like Telnet, is a way of navigating the Internet, in this case one meant to facilitate transferring files from one computer to another. The firewall was not configured to ask for passwords on FTP. Info slipped into the supercomputer division.

In Scott's experience, such lapses were typical of the Internet. Firewalls were touted as the next great thing, the solution to security problems, but they were only as good as their operators. Many inexperienced sysadmins lacked the necessary know-how. And experienced sysadmins often did not have the time to adjust their firewalls continually to combat the latest cracker techniques. If firewalls were not configured properly, they became little more than electronic Maginot lines, easily outflanked by clever invaders. The Intel firewall, which blocked Telnet but ignored FTP, was an example.

At Intel, Infomaster went through his paces—scanned the e-mail for words like "password" and "account," checked the .rhosts file, looked for world-exportable directories, and checked the password file. He copied the password file and sent it with FTP to his electronic warehouses at MIT, Portland State, Texas A&M University, and the State University of New York at Buffalo. Then he ran the password file through Crack. The incredible thing was that he Cracked the file on the network of Thinking Machines, Intel's rival in the race to create the world's fastest computer. Concluding that Intel might not wish to have its password files on its competitor's computer, Scott once again ended his pose of neutrality. He checked the Whois database and called the Intel sysadmin.

Hey, folks, your network has been sliced to ribbons. Someone's got in and cracked your password file.

The response was going to be fun, he thought. He envisioned his electronic mailbox full of astonished messages, a galvanic burst of phone calls, corporate fury of volcanic dimensions.

Instead there was a brief, noncommittal thank-you.

Pretty cool customers, Scott thought. The next night, as usual, he watched Infomaster. After hopping through a variety of networks, the cracker jumped back into Intel. Not a lot seemed to have been done on the security front, Scott noted. Standing just behind the cracker, so to speak, he watched Infomaster reading employees' e-mail—including a warning about a break-in that had compromised passwords. Of course, if employees had changed their passwords, Infomaster could vacuum up the changed password file and run it through Crack again.

Unable to credit his eyes, Scott called again. After some back and forth with the company directory, he reached the security office.

He's still in your system, Scott said. He's reading your warning about the attack. Did you actually do anything to block him, or did you just send out that warning?

Now he won a longer response: We appreciate your concern, thank you very much. An obvious brush-off, in Scott's opinion.

He called a few more times and elicited the same reaction.

It's your network, Intel, Scott thought. You're the guys whose company depends on keeping secret your corporate information about chip design and manufacture, not me. You're the ones who bought a bunch of firewalls at umpteen dollars a pop and didn't configure them right, not me.*

In a fit of curiosity, Scott grabbed Info's copy of the password file from the Thinking Machines system and ran it through Crack for a day. The passwords weren't bad—the Intel system did not permit obvious choices. But you had to wonder what would happen when Infomaster told his buddies about the holes in the company firewall.

Information like that had a way of getting around.

Tysons Corner
June 1992

Jim Settle was out of the office when Beth Barnett appeared at the National Computer Crime Squad in April. She was odd woman out—everyone else had been there since February. But she wasn't

---

* Given Intel's apparently relaxed views about security, Scott was appalled to learn that in November 1993 the company charged Randall Schwartz, a consultant at its supercomputer division, with using Crack on the same password file lifted by Infomaster. Among the odd features of the incident, in Scott's view, was that Schwartz had never removed the file from Intel. He had run Crack on the division's own network, trying to demonstrate its lack of security. Indeed, he turned up forty-eight weak passwords, one of which belonged to an Intel vice-president whose choice was "pre$iden"—presumably a psychologically revealing reference to "president." (Always, Scott said, it was the bigwigs who were the worst security problems.) In July of 1995 Schwartz was convicted. He was sentenced to 480 hours of community service, five years of probation, ninety days in jail (deferred until 1998), and $68,471.45 in restitution.

really a newcomer. Having worked on the phone outage and Masters of Deception investigations, she already knew most of the squad, especially Kintigh and Kolouch.

She went down the hallway, knocking on doors and reacquainting herself with the guys.

Kolouch gave her his familiar tense grin. Couldn't stay away, could you? he said, shaking his head in stylized disbelief.

Barnett could hardly believe she was back in Washington. After wrapping up the Masters of Deception datatap, she'd planned to return to Birmingham after a weeklong training session at Quantico. At the academy she learned that she had been permanently transferred to Settle's new squad. She had managed to wangle extra time to wrap up her affairs before coming to Washington Metro.

Almost immediately she realized that Settle was generating frenetic activity. In an effort to bring Barnett and the others up to speed on computer networks, an area about which many of the ten squad members were ignorant, he was subjecting the group to a grueling marathon of educational seminars. Between lectures, there was a parade of meetings with computer-security experts and with law-enforcement representatives of every stripe—part of spreading the good word about the existence of the squad, a high-priority goal for Settle.

Meanwhile, Barnett was also supposed to do her job: investigating computer crime. But despite Settle's efforts to create excitement, most companies still refused to report computer crime, leaving the squad members stuck mostly with anti-hacking scut work. Chafing under the tedium, some maneuvered for transfers— including Dennis Kintigh, whom Barnett saw in his office one day in early June stacking papers into cardboard boxes.

Straightening up your office? Barnett asked.

Moving to Albuquerque, he said. He had obtained an "office of preference transfer"—meaning that he was senior enough to switch jobs if he wanted. I don't want to spend my day in front of a monitor, he told her. I could have stayed in computer science and done that. Some exciting drug cases were happening in New Mexico. That was more like what he wanted to do. Then he casually handed over an inch-thick file labeled "Portland." Would Barnett look at it when she had a moment?

She dropped it in a drawer without a glance.

A few days later, Settle walked over with his usual abrupt stride and summoned her to his office. Unlike any other manager she had ever known, Settle kept his desk facing the wall. According to some management theory, orienting his desk in this way emphasized the lack of formal hierarchy in his staff.

Across town at FBI headquarters, Settle explained, Richard Ress, a former FBI sniper who was now their liaison with the white-collar crime division, was walking the T-3 through the bureaucracy.

Who's running a tap? she asked.

Settle frowned at her. Didn't Kintigh give you the file?

She had entirely forgotten about it.

Settle shook his head. It's your case, so you better bone up, and fast. By the time the T-3 comes through I want you to be able to hit the ground running.

Barnett couldn't believe it. In its entire history, the Federal Bureau of Investigation had operated two datataps. One agent had been stuck with both: Beth Barnett.

She found the file and glumly settled down to read. Most of the information detailed how these hackers had run amok for more than a year through Portland State University, but they had been to many other places, too. A *lot* of other places—universities, of course, but also corporations, phone companies, and government sites. A list of locations made by MIT included hundreds of sites.

These guys made the Legion of Doom and Masters of Deception look like dabblers.

A name jumped out: Matt Singer. All this was caused by one guy? Why would anyone do it? What did he *want*?

### Cambridge

Nick Papadakis was not supposed to contact Agent Hegarty directly. All communication was channeled through Lieutenant McCoy of the campus police. Which meant that Nick was supposed to wait hours for Hegarty's response when Nick discovered evidence on the sniffer logs that the cracker had, in fact, been breaking into government networks. Nick saw little reason for the delay—he wanted to know if the evidence was important enough to be sent immediately to the FBI. McCoy was equally firm about the value of official supervision over encounters between MIT employees and outside police agencies.

You're not adding any value here, Nick told McCoy. It's time to snap this link.

A confrontation, doubtless inevitable, ensued, complete with shouting, scarlet faces, and desk pounding.

In the end, the annoying extra step vanished. Mike Patton and Nick could telephone Hegarty directly.

That was it for the interesting news.

Once he had finished tinkering with the sniffer code, the logging itself quickly got old. The prospect of confronting twenty megabytes of Infomaster every morning dimmed Nick's usual zestful anticipation of the day to come. The logs were always the same, hour after hour of behavior so remorselessly motiveless that he wondered if the cracker were mentally disturbed. When a friend announced that he was visiting Oregon, Nick e-mailed a sincere request: If you run across someone named Info, would you break his fingers for me?

Mike had been dealing with CERT. At first the two men had been reluctant to report the incident. What are we going to say? they asked themselves. There's somebody out there doing the eight most common things you can think of, over and over again, eight hours a day? In the end, though, that was exactly what Mike recounted. We have been observing what appears to be a single individual in the following pattern of behavior, Mike said to CERT staffer Moira West. And then he listed Info's few tricks.

We've seen other reports like this, West said. Could you send me details?

Funny she should ask. MIT had a few hundred megabytes of logs.

After FTPing them to CERT, he asked for her West reaction.

Hmmm, she said. Interesting.

Any news?

We're working on it, she said.

Inscrutability was evidently part of the agency's stock in trade.
He felt better when CERT finally issued a bulletin.

---

CA-92:14        CERT Advisory
June 22, 1992
Altered System Binaries Incident

------------------------------------------

The Computer Emergency Response Team/Coordination
Center (CERT/CC) has received information regarding a series of
significant intrusion incidents on the Internet. Systems administrators should be aware that many systems on the Internet have
been compromised due to this activity. . . .

------------------------------------------

I. Description

The intruders gain initial access to a host [computer] by
discovering a password for a user account on the system, [or]
exploiting . . . any ".rhosts" files on the system. The intruder then
connects to the system using [a remote log-in] and attempts to
become root on the compromised system. . . .

II. Impact

Having gained root access on a system, the intruders may
make unauthorized changes to system binaries [that is, programs]
that can capture account information for both local and remote
systems. In addition, the intruder adds "+  +" to any ".rhosts"
files to which the intruder has access [in Unix, the two plus signs
let anyone on the Internet enter as root]. . . .

III. Solution

A. Check your systems for signs of intrusion due to this
incident.

B. Take the following steps to secure your systems. . . .

By the time of the CERT advisory Nick was examining the
sniffer logs intermittently, a day here, a day there, tracking Info only

when jogged by conscience or, more likely, encouraging words from the FBI. Then he'd guiltily scroll through the logs. Within half an hour his eyelids were drooping and he was so stupefied with the boredom of wandering in this digital swamp that he would not have noticed if Infomaster was reading the e-mail at whitehouse.gov.

We really appreciate your work, Hegarty said. It's tremendously useful.

Hegarty, too, seemed burdened by the case. Whenever the agent came to the Laboratory for Computer Science to pick up a floppy, he looked at the small plastic square as if it were exuding a bad smell. Nick was also sending a second copy of the logs to an agent named Rasmussen in Portland; Rasmussen's lack of enthusiasm for computer files was equally obvious.

The agent told Nick where the cracker was coming from: the Portland branch of the Bureau of Land Management. The branch had installed a computerized voice-mail system that, in addition to its other features, allowed incoming callers to reach outgoing AT&T lines. More than likely, Infomaster was making a local call to the BLM, which meant that he was not, say, working for a Chinese triad. In return, Nick told Hegarty which new networks Info had visited at banks, Internet service providers, and the Department of Energy.

Hmmm, Hegarty said. Interesting.

Any news?

We're working on it, Hegarty said.

Nick couldn't see this alleged work. From what he could see, Hegarty might as well be dropping the floppies in a Dumpster. In truth, Nick didn't believe that the FBI was dragging its heels— Hegarty was to all appearances a hardworking, conscientious, and utterly straightforward man. But his labor was not producing any manifest effect.

We're taking this case very seriously, Hegarty said.

Considering what he had seen from the Bureau, Nick found this a depressing statement.

I know it's difficult, tedious work, said Special Agent Hegarty. Please keep with it.

Nick considered his options.

In mid-July he telephoned Hegarty to inform him that the Laboratory for Computer Science was no longer going to keep cooperating. If the Bureau wanted to catch this guy, it would have to do it without further input from Nick Papadakis. The agent protested, but Nick was adamant. He was going to stop devoting time to this subject. Any other course of action would have been irrational.

Jsz told Info it was time to escalate. Instead of installing Trojan horses and hoping to snare passwords, why not develop a tool that would monitor *everything* taking place on a computer? To do that, Jsz was thinking of a new kind of program: a sniffer.

Like the sniffer written by Mycroft for MIT, Jsz's sniffer ran in the background on a computer, reading every packet that passed in or out. It could be set to strain through the cacophony for packets of any sort—groups of sixteen numbers, say, if Jsz wanted VISA or MasterCard numbers. Or keywords suggesting mergers and acquisitions, if he wanted to make a killing on the market.

Jsz, like Info, was not terribly interested in such moneymaking schemes. He wanted something more fundamental: access. Money, power, notoriety—access was better than any of them. For this reason Jsz had designed the sniffer to filter the streams of data for packets representing the beginning of a session on the Internet— the point at which one computer contacted another. When the program found such packets, it would record the first 128 keystrokes and copy them into a file. The first keystrokes contained two items of interest to Jsz and Info: the account name and the password. In other words, Jsz's program would pluck out passwords on the fly.

Info's log-in Trojan also recorded passwords. But the sniffer would be much more powerful, because it could take advantage of the TCP/IP software at the heart of the Internet. When the packets in a message travel from one computer to another, they move from the originating machine along a feeder line to a router, a specialized traffic-directing computer. The router reads the forwarding address on each packet and shunts it to the next stop on the way. The next stop is usually a second router, which sends the packet to a third, and so on, until the packet arrives at its destination. Because of their traffic-directing role, routers are scenes of furious activity; huge numbers of messages stream through them, few of which are generated by the routers themselves. The beauty of a sniffer, Jsz explained, is that it can be installed in a router. There it can monitor the communications of tens, or hundreds, or even thousands of computers—the number depending on the individual router. By scanning, in effect, a large number of computers, the program will quickly pick up many more passwords than any log-in Trojan could obtain on a single computer.

The sniffer would be especially effective if it were installed on the routers connected to the superfast communications lines called "backbones." Initially put together by the National Science Foundation, the backbones are the interstate highway system of the Internet. In 1992 most of the backbones were run by a nonprofit corporation called Advanced Networks and Services, a collaboration among IBM, MCI, Northern Telecom, and other communications firms. Other backbone lines were managed by Sprint (Sprintlink), Bolt Beranek and Newman (BBNplanet), and General Atomics (CERFnet), which had formed a consortium called the Commercial Internet Exchange.

Because these organizations ran the backbones, a large portion of the traffic on the Internet passed through them. Bank transactions, stock market information, credit reports, corporate strategies, top-secret research, notes about adulterous assignations, marketing numbers, data on utilities and waste dumps and building construction—all passed through the backbones. The backbones, Jsz and Info decided, should be the target for the sniffer.

Jsz wanted Info to do the grunt work of breaking into networks and testing the sniffer. Info didn't mind. After all, he couldn't program like Jsz. The project would take a long time, because Info would need to try out the sniffer on a number of small, unimportant computers. Only when the program seemed bulletproof could they assault the backbones.

Naturally, the networks that ran the backbones were security conscious—Info had already discovered that their sites bristled with firewalls. When he tried Telnetting in, he didn't even get a chance to log on. The screen simply reported: Connection refused. The firewalls also bounced FTP and the other ways he knew to move data back and forth on the Internet. How was he supposed to get in?

Almost always, the only network service allowed through such stringent firewalls was the most fundamental: electronic mail. Without e-mail, joining the Internet was pointless, and it was unthinkable for the organizations that maintained the network not to be connected. Thus the best way to slip through the firewall would be to employ Sendmail, the e-mail program. With such a method, Info and Jsz could, in theory, tunnel into heavily guarded fortresses like Sprint and MCI. Once there, they could implant sniffers on the backbone.

If Jsz and Info could figure out how to use Sendmail to get root access, they would be able to run their audacious hack. In an electronic sense, they would be able to wiretap the entire United States.

# 12

# THE
# NEVER-ENDING
# STORY

a single person is now capable of effectively shutting down an entire business as retaliation. this can probably be considered the ultimate lesson in "give me good service or else". rather than put a brick through their window, you now have the ability [with a computer] to anonymously and very effectively attack the company which screwed you over. . . . if [computer attacks on businesses] can be done quickly and efficiently, what else can be done? how about if someone focused their attacks toward government or military computers? do you feel safe knowing the government is at the whim of hackers who are generally displeased with governmental actions? you should be scared, very scared.

—"JOHNNY," AKA THE UNAMAILER, CRACKER WHO DISABLES PUBLIC
FIGURES' INTERNET ACCESS WITH FLOODS OF FAKE MESSAGES, LETTER TO THE
ON-LINE *NETLY NEWS,* SEPTEMBER 30, 1996

Brent Rasmussen was one of the few agents in the FBI who had ever crossed paths with a hacker. In the late 1970s, while stationed in Kansas City, he learned that persons unknown had taken over the computers at the White Sands Missile Range, the big weapons-testing ground in New Mexico. No one knew how to stop the attack, save by shutting down the Pentagon network—an unthinkable course. In desperation, an FBI counterintelligence team sent the intruder a message: What do you want? The hacker replied with a nonnegotiable demand. He would stop menacing the nation's defense if the FBI gave him a brand-new white Corvette.

By coincidence, a local assistant U.S. attorney had a Corvette of the right year and color. Rasmussen, the prosecutor, and several FBI agents made the drop where instructed: a Long John Silver's fast-food restaurant in a strip mall south of Kansas City. Hidden in their cars, the agents watched until the hacker came to claim his reward. When he showed up, Rasmussen could hardly credit his eyes: it was the teenage cook at the restaurant.

Afterward, Rasmussen thought it was one of the most preposterous cases he had ever investigated. But it had taught him two lessons. The first was that criminals with computers could threaten the security of the United States. And the second lesson was that if there was one thing on earth he never wanted anything to do with again, it was computers.

Portland
June 1992

While the T-3 made its way through the bureaucracy, Rasmussen decided to take a firsthand look at this Matt Singer—or Infomaster, as he called himself, although sometimes he was known as Phantom Dialer or Phantomd, and maybe also Grok, or Jsz, or— this from the NASA report—Rokstar. Rasmussen drove to the address Janaka had provided, parked down the block, sat in his car, and waited. And waited. Hours later, it was apparent that the man didn't get out much.

Incredibly, Janaka called the next day to say that Singer was on campus. Rasmussen met Janaka at the Portland Center for Advanced Technology and accompanied him to the student union. After a bit of searching Janaka pointed him out. Rasmussen caught a glimpse of a short, scrawny young man with a beard—a classic hacker profile, Janaka said. Even at a distance, they could see that his glasses were askew.

Rasmussen called Barnett soon after Kintigh's departure. From her voice, Barnett sounded like a teenager, but she fired off a barrage of professional questions about the datatap. The T-3 was before a federal judge in Portland, she explained; Settle had told her that approval was expected any day. In the meantime she was arranging for the equipment. Maybe, Rasmussen decided, Barnett's arrival wasn't the worst thing that had ever happened.

Soon after, Doug Schmidtknecht from the FBI's Engineering Research Laboratory in Washington showed up, accompanied by crates of electronics. A friendly type who attacked his work with relish, Schmidtknecht set up a command post in the Portland FBI office. An ever-growing ziggurat of high-tech gadgetry blinked and muttered in Schmidtknecht's temporary office—Rasmussen couldn't imagine how much money the agency was spending on it.

That was the way of the FBI, though. When the Bureau finally decided to act, the layers of bureaucracy that adhered to every FBI action like chewing gum to a sneaker magically dissolved away. Although it would usually take intervention by the Lord Almighty to get the agency to cough up a train ticket, when a big case heated up, agents had only to *think* cellular phone or surveillance plane or extra team members, and they happened, just like that. The FBI was like a battleship—it couldn't turn fast, but when it was pointed in the right direction, look out.

For his part, the anxious Rasmussen wanted to get moving as fast a possible. He kept asking Schmidtknecht for assurances that the equipment would be ready and working when the T-3 came through. Everything will work fine, Schmidtknecht said, when it's time to throw the switch.

Oh, *right*—that was Barnett's reaction to Schmidtknecht's prediction. Her scoffing drove Rasmussen to step up the frequency of his checks on the technician.

Anything I can do to help, he kept saying. I want this to be ready the instant we get approval, and that's coming down the pike any moment. So just ask. Anything.

You can get me some audiotapes, Schmidtknecht finally said.

Rasmussen had a few cassettes in his desk for taping interviews. How many do you need? he asked.

At least a hundred, Schmidtknecht said.

A hundred?

Two hundred would be better.

Two hundred tapes? said Rasmussen.

Please. And they have to be 120-minute tapes—Type I, not Type II.

Rasmussen opened the yellow pages. It turned out that Type I, 120-minute tapes were not popular items in the nonwiretapping world. Most music and video stores carried no more than a handful of them. Eventually, he found a small store just outside Portland with a clerk who had just received a shipment of these tapes. Rasmussen asked the kid on the phone if he would hold them.

For how long? asked the kid.

Twenty minutes.

I don't think you have much to worry about, the kid said.

Rasmussen emerged from the store cradling a dozen cases of cassette tapes. As he put them in the trunk, the dreadful truth occurred to him: within days, he was going to be reading whatever ended up on these tapes.


Cambridge

Although not many of his fellows in the Laboratory for Computer Science knew it, Mycroft was on the board of Free-BSD, an international project that worked, like the Free Software Foundation, to create a version of Unix without code from AT&T. He was not especially troubled by the thought of crackers. As long as they didn't cause too much bother, he let them alone. He certainly had never imagined reporting an incident to the police.

Info was something else, though. In years of intense involvement on the computer scene, Mycroft had never seen anything like his attack—its relentlessness, its repetitiveness, its burgeoning scale. He could understand why Nick had wanted to call the FBI.

He didn't like doing it, though. And while the logging continued he went to #hack, looking for Infomaster. Every now and then Mycroft found him. And then, speaking as straightforwardly as possible, Mycroft warned the man not to keep going. They're watching you, he said. I know this for a fact. You better get off your box for a while, know what I mean?

To Mycroft's amazement, Info ignored him completely. Maybe the reaction was rational—after all, the cracker had been operating in this brazen way for more than a year with no adverse consequences. But Mycroft suspected that the answer lay beyond calculation. It seemed possible that Info did not stop because he could not stop. Cyberspace had become his preferred environment, and he was unable to abjure it for a shadow existence in what hackers called the SCReW—the so-called real world.

Portland
Summer 1992

When Steve Singer was in high school, he worked in a computer company. The company let him create a game on its computer network. The game was a MUD—a Multi-User Dungeon. Originating in the elaborate fantasy-adventure game Dungeons and Dragons, MUDs are simulated environments, usually big castles or underground mazes. No images are involved; players navigate the environments by typing commands. To use a prosaic metaphor, MUDs are like conference calls, except that the interaction is entirely through the written word and the callers agree to pretend that they are together in an imaginary space. Players assume imaginary identities in the MUD, and some addicts spend hours every day in these virtual environments. Steve's MUD was called the Never-Ending Story, after the cult novel of the same name.*

Attracting a coven of dedicated users, the MUD grew to encompass more than three thousand virtual rooms, each with its own elaborate description. A world of its own, the Never-Ending Story was an environment in which all puzzles could eventually be solved, no interactions caused real harm, and participants could always go back and fix what they had broken. Steve immersed himself in it whenever he had the chance. Sometimes he wouldn't play for one week and the next week the MUD would fill up every free moment. After leaving the job, he moved the Never-Ending Story to Portland State, where Janaka tolerated its existence as long as it did not use too many computing resources. Despite the fracas with Steve's brother, Portland State let the MUD continue.

That summer, Steve spent a lot of time at his mother's home. He wanted to use his brother's computer to play the MUD, which forced him to confront the fact that Matt was still up to his shenanigans. He decided to force the issue. Almost literally pushing his brother out of his chair, he announced that for a while the machine was going to be used solely for MUDding. Matt complained furiously, but gave in to his brother's unwonted insistence. After all, Matt, too, enjoyed the MUD. And he knew that his brother's attention would lapse, and that he would eventually be able to pick up the threads again.

Tysons Corner
Summer 1992

To Barnett's surprise and pleasure, Schmidtknecht was as good as his word. After the datatap was authorized, he had the electronics working within twenty-four hours. The wiretap was

* MUDs come in many slightly different varieties—MOOs (Multi-User Dungeon, Object-Oriented), MUCKs (the name is a punning variant, not an acronym), and the popular TinyMUDs, for example. Technically, the Never-Ending Story was a MUSH (Multi-User Shared Hallucination). The distinctions among the various types of virtual world are more important to their aficionados than to anyone else.

physically located in a phone-company switching station in Portland. From there, the intercepted data were then relayed by phone
line to the FBI field office in Portland, where Rasmussen and
Schmidtknecht monitored the data flow for readability and recorded
the transmissions on cassette tapes. In Washington, Barnett had
arranged to create a secure telephone link—a line that couldn't be
tapped—between Portland and Washington, over which Schmidtknecht sent the intercepted data. The transmissions trickled in for
the first few days, as Schmidtknecht worked out the kinks in his
equipment. Then, suddenly, the volume picked up, and she was
deep in the case.

Having heard so much about the threat posed by the Portland
hacker, Barnett was puzzled to find that the transmissions consisted almost entirely of cheery typed conversations about traveling
through a fairy-tale world. Now and then the suspect Telnetted to
other networks, but on these systems he had entirely legitimate
guest accounts, a hospitality provided by any number of universities. But the great majority of the transmissions concerned spells,
monsters, potions, and swords. Baffled, Barnett spent the day
scrolling through fantasy blarney.

Sure didn't look like the evil mastermind of the Internet.

Barnett decided to ask Steve Nesgoda if something had been
lost in the translation.

Nesgoda was a member of the FBI's Computer Analysis
and Response Team, the technical group that extracts data from
seized computers. With two CART colleagues, he removed all
material from the datatap transmissions that could be considered
personal and of no likely use to the investigation. Known as
"minimization," this process, standard on all FBI wiretaps, seeks
to avoid unnecessary invasions of privacy. Minimization is performed by technicians who are not otherwise involved in the
case, and who are thus unlikely to exploit information in the
transmissions. As a rule, case agents never see the raw transmissions; they work only with the filtered transcripts that the minimizers throw over the Chinese wall separating minimizers and
investigators.

What is this junk? she asked Nesgoda. Am I missing something here?

He's just playing games.

What sort of games?

I don't know. Just games. It's pretty much all he does.

Barnett didn't push for more; contact with the opposite side of
the Chinese wall was strictly regulated.

The game, she learned, was a MUD, a virtual fantasy environment that some people found deeply attractive. One of these people,
alas, was the guy Barnett was tapping.

As the transmissions poured in, Barnett began to get a feel
for the amount of time that Matt Singer spent at the keyboard.
She was appalled. Ten or twelve hours a day was standard, and
he often did more. At first, Schmidtknecht, Rasmussen, and Mike
West followed his progress live in the office. That quickly became
unfeasible—he sometimes stayed on-line through three shifts of
observers. Indeed, the datatappers gave up completely after the
suspect finished an epic thirty-hour session with a three-hour
string of "H"s when he apparently passed out from exhaustion
and his face dropped onto the keyboard. On waking, he had
resumed work immediately.

Even after minimization, the sheer mass of information was
breathtaking. Each morning Nesgoda burdened her in box with a
stack of paper that would have dismayed Marcel Proust. Within ten
days the transmissions filled half of a four-drawer file cabinet. They
were so voluminous that Schmidtknecht abandoned his plan to
send the material to Washington over a special modem line. Even
at a speed of 9,600 baud, about a thousand characters a second,
transmitting all the data took hours. Unwilling to spend almost as
long sending the data as the suspect had taken to generate it, the
defeated Schmidtknecht reverted to the low-tech practice of sending
floppy disks by overnight mail.

Nesgoda and his colleagues at CART had it easy, relatively
speaking. They didn't have to understand the material, they only
needed to look for and delete personal information. Barnett, on the

other hand, needed to scrutinize every step the suspect took. Because of the volume of the data, a single session could take several days to analyze, even a week. Fortunately, she was helped by squad members Levord Burns and Ken Welch. Nonetheless, she was continually falling behind. And it was such stupid stuff! Working in a haze of tedium, Barnett followed the suspect's bumbling, misspelled progress through the imaginary world of the MUD.

At the same time, she was being bombarded by angry male voices. Rasmussen, Settle, Silverman—all were furious at the maddening lack of progress. Forced into the unaccustomedly passive role of waiting for the experts to interpret the datatap, Rasmussen couldn't fathom why Barnett was days behind Singer's current activities. The thought that Singer might be committing some awful crime while actually being monitored by the FBI horrified him. He didn't want to know what the suspect was doing last week, he wanted to know what he was doing *now*. I don't know what he's doing now, she kept explaining. Four days ago, he was just playing games. Thanks, Rasmussen said. Thanks a *lot*.

Meanwhile, the increasingly impatient Settle demanded daily progress reports. Silverman, for his part, seemed to regard the disappointing haul as a personal affront—a conspiracy by Washington bureaucrats to obstruct his investigation. I have to go before the judge to justify this T-3, he growled. Am I supposed to tell him we violated Singer's privacy to watch him play *games*? You've got to come up with something better than this.

What was Matt Singer up to, anyway? Why was every sysadmin in the nation convinced that he was hacking the Internet to pieces, and the FBI only saw him play games?

Still sufficiently green to feel intimidated by federal prosecutors, Barnett endured the harassment in silence. But the case was getting to her. She was house-sitting in Maryland for friends who were away for six months. The arrangement saved money and provided nicer digs than she would otherwise have been able to afford, but it also saddled her with a hellish commute along the Beltway. Then she put in twelve hours a day on the datatap transcripts, studying every command, scrutinizing every message exchanged with on-line pals, desperately trying to espy some tiny morsel of digital malfeasance.

On top of that, the tap didn't free her from other obligations. She still had to keep an eye on several other cases she had launched, one of which concerned the Coast Guard network, whose security chief was raising a fuss way out of proportion to the attempted attacks. She had to attend the seminars and workshops on Unix and networks that Settle was forever arranging. And she had to meet the politicians, agency heads, security experts, and law-enforcement representatives that Settle—who never rested from his self-appointed mission to raise the squad's visibility—had asked to come by.

At the time she was falling furthest behind Singer, the office hosted a slew of Italian security experts, including the entire computer-crime division of the carabinieri, the Italian national police force. Settle pulled out all the stops for the Italians. The visit culminated in an Italian-American computer-crime cookout at his home in Alexandria. Clutching a disposable plastic tumblerful of mint julep, Barnett saw sections of that day's transcripts scrolling before her, as if on a teleprompter.

Her temper snapped on the particularly hectic day when Josh Silverman called to heckle her for maybe the third time in a single afternoon. What do you want me to do, make something up? she shouted. Silverman, taken aback, eased off.

The next day Rasmussen called to tell her that the tap had stopped working. Apparently, Singer had switched to a different type of modem, and Schmidtknecht's equipment could not interpret its signals. For a week, no new data arrived.

As if he'd read her mind, Jim Kolouch stuck his head in her office and asked her how it was going. Badly, she said. The modem was broken and she was going to lose her mind, her job, or both.

It doesn't matter whether the wiretap works or not, Kolouch informed her. It doesn't even matter whether you catch him hacking or not.

It doesn't?

No matter what happens, the most you ever get out of this case is one lousy conviction, and it won't even be yours, it'll belong to the office of origin—Portland. And they'll never convict this kid, anyway. He's a loser. The case is a loser. Dump it.

Kolouch disappeared with a cheery wave, leaving Barnett staring at the doorway.

Thanks for the support.

The next time her phone rang, she resolved not to answer it. But she picked up the receiver anyway. It was Rasmussen—the wiretap was working again. Schmidtknecht had peeked at the material, and Singer appeared to be getting busy.

Santa Fe
August 1992

This again? Scott Yelich thought. Someone had Trojaned the log-in program of his network just before midnight on August 12. He spent the day monitoring his system, waiting for the cracker to come for his captured passwords. Around midnight the culprit appeared: Infomaster.

Him? In a way, Scott was pleased—Info was amusing to have around when Scott didn't want to strangle him. The cracker had disappeared from the scene for a while. In recent days, Scott had heard that he was back. Now here he was. His new log-in Trojan was better than his previous version, and more cunningly concealed. Grok had undoubtedly provided it. The new program encrypted the name of the directory into which it dumped passwords, hiding the information from Strings.

While the cracker was looking futilely in the network for his passwords—they had been deleted, of course—Scott dropped a standard log-in admonition in front of him.

## WARNING:

[The think tank's] equipment is to be used only in
conjunction with work approved by the Institute

and is available for the sole use of authorized
users. Equipment use is monitored.

In other words: Hey, buddy, you're caught.

Beat me, Info typed, and logged off.

Scott switched to #hack and waited to see if the cracker would
appear. It was a busy night for the Internet Relay Chat channel—
every member of the Masters of Deception and Legion of Doom who
had avoided arrest seemed to be on-line. The messages were short,
rapid, badly typed, a typographical hodgepodge that was the on-line
equivalent of trying to converse in a crowded bar. Only a practiced
user could decipher the silently scrolling cacophony. As soon as
Info logged on—he had Telnetted to a machine at the Free Software
Foundation—Scott sent him a greeting.

```
<scott>  [My system's] login [program] was
         modified last night
         your backdoor was installed.

<info>   Oh. Only for two minutes.I put it back
         afterwards. .
```

No, Scott thought with a sort of mental rolling of the eyes, you *didn't*
put it back afterward. But he'd put the guy on notice now, and could
afford to be friendly.

```
<scott>  I've been really busy the last two
         months. . . . has anything new appeared
         at mit?

<info>   Not really. Oh check this out. .
```

Info sent Scott a file:

## NASA SCIENCE INTERNET - SECURITY
## BULLETIN NUMBER: 92-08

### 2-JUNE-1992
SUBJECT: **ALERT** Compromises of UNIX Systems

-----------------------------------------------

### NASA/NSI DISTRIBUTION:
***Official NASA Use Only***
FIRST Restrictions: RESPONSE TEAMS ONLY

This is a heads-up message for all UNIX system administrators. Several compromised systems have been discovered at multiple NASA centers. You are advised to pass this memo along [to] other system managers as well as your management so that as many people can be informed as possible.

The attacks are taking the form of trojan-horse versions of the /bin/login program replacing the actual program that is part of UNIX.

The activity appears to have been active for at least the last 2 weeks. . . .

The alert warned sysadmins to look for a hidden file called /usr/spool/secretmail/.l, which was the name of the file in which Infomaster's log-in Trojan stored passwords.

Scott thought the advisory, like many official security bulletins, was a crock. "The activity appears to have been active"—who wrote these things, anyway? And saying that the problems had been occurring "for at least the last two weeks"—it was *eight months* since NASA had discovered the attack. Not to mention that the subject of the warning was in possession of a document that was supposedly restricted to the computer-security agencies that made up FIRST—the Forum of Incident Response and Security Teams, an international umbrella group that was a kind of electronic Interpol.

It turned out that NASA had also produced a second bulletin, which Infomaster zapped to Scott. It, too, was restricted to FIRST members, although it consisted merely of the early CERT bulletin, which was publicly available. Not nice at all, Infomaster wrote about the bulletins.

Scott thought his reaction was bizarre. What did he mean "not nice"?

<info>    That nasa and cert sent out advisories on me. .

<scott>    what do you expect? [ . . . ] you've been making waves at a few sites.

<info>    I guess i need to be more careful.It's obvious there talking about me [because] / usr/spool/secretmail/.1 is the defualt [file name for the captured passwords] on [m]y backdoor login i made.THat's what i usually use [ . . . ]

<scott>    I've been hearing a lot about activity on the net . . . i've figured it was you.
but I hadn't seen you for a long time, and then I noticed the binaries changed last night . . . very strange.

<info>    . . . Hmm . . . Tell me more.Alot of activity on the net?

<scott>    yeah, the cert notice. . . etc.

<info>    [ . . . ] Strange that it [the CERT notice] came out in june[. . . . ] Did that cert advisary actually show up in the official cert advisories . . . Oh boy . . .

<scott>    uh huh
it was quite explicit.
but was old.

&lt;info&gt;    Great.Though that was a couple of
          months ago. I mean great sarcasticaly of
          course.TIme to do some changes on my
          login program.

By now it was 2:30 A.M. Scott had learned what he wanted to learn.
Besides, he had a lot of work. In two weeks he was going to Hong
Kong to teach a security workshop.

&lt;scott&gt;   [ . . . ]oh well, time for bed.
          back tomorrow
          be good kiddies, big brother is logging.

When he went to sleep, Info was still working.

# HONG KONG
# HEIST

Using encryption on the Internet is the equivalent of arranging an armored car to deliver credit-card information from someone living in a cardboard box to someone living on a park bench.

**—GENE SPAFFORD, DIRECTOR, COMPUTER OPERATIONS, AUDIT, AND SECURITY TECHNOLOGY (COAST) PROJECT, PURDUE UNIVERSITY**

College Station, Texas
August 1992

Doug Safford picked up the telephone to hear a voice politely informing him that one of his machines was being used to attack a machine at Ohio State University. Would he please do something about it? Safford was the sysadmin of the supercomputer center at Texas A&M University; the voice belonged to the sysadmin of the supercomputer center at Ohio State; the source of the attack was a Sun SPARCstation in the locked office of an electrical-engineering faculty member who was out of town.

Safford tapped the shoulders of his two assistants, Doug Schales and Dave Hess. All three had studied computer security at

Texas A&M, but until that moment they had never put their book learning to the test. Now circumstances had provided them with an opportunity. Unfortunately, the obvious first step—examine the SPARCstation—was not possible. Because the owner of the machine was absent, they had no legitimate access to its hard drive. But they could monitor its connection to the Internet.

To their chagrin, they discovered that not one but several crackers were using it as a base. In addition, outsiders had grabbed root on another half a dozen machines, filled them with files, and installed a bulletin board. Transmissions flew in and out at an amazing clip.

How could the people who worked with these computers not have noticed the activity? Easily. Unix, with its system of file owner-ship, discourages average users from poking around the boxes, be-cause most files don't belong to them. Not that users usually want to explore their machines. Most regarded the contents of their hard drives as incomprehensible "computer stuff."

Who was attending the electronic cocktail party at Texas A&M? Safford, Schales, and Hess were able to observe only the time and duration of the connections, not what transpired. Wanting to know more, the sysadmins—like Janaka, Nick, and Scott—spent a few hours hacking together a keystroke-recording program. Ohio State had called them on the afternoon of Tuesday, August 25. By early Wednesday they were recording the crackers.

Almost as soon as the program was running they observed a cracker tag team attacking Kent State University, where the mathe-matics department left its many Hewlett-Packard workstations al-most completely unguarded. The team members were one Info, who was aggressively hardworking, and a buddy, a programming-oriented chap who went under the moniker of No Means No or NMN. The Texans didn't know it, but both were familiar figures in the computer underground. Or maybe all three—for although No Means No was a real person who was said to be from Maryland, many crackers believed that the increasingly notorious Jsz liked to borrow the handle for his exploits. Nor did the Texans know that they had stumbled across an early iteration of Jsz's long-held dream of moving beyond the simple guessing of dictionary words in Crack.

CrackerHack, as the program was called, matched passwords against every combination of letters and numbers from A to Z and from 0 to 9. Because the number of random combinations was much larger than the number of dictionary words, the program would inevitably take more time to crunch through all the possibilities. To speed up the process, Info and No Means No were attempting to run CrackerHack simultaneously on all the Kent State machines. They copied a password file to each one, then set up CrackerHack to sift through part of the range of possibilities—aaaaaaaa through cccccccc on one box, for example, and dddddddd through ffffffff on the next.

The password file belonged to a Sun workstation with the address tec.army.mil—the Topographic Engineering Center of the Army Corps of Engineers, a complex in Alexandria, Virginia, dedicated to research on satellite mapping. TEC prepares secret ultra-detailed maps of the world for military and intelligence purposes. The Texas A&M sysadmins were not defense experts, but they suspected that this facility was of the sort routinely described as being essential to national security.

The crackers had managed to burrow into TEC deeply enough to grab password files, but apparently had been frustrated in their effort to obtain root. The only barrier between the crackers and full control of the network was the root password, which appeared in the TEC password files under the encrypted form "du02.uTE35sp2." Unfortunately for Info and No Means No, du02.uTE35sp2 seemed not to be formed from a dictionary word—that is, the root password was a string of random typographical symbols. Crack could not break such passwords, because they were not in a dictionary. Hence the attempt to hitch up CrackerHack, which employed brute force to enumerate all possible passwords.

In theory, the brute-force approach is next to impossible. The number of possible combinations is so vast that Info and No Means No would need to run CrackerHack on many machines. The dozen computers at Kent State could only be a start. They would need to harness more than a hundred others. And any cracker would have to be insanely persistent to break into that many machines and run a program on them. Nobody would be crazy enough to try that, right?

In any case, the sysadmins realized, Info and No Means No were having trouble with CrackerHack even at Kent State, either because it was poorly written or, more likely, its Sun-oriented code —it had attachments with source code from Solaris and SunOS— didn't mesh well with HP-UX, the notoriously cranky Hewlett-Packard version of Unix on the Kent State machines.* Another source of trouble was the crackers' abysmal typing skills, painful to watch. To start CrackerHack, the two crackers first had to translate the source code—it was written in the common programming language C—into a form the computers could read, a process called "compiling." To compile CrackerHack, they needed to type "cc ch.c" —that is, the name of the compiling program (cc, for "C compiler") and the name of the CrackerHack program (ch.c, for "CrackerHack in C"). Maddeningly, Info kept typing "ccc" or "c.c" or "hcc," which caused the machine to emit querulous complaints about syntax errors. And because the crackers were at the end of a chain of connections—Info came to Kent State from Texas A&M, to Texas A&M from the Free Software Foundation, and to the Foundation from Lord knew how many other machines—the accumulated network delays meant that each failure manifested itself with nail-biting slowness.

Even as the crackers struggled with their own spelling, they used their private bulletin board to boast about their next scheme, a plan that to Hess felt like an equal mix of the absurd and the frightening. Info and No Means No wanted to create a "worm," a

---

* "HP-SUX (H-P suhks) *n*. Unflattering hackerism for HP-UX, Hewlett-Packard's Unix [version], which features some truly unique bogosities. . . . Hackers at HP/Apollo (the former Apollo Computers which was swallowed by HP in 1989) have been heard to complain that Mr. Packard should have pushed to have his name first, if for no other reason than the greater eloquence of the resulting acronym."—The on-line hacker Jargon File, version 3.3.1, January 25, 1996.

term borrowed from John Brunner's *The Shockwave Rider,* a science fiction novel popular with hackers. In Internet parlance, a worm is a program that automatically crawls from machine to machine over a network, making copies of itself as it goes. The worm that Scott Yelich saw sweep the Internet in 1988 is the most notorious example. Multiplying with incredible rapidity, it clogged up hundreds of computers across the nation. The worm, which was created by a Cornell University graduate student, had no purpose; a misdirected prank, it simply took advantage of one of the ubiquitous holes in Sendmail and spread everywhere. But No Means No had an idea for a new kind of worm that was not a prank. The explanation spilled across Hess's computer screen, expressed in the mix of typos, technobabble, and sideways smiley-faces (the :) symbols known as "emoticons") that is the hallmark of digital communication.

### NO MEANS NO
i wanna discuss the worm its been goin through
my head alot
So heres what i say it does:
You instal it on a system, and give it
username/pass[word] info for another syste,m
(basically you need 2 systems to start it) Its got a
tail and a head basically. and does this: The
head tries to gain access to anothewr system
while the tail does all it can yto install
backdoors, mail .logs,mail etc/passwd files, etc
. . . until it is told to abort. . it aborts when: It
aborts when the head gains access to a 3rd
system, when it does the old head becomes the
tail and the old tail is told to self destruct.

### INFO
Sounds like a plan. . . .

### NO MEANS NO
so it moves its way through every system forever. .
i will have detection routines so if a tail or head

gets killed (from a shutdown or killed process) it
will sprout a new head and MUTATE into 2
wworms
so basically there will be worms ALL OVER THE
FUCKIN PLCE man
In time that is . . . we will have every fuckin
system. . it could run for months or years until it is
fully detected and exterminated

### INFO
We will create the very first AI Cyberworm

### NO MEANS NO
It will be a VERY COMPLICATED program i tell ya

### INFO
It sound's like it will be pretty complicated.I can
envision a few things myself. . If where lucky and
do it right nobody will be any the wiser :).

### NO MEANS NO
Unmatched. and be pretty fuckin large because it
will carry tools like program crackers that mail
results etc. . so if the tail gets kileld it leaves
behind running poograms and backdoors and
password crackers that mail the restults, like
shit. . it digests the system and leaves tracks

### INFO
*CACKLE* [ . . . ] It will be like an auto spreading
hacker virus

### NO MEANS NO
Hehehe . . . . . I like that. . . . . . . .

### INFO
yep! *GRIN*

*GRIN*, indeed. The crackers never got CrackerHack running
that night. After three hours of fruitless effort, No Means No thought
about quitting.

### NO MEANS NO
Dude this is TOO frustrating. things just arent
working let me call tommorw when i wake up. . i
also completely do not understand why you cant
install it. . i write programs, i give ideas, and you
also want me to go through and put the stuff up?

### INFO
Ok. .Good night.See you on [the Texas A&M
machine] in the morning or afternoon.

### NO MEANS NO
[ . . . ] who gives a fuck im going to bed man i am
frustrated as fuck and i cant beleive i stayed up
all fucking night and accomplished 0
life is just total shit lately fuck it all good nigth, c
u tommorw

Info was reassuring.

### INFO
Give me the exact instructions and i will put it on
all the hp's [Hewlett-Packard computers]. . I am
sorry you are so frusterated . . . Well.MAybe
getting some sleep will make you feel better.

To Hess's eye, Info seemed to have some understanding of the prin-
ciples of psychology. He was a leader of the troops, reassuring No
Means No today in the hope of obtaining further effort tomorrow.

### INFO
BUT it sould crack it. . its running right now, it
could crack it [the root password] tonight, could
crack it next week, who knows.

### NO MEANS NO
Good luck and sorry if i seemed like an asshole. .
nothing personal man. . im just in that bummed
mood today i guess., blah

### INFO
I have had does like that.Lack of sleep will also
do weird things to some people.Just get a good
night's rest and we will hva have fun tommorow.

No Means No quit at four in the morning. Rubbing his eyes, Hess
watched Info continue, tirelessly reading other people's e-mail in
between bouts of trying to compile the program work. He was still
working when Hess at last went to bed.

Info could understand No Means No's frustration, but that didn't
mean he, too, was going to quit. Things had always come hard for
him—very hard. But he had learned that if he worked long enough
he would eventually come through. Patience was the cardinal virtue.
If one attempt was unsuccessful, he stepped back, took a rest, and
tried again. Or he went on to something else, then came back. When,
after another hour of trying CrackerHack, he concluded that something he didn't know was preventing him from running it success-
fully, he turned to another subject while awaiting more data.

Info was in excellent spirits. After months of fracas about his
hermitic habits, he and his brother had moved to his father's house
in northeast Portland. The setup there was made to order. His father
and stepmother both worked the night shift at a mental hospital.
Info began waking up with them at midnight. The whole household
went on backward time. Except for Steve. But because his brother
refused to alter his schedule, Info suddenly had his computer back

to himself. Every night he waved as his father drove to work, downed a midnight breakfast of potato chips and Doritos, then got on-line. When his father returned, clumping up the wooden steps, it was a signal to Info that he might consider getting some sleep. Or he might not, if he was finding material that interested him.

For the first time in his life he was being left alone long enough to get something accomplished.

When he joined #hack early in the morning of Thursday, August 27, lo and behold, there was Scott, acting friendly as usual. Scott was a pain in the neck who always asked Info for new tricks and never gave anything back. Info had taken his stash of cracker tools to redress the balance, except it turned out to be useless—everything was encrypted. Since then Info had returned many times to Santa Fe, always hoping to return at the magic moment when Scott had decoded his tools, a necessary step to using them. That hadn't happened yet, but Info was willing to wait.

Scott greeted him right off the bat.

<scott>   learned any new tricks?

<info>   No not really.

<scott>   I got a few. . . .I haven't had time to
          check them out.

This was one of Scott's standard lines. He had all this great new stuff, except that somehow he didn't. Still, there was always hope.

<info>   Cool what are they. . . .Spill the info
         scott.

Info was constantly on a low-intensity prowl for information about Sendmail, which was necessary for his long-term backbone-sniffing project with Jsz. Recently rumors of new Sendmail bugs had appeared on #hack. If Info acted like he already had them, maybe he could learn about them from Scott—assuming, of course, that Scott actually knew anything.

> &lt;info&gt;   I have been messing with sendmail
> without much luck getting any of the
> holes to work. .
>
> &lt;scott&gt;  I haven't had a time to try them.
> Basically they look like standard shell
> escapes.
>
> &lt;info&gt;   That's telling me a lot :) . . . Can't you at
> least tell me the basics of what the holes
> are.HAve there been advisories
>
> &lt;scott&gt;  I don't know if this works.
> It's for new sunso
> sunos
> but I don't have access to new sunos
> [source code]

Info ignored this broad hint about whether the underground had
the source code for the latest release of the standard Sun operating
system. As he often did, he checked to see who was on-line. Surprisingly, the hacker who called himself Scott was not on-line from his
usual location in Santa Fe. Instead he was at a different address:
cssul l.ust.hk.

> &lt;info&gt;   Hold it once second. .You aren't the
> scott. Wait . . . How can this be. Where
> are you?

An address ending in .hk was . . . the United Kingdom? No, wait,
not .uk, it was .hk—Hong Kong? Was Scott in Hong Kong?

Scott explained that he was co-teaching a security course at
the new University of Science and Technology up in the hills of
Kowloon. He'd brought a few floppies' worth of his cracker tools and
was having the workshop students work with them. One of the tools,
in fact, was Info's most recent log-in Trojan—the Grok-improved

program he had installed on Scott's network just two weeks before. It breaks the system horribly here, he told Info. Can't use it at all.

They spoke desultorily for at least three hours, Info badgering Scott for news about Sendmail in one window on his screen while checking the results of his password cracking at Kent State in a second. Then, pleading exhaustion at the end of a hard day, Scott logged off.

When he was certain that Scott had retired, Info Telnetted into the university at Hong Kong. If Scott was letting students use his cracker tools, he must be decrypting them. Somewhere in the University of Science and Technology, then, sat Info's goal—unscrambled copies of Scott's cracker tools. It was just a matter of finding a path. A technical school would have a big network with many machines. One of those machines, he knew, would have a hole. By now the sky was the clear, pale blue of high summer. His father was back from work and he'd been at the keyboard for more than twelve hours. In ordinary circumstances he might think of sleep, but these were not ordinary circumstances. He began knocking on doors in the university network.

Twelve hours later, he had root access.

Exactly as he had hoped, the files were unencrypted for the students to use. As an experiment, he ran a routine that wiped out his entries in the logs of the Hong Kong network. He disappeared from its view.

Within an hour, he was downloading Scott's programs from the students' computers to his own stash at Texas A&M. Because his modem was slow, the transfer took a long time. He didn't mind. Charged up with success, he was still working away in the first light of dawn on Friday.

He went to bed about the time that his father came home. He'd been on-line for two days straight.

When he awoke that night, he went immediately to his machine. He slipped into Portland State, then Telnetted to Texas A&M, ready to explore Scott's programs further.

He could not get into Texas A&M. The network was shut down. His new tools were out of reach.

• • •

After a night of cracker-watching, Doug Safford, Doug Schales, and Dave Hess had enough information to order a total shutdown and cleanup at the Texas A&M computer center. On Friday morning, August 28, they purged the network of Trojans, .rhosts files, illicit copies of Crack, root-grabbing programs, and the other epiphenomena of the invasion. After working all day to clean up the pillaged boxes, the three men switched on the network and went home.

Within hours, emergency calls from assistant admins dragged the three men from their beds. The crackers were back. Amazed, the sysadmins returned to their logging programs, which they had continued to run. Quickly they found a hidden file with hundreds of captured passwords. Alas, they had grossly underestimated the number of compromised machines. They had thoroughly disinfected a few boxes, but many others were Trojaned.

Furious and embarrassed, the sysadmins regrouped. What to do? The crackers were more sophisticated than the sysadmins had initially guessed. Info, the chief attacker, couldn't spell but he certainly knew how to break into the Texas network. The sysadmins also faced figures like No Means No, who seemed to be a capable programmer, and the mysterious Scott From Hong Kong, whose role was bafflingly ambiguous. What was he doing with all those cracker tools, anyway? Meanwhile, at the university, the professorate was in a state of revolt, demanding that their machines be physically disconnected from the network.

After long discussion, the sysadmins decided to install a kind of filter—like a firewall, but not as complete—that would cut off the university from Telnet altogether. Each machine would then be reinspected, inoculated with corrective programs if infected, and permitted to add Telnet on a machine-by-machine basis. On Monday afternoon they presented the plan to the administration, which gave it the thumbs-up. Writing the filter took all night. Installation was complete by the end of the afternoon of Tuesday, September 1.

• • •

It hadn't taken long to slip back into Texas A&M after the network reappeared on-line Friday night. The sysadmins, Info decided, must have found his log-in Trojan. But they had not found all of his back doors. He continued experimenting with Scott's tools and working with No Means No until the evening of Tuesday, September 1, when he was abruptly cut off again. This time the barrier was for real. He couldn't Telnet into the university at all—they'd blocked the service entirely. He tried everything he could think of, and still couldn't get in. He had lost access.

By a stroke of good fortune, he came across Grok on #hack. They hadn't talked to each other for a couple weeks, which meant that Grok was likely to be favorably disposed toward him. In addition, they went a long way back. Grok had given Info his first Trojan. In return, Info had given Grok the source code to Solaris. And he had passed on Dan Farmer's e-mail to him. Now he had something else to give Grok—Scott's decrypted cracker tools. The only problem was that they were locked up at Texas A&M.

No problem. Grok had recently discovered—who knew how— a brand new hole in Sun's version of Sendmail. It was incredibly simple to use. You just sent blank e-mail, then e-mailed root commands with a pipe symbol in the address. In fact, Grok told him, the same hole had turned up years before and been fixed. While working on another bug, the folks at Sun had inadvertently re-created this old favorite.

Info and Grok e-mailed themselves a root account.

The funny thing was that Grok hadn't needed to trot out the Sendmail hole. Only after they were inside the Texas A&M network did they discover that the sysadmins had blocked only Telnet. Like the Intel system, the Texas network was wide open to FTP—File Transfer Protocol, the Internet service that is usually employed to send files from one computer to another. Grok knew how to use FTP to slip past the filter and install another back door.

So they did that, too.

• • •

Early in the morning of Friday, September 4, CERT called Texas A&M. Hess couldn't believe it. Another university was under attack from a machine at Texas A&M, which meant that the crackers were back. They were like digital kudzu—impossible to eradicate. Again, the three men stayed up all night, exhaustedly poring through their logs. The crackers had broken in with FTP, a possibility that the sysadmins had not considered. In addition, they were using programs that concealed their presence. One of them prevented Ps, the program that lists the processes running on a computer, from showing the intruders' activity. If they were running Crack, sysadmins could ask what programs were active and never learn the true answer.

Again working all night, the weary Safford, Schales, and Hess redesigned the filter from a new point of view. From now on, the filter would automatically refuse all connections. Only after it was specifically instructed to accept a request would it permit entry. The work was finished by five in the morning on Saturday. It seemed to lock out all unauthorized entry.

The crackers apparently were stymied. Indeed, surprisingly, they exerted no effort to return. Wondering what the crackers were doing, the sysadmins spent a few days adapting their filter into a set of security programs that they gave away in good hacker fashion.

Meanwhile, the three sysadmins prepared a long memorandum about the incident to CERT. Appended to their report was a list of forty-five machines the crackers had broken into, culled from the first 5 percent of the logs. The tally included sites of every description: Kent State, of course; the Topographic Engineering Center; the University of Maryland; Portland State University; the Consiglio Nazionale di Ricerca, the Italian national nuclear physics center; and ANS (Advanced Networks and Services), the consortium that ran much of the Internet backbone. The biggest corporation on the list was Harris, a large Florida-based defense contractor.

Reading the list over, the sysadmins wondered what the crack-

ers had *done* in these places in all the time they operated unde-
tected.

After leaving Portland State University, Mike Wilson, the big-
boned student sysadmin, went to work at Lawrence Livermore National Laboratory. He continued to be interested in computer
security, which was why he attended a lecture on the subject soon
after his arrival. The speech covered a variety of potential computer-
security threats, one of which jolted Mike sufficiently that he lost
track of the lecture and sat in the audience with his eyes wide in
private alarm.

The threat involved what is known as flash-ROM. ROM—read-
only memory—is the kind of computer memory that resides permanently on a chip. In a personal computer, ROM chips instruct the
microprocessor how to perform actions such as connecting to a
hard drive. Flash-ROM chips are ROM chips that can be permanently stamped with a program in a factory. The lecturer pointed
out that the ROM software originally resided in a network at the
chip factory. If crackers entered that network, they could alter the
program—and all of its millions of flash-ROM copies.

The lecturer cited several examples of flash-ROM chips that
should not be altered. Mike was thrown into his reverie by an example he thought of on his own: automatic braking systems in automobiles. These systems use the software in flash-ROM chips to monitor
drivers' actions, regulating brake pressure to prevent skids. As the
talk continued, Mike's interior theater was occupied by a vivid picture of millions of cars programmed to lose control the five thou-
sandth time the brakes engaged. How many deaths would occur
before someone figured out the problem?

Later he looked up the names of the manufacturers of automatic braking systems. One of them was Bosch, a German conglomerate. Another one was Harris, a large Florida-based defense
contractor.

# 14

# BREAKING THE
# BACKBONE

When we were designing the Athena system [at MIT], we knew the network represented a major security threat. Quite frankly, we assumed that our students would quickly figure out how to program campus workstations so that they would act as efficient password-grabbing machines. To reduce this danger, we developed the Kerberos authentication system. . . . This name sake of the great three-headed dog that once stood guard at the entrance to the underworld is the heart of Athena's security. Unlike its predecessor, however, our cybernetic watchdog has yet to fail in its vigil.

—JEFFREY SCHILLER, MIT NETWORK MANAGER, *SCIENTIFIC AMERICAN,*
NOVEMBER 1994

As far as Info was concerned, Grok's demonstration of the Sendmail bug at Texas A&M could not have come at a better time. Jsz had almost finished his sniffer. Using the hole in Sendmail, they'd be able to slip the sniffer past the strongest firewall. They were both rueful about how Grok had discovered the hole—reading Dan Farmer's e-mail, which Jsz had lifted and sent to Infomaster, who had in turn passed it on to Grok. For months the crackers had been trying to figure out how to exploit Sendmail, and the entire time the answer had been sitting on their hard drives.

To test the sniffer, Info broke into a network, installed the program, and returned to the network to collect the results, which he fed to Jsz, who used them to revise and correct the code. When Jsz sent the next version of the program, Info broke into a new system to test it, in the long, iterative sequence of improvements characteristic of software design. As expected, the program was buggy at first. Sometimes it froze and recorded nothing. Sometimes it crashed the machine. A few times Info discovered to his horror that it had wiped out every file on the box on which it was installed.

Other problems surfaced as well. Because Jsz based the sniffer on SunOS and Solaris source code, the program was limited to Suns. Indeed, after a series of lockups Info concluded that the software could not abide other flavors of Unix. Fortunately, Sun was everywhere on the Net.

Exasperatingly, Info himself created difficulties by purchasing a new, faster modem. Unfortunately, he couldn't make it talk, so to speak, to his computer. In such situations, as sysadmins often complain, years of expertise are little help: setting up modems on personal computers involves, among other things, establishing an "initialization string"—a line of opaque commands. The commands are "explained" in manuals that to most people read as if translated from the Icelandic. For two weeks Info struggled with the manual, during which time his machine constantly stalled and the modem transmitted nothing but gibberish. When he realized that the new modem was hindering the development of the sniffer, Info gave up on the new device and returned to his old modem.

After testing the sniffer on machines throughout the Internet, Info decided to install the software on the backbone. He had explored the edges of Advanced Networks and Services, the MCI-IBM–Northern Telecom consortium that operated the most important of the backbone lines. At the heart of the ANS network was a group of large routers—computers that directed the flow of data packets like so many electronic traffic cops. Each router was serviced by a subnetwork of attending machines, the whole forming an electronic archipelago of impressive scale. The system was bristling with firewalls. Not only did firewalls stand guard between every router and the outside world, but ANS had installed them between the routers, isolating each subnetwork in a protected zone of its own.

The firewalls had rejected everything Info threw at them. But even if he had been able to break through the protection, he could not have created an account for himself or endowed an ordinary account with root privileges, because the networks had software alarms that alerted sysadmins when users performed actions like creating accounts or seizing root.

That was where the Sendmail bug came in. Like all Unix programs, Sendmail is "owned" by an account, in this case usually an account with a name like Operator or Mail. Because Sendmail must be able to put messages into every user's electronic mailbox, Operator or Mail must have root access. Every time users send a piece of e-mail, they in effect temporarily become Operator or Mail, which means that they have root access. They lose that access when they finish sending mail and go back to their ordinary identities. In theory, Sendmail prevents users from doing anything with that root access but sending mail. But the Sendmail bug let Info employ the program's root privileges for other purposes.

The alarms on the backbone network were designed to go off if anyone seized root. But because Sendmail—or, more precisely, the Operator or Mail accounts—already had root privileges, Info didn't trip the alarms. He was effectively invisible.

For a little while, anyway. He was sure that the sysadmins of Advanced Network Services scanned for intruders frequently. They would surely notice rogue programs if they ran for long periods of time. As a result, he ran the sniffer in bursts—an hour or two at the most.

One by one, he slipped into the backbone subnetworks, installed the sniffer, and left the system. A little later, he returned and removed all traces of his handiwork, including the sniffer log.

The sniffer copied the first 128 characters of any session into a hidden, encrypted file. Because the backbones carried huge amounts of electronic traffic, the files grew rapidly. After an hour, they contained tens of thousands of 128-character entries, most of which were names and passwords.

Working diligently through October and November, Info installed sniffers first on ANS, then Sprintlink and BBNplanet. In each system Info monitored a tiny slice of the backbone traffic for a short interval. But that was enough to let him accumulate about sixty megabytes of sniffer logs with hundreds of thousands—perhaps millions—of passwords and account names. Military networks, government systems, commercial communications—everything passed through the backbone, where it became prey to the sniffer.

Like all crackers, Info regarded the phrase "Internet security" as an oxymoron; anyone who entrusted vital data to the Internet was, in his opinion, a fool. Regarding the sniffer logs as his greatest treasure, he wouldn't entrust them to a machine like mit2e.mit.edu, which was always connected to the global network. Instead, he stored the logs on his own computer.

Info had two hard drives of two hundred megabytes apiece—a lot of capacity by the standards of 1992. Nonetheless, the sniffer data overloaded his system. His programs had so little room to operate that his machine was constantly stalling.

Not that Info was complaining. He was done forever with searching electronic mail for the word "password." Nor would he need to hunt for .rhosts files or people who used the same password for several accounts. He could throw away all the versions of Crack that he had ever tried. From now on, when he wanted to enter a system, he simply picked through the sniffer logs until he found the name and password of someone who had logged onto the system while the sniffer was riding the backbone.

Infomaster had justified his handle. He had access to everything. Never again could anyone shut him out of his electronic world.

From Beth Barnett's point of view, the end of the MUD was a mixed blessing. On the one hand, the suspect began visiting many other networks—universities, mainly. On the other hand, she didn't understand what he was doing there. In itself, unauthorized entry into a computer network violated federal law. But electronic trespassing was not the kind of crime that would excite Rasmussen, Settle, and Silverman. They wanted to know whether Singer was up to something more sinister, as his repeated attacks on government sites and penchant for supercomputers suggested. And the plain fact is that she didn't understand Unix well enough to know the answer.

Her transfer to the computer-crime squad had placed her in an embarrassingly false position. Before joining the Bureau, she had done low-level programming with languages such as BASIC on MS-DOS personal computers—experience that was irrelevant to Unix systems and their associated languages, C and PERL. In addition, the FBI had taken her away from computers for three years, stationing her in Birmingham, Alabama. The posting had broadened her experience as a crime fighter but knocked her off-line as a computer expert. She knew less than her nominal subordinates in the minimization group on the other side of the Chinese wall. Absurdly, she was boning up on the fundamentals of computer networks at the same time that she was effectively running a major computer-crime case. It was like trying to learn to drive while racing a Formula I car.

To learn Unix, she consulted a slim paperback called *Unix in a Nutshell*. By the standards of computer manuals, the text was lucid, even friendly. Nonetheless, *Unix in a Nutshell* was of little help. The book explained how to approach Unix properly. But to understand what hackers were doing, she needed to learn how to use it improperly. For instance, *Unix in a Nutshell* neglected to explain the art of seizing root. The index did not have entries like ".rhosts files, manipulation of," or "directories, world-exportable, abuse of."

Little wonder that she was almost two weeks behind in the transcripts.

Unix was not the only problem. Soon after Singer recommenced hacking, he bought another modem, which Schmidt-knecht's equipment could not understand—the transcripts looked as if Singer were receiving nothing but gibberish. When she told Settle what was happening, he came up with a theory: the hacker was doing his illegal work on a special modem that was equipped with some kind of stealth capability, saving his game playing for the modem that transmitted *en clair*. Although Settle convinced himself of the validity of this theory, Barnett had doubts. Singer proved her correct. He stopped using the stealth modem entirely. Which left her back where she had started. What was he doing in the networks he entered?

She was struggling through a new set of minimized transmissions when she found a note from someone on the other side of the Chinese wall: *Hey, Beth, look at this!*

The lines of text after the note consisted of a log-in procedure followed by a stretch of letters and symbols that meant nothing to her.

Unix strikes again.

Unable to understand the reason for the annotation, she consulted Levord Burns. What's he doing there? she asked, pointing to the commands.

He's porting root, observed a gravelly voice from behind their chairs. Startled, Barnett whirled around to see the thin, bespecta-cled form of Dave Icove, from the FBI's Engineering Research Section in Chantilly, Virginia. Icove was the kind of Unix power hitter who should have been in the computer-crime squad. Naturally, his expertise made him too important to take part in actual crime fighting; instead the Bureau used him to develop new software for criminal investigation. He dropped by Tysons Corner now and then to gossip.

Porting root? asked Barnett.

Hopping from one host where you have root privileges to an-

other where you don't. Except you take the privileges with you. It's
SOP for these guys.

Why's he doing it?

Probably wants to put in Trojans and back doors. Yeah, look
here, see?

As Icove explained the next commands, Barnett realized that
she was observing illegal activity of the sort that would please Rasmussen, Settle, and Silverman. Editing a .rhosts file, copying electronic mail, installing software . . . it was all here.

Barnett had been praying for this moment for a month, but
now that the moment was upon her, she felt strangely restrained.
Too many people were depending on this. Settle wanted to nail a
major-league hacker for his squad. Rasmussen wanted to stop waiting by the phone and kick down a door. Silverman wanted to face
the judge with a real crime. And Barnett, for her part, wanted to go
to sleep at night knowing she didn't have to wake up the next morning and face another day of Matt Singer transcripts.

Another two weeks of interceptions were piled in her office.
She hoped that Singer had continued to work in that time, which
would provide law enforcement with enough evidence to build an
overwhelming case. She also hoped that Singer hadn't done something catastrophic, because that would bear out everyone's worst
fear—that the suspect would plan and perform some evil act while
under the scrutiny of the Federal Bureau of Investigation.

Instead, Singer hardly hacked for the entire time. Out of his
computer came nothing more than MUDdery and harmless mean-
dering through the global network—infuriating Settle, who had the
smell of blood in his nostrils. He was more impatient than ever for
Barnett to prove that Singer was not merely shoehorning his way
into a few university computers, but that he was stealing something
important.

Rasmussen, too, was exercised. Whenever Barnett was pulled
out of the office by one of Settle's daylong seminars, she returned
the next morning to find two or three messages from Rasmussen.
Then he'd call again before she had worked up the patience to return

any of the calls. Over and over again, they had the same conversation.

I left you a message—didn't you get it?

I was out.

I guess you have a right to take a headache day.

It wasn't a headache day, whatever that is.

Look—can you tell me what he's doing now?

I'm not working on where he is now. I'm on where he was almost two weeks ago. It'll be two weeks from now before I can tell you where he's going for today. If you need to know immediately, why don't you see if you can get some help from MIT?

This usually silenced him—the school had made it clear that it would expend no more resources on hacker chasing. CERT, too, was useless. The agency treated FBI agents as if they were spies. Rasmussen eventually caved in: All right, where was he two weeks ago?

Toward the sixth week of the datatap Barnett was finally able to produce a satisfactory answer. It looks, she said, like he was getting into Los Alamos.

*Los Alamos?* Beth, that was something you should have told me right away. Don't you know what they got out there? You can't sit on that kind of thing for two weeks.

Brent, she said, gritting her teeth. I didn't know he was there until today.

Silverman wasn't happy, either. Now back in Washington, he, too, called constantly for information. When, at last, she was able to provide him with the news about Los Alamos, he reminded her that mere entry into a government lab was not enough to ensure a conviction, notwithstanding the nuclear weapons data at the facility. Simple entry was not even enough to be certain the judge would continue to approve the datatap. To prosecute, Silverman would need a penetration that clearly showed the hacker meant business.

Just what does it take, exactly, to make you happy? she snapped at him after one such telephoned complaint.

You know what I need, he barked back. I need alterations, I need deletions, I . . .

I've *given* you that, Josh. What's your problem?

What are you talking about? You haven't given me anything like that.

Did you read the summary I faxed you yesterday? she asked.

I read it, he said, sounding a little tentative.

Take a closer look, she said.

Silverman called back ten minutes later. Okay, he said, it's there, but you *buried* it.

Excuse me?

Silverman explained that he expected important findings to be prominently featured at the beginning of each day's summary. Barnett had been constructing long, formal memoranda patterned after the T-3 affidavit; the details of each break-in were more or less tacked on to the end.

Don't hide the good stuff, Silverman chided.

You're supposed to be reading the whole summary, not skimming the beginning.

Silverman failed to appreciate this observation.

When further words were exchanged, Josh Silverman, Scott Charney, Jim Settle, and Beth Barnett met in Tysons Corner. Charney and Settle pressured their young colleagues into a truce of sorts. Silverman agreed to back off a notch; Barnett promised to write a few paragraphs at the top of each day's summary that explained the most salient points—in effect, to write summaries of the summaries.

But some of the acrimony remained. After the meeting, as Silverman was walking out the door, Barnett called his name. He turned around.

She tossed him a copy of *Unix in a Nutshell.*

Cambridge
December 1992

Early one cold morning, Ted Ts'o received a call for assistance. An assistant to Jeff Schiller, MIT's network manager, Ts'o spent his days tweaking one of the world's most complex computer networks.

He was accustomed to sudden demands for help. But this one was a distinct surprise.

The center of Ts'o's working life was Project Athena, the biggest, most expensive research project in MIT history. Athena was what happened, as Schiller liked to put it, when people created a computer network from the ground up. As a rule, networks have been created atop previously existing institutions; most warehouses, for example, simply translated their current record-keeping systems into digital form. Athena was an attempt to go the other way—that is, to imagine that the network existed first, and then to graft institutions like warehouses onto it. Athena began in 1983 and cost about $120 million.

Athena was also intended to prove Schiller's belief that encryption, properly applied, was essential to solving the problems of computer security. All communications within the Athena network were passed through Kerberos software. When users logged onto Athena, Kerberos issued a "ticket" that encrypted their names and passwords with a mathematical key created especially for that session. By such means, Schiller argued, the vulnerabilities of Unix could be obviated.

The weaknesses of even the best-protected system were thrown into relief on the day in December of 1992 when Ted Ts'o got a call for help and discovered that the disk in one of Athena's dial-up servers was choked with files from a cracker. The dial-up server was, as its name indicated, a server that could be contacted by telephone and modem from outside MIT. On the server were a variety of cracker tools, including a Trojaned version of Telnet that logged passwords as they came in. Ts'o guessed that the cracker had installed the Trojan at least two months earlier—and forgot to return for his passwords. Throughout October and November, the program had merrily collected all the passwords and account names flowing into the busy server. Eventually, the interceptions had filled up every scrap of empty space on the hard drive. The box had promptly crashed, which was why Ts'o had been called in.

Ts'o had little trouble imagining what had happened. The cracker had found a user with two accounts, one at MIT and one somewhere else. The user had the same password for both accounts —something that sysadmins at neither network could prevent. With the password, the intruder logged on in the guise of the authorized user. Then he got into a program called Rdist, which keeps a group of machines in synchronization by copying master versions of a file from one machine to many others. Unfortunately, the program can only jump from machine to machine if its "owner" has root access and is listed in files like .rhosts. In 1991, CERT had warned about a problem with .rdist—and somehow Infomaster had found a machine on the campus that had not been patched. With that, he seized root, grabbed the source code for Kerberized Telnet, doctored the code, and used his root access to replace the log-in program with his Trojan. The only mystery was the cracker's failure to return for his passwords.

The next question was the number of potentially compromised accounts, which was equivalent to the number of accounts that had Telnetted to the dial-up server while it was Trojaned. After a few hours of dusting off old records, Ts'o calculated the number: more than four thousand. Ugh, he thought. He was going to have to notify all four thousand people of the problem and get them to change their accounts—an odious clerical task. Worse, he would have to tell Schiller that their fully encrypted system had been Swiss-cheesed in the most classical fashion.

In point of fact, Schiller took the news with relative equanimity. With suggestions from Ts'o, he put together a campuswide alert about the incident that was printed on December 14—printed, rather than distributed by the customary e-mail, because they didn't want to alert the cracker. The only explosion had occurred when Schiller surveyed the cracker's handiwork and discerned that the captured passwords resided in a hidden directory called "secretmail." A Trojaned Telnet that set up this directory had not only been the subject of advisories from CERT, CIAC, and NASA, but it had been seen before at MIT, by Nick Papadakis and Mike Patton at the Laboratory for Computer Science.

This is the guy we reported to the FBI six months ago, Schiller thought. He's still out there.

Unlike others at MIT, Schiller had an uncomplicated response to cracking. He thought that it was wrong, that it was illegal, and that it should be punished. On the other hand, he had complicated feelings about law enforcement. As a teenager he had once been roughed up by some local cops—an experience guaranteed to turn the most ardent supporters of law and order into skeptics of police power. He also had violently colored views about the importance of privacy and the predilection of the state for snooping. But his job at MIT kept him in frequent contact with agencies like the FBI, and he had come to respect many of the agents with whom he worked. Vexed by the months-long attack on Athena, he took the occasion of one of his conversations with the new FBI computer-crime squad to ask in his politely tenacious way what had happened to the investigation begun by Nick Papadakis. Partly because of the power of the MIT name, he quickly reached the FBI agent who was in charge of the investigation—a woman named Barnett.

Here is a guy who has stolen thousands of passwords from us, he said. He has broken into the electronic homes of enough people to fill a small city. And that's just at MIT. We know he's done the same to many other systems—six months ago, we had evidence he had hit thousands of them. He's still out there, evidently. So what's going on with you people?

Tysons Corner

Jeff Schiller's calls were invariably polite, but they were almost as unnerving to Barnett as the calls from Rasmussen and Silverman. Everyone wanted her to deliver something she didn't have.

Then, more than forty days into the datatap, the case exploded. Like a recovering alcoholic who suddenly falls off the wagon, Singer went on a hacking marathon. Moving with incredible swiftness, he slipped into one system after another. In each he gained access easily; indeed, he seemed already to have stolen accounts on all of them. As the number of break-ins mounted, Barnett wondered if the hacker were operating from a nationwide list of accounts. He wasn't guessing anymore. Instead, he used accounts and passwords he already knew to walk boldly through the front door.

It was about this time that Barnett came across another note from minimization: *Beth, here's your case!*

Having had another few weeks of cramming, she was better at following the standard hacking routines. Calling Levord Burns over, she needed only a few minutes to recognize that the suspect had broken into the Naval Research Laboratory, an R&D center just outside the Beltway, and the Ballistic Research Laboratory, a facility operated by the Department of Defense in Aberdeen, Maryland. In both places, he rifled through files, established phony accounts, emplaced back doors, erased his tracks, and left.

Barnett called the sysadmin at Naval Research, who denied that any break-ins had occurred. No security lapses here, the sysadmin said.

She asked if she might pay a visit to the center.

At the laboratory, Barnett and Burns were greeted by a delegation of skeptical navy officials. They conducted the two FBI agents to a conference room, where copies of the transcript were passed out. As the officers flipped through the pages, the volume of conversation fell. By the time the last person finished the last word, the room was silent.

I think we have a problem here, a sysadmin said.

At the ballistics laboratory, the two agents met with Les Aker, an easygoing computer manager. Like the navy officers, Aker looked on skeptically as Barnett spread the transcript on the table. Working his jaw, he scanned silently through the typed exchanges. Then he said: Oooooh.

Barnett and Burns looked at each other. Oooooh?

The hacker, Aker said, had gotten right next to some black systems.

"Black" systems, he explained, were those with classified information. Researchers weren't allowed to connect black machines to the Internet. Instead, they were supposed to use a separate system of "white" machines for sending and receiving e-mail. But it was hard to keep the machines completely separate when people were constantly jumping back and forth between the two. In effect, Aker said, the white machines often became off-white, or even gray.

The off-white machines had been penetrated by Singer.

As Aker made clear, the compromised boxes would be unlikely to be holding any classified military data at the exact time that Singer was inside them. It was extremely unlikely that the first breach of security (secret data on the white systems) would occur at the same time as the second (hackers penetrating into white systems). The coincidence would be incredible. On the other hand, nobody wanted to imagine that military security depended on luck.

Now that they had watched the suspect sneak into defense systems, Settle consulted with Scott Charney. The question was, Should they roll this guy up now? The answer wasn't obvious: the Justice Department wanted to set a precedent with a big, fat case, suggesting that Settle's crew should wait until a serious offense occurred, but on the other hand, the FBI couldn't let him commit major mayhem while agents were watching his every move.

Settle was worried by the increasing severity of the attacks. The incident had escalated from MUDs to universities to corporations and military installations. And somehow this Infomaster was stealing passwords at an ever-greater rate. Alarmingly, he had obtained a bunch of account names and passwords that let him into the ATM networks—the private linkups among banking computers that carried America's financial lifeblood.

Settle informed Barnett that the Bureau was going to visit this Matt Singer.

# 15

# HARD CASE

Eight o'clock in the morning, two days before Christmas. Winter in Portland: the drizzle turns the dawn air to pewter. Not much traffic this Wednesday morning—it's almost possible to hear the droplets fall. By Northwestern standards, the neighborhood is ancient: bungalows from the Hoover administration, separated by thin cement driveways and skinny strips of lawn. Not many lights shine from the houses. The kids are out of school and their parents are finding reasons not to go to work.

Sitting in a parked car is a well-built man with fair Scandinavian features, level blue eyes behind steel-rimmed glasses, and a perfectly cut cleft in his chin. He is wearing a dark suit and an overcoat, attire more formal than is customary in this part of town. Brent Rasmussen is carrying a portable radio and a 9mm pistol. So are the other FBI agents waiting in vehicles along the block.

The agents are watching a second-story window. The window is covered by a shade. Through the shade the viewers can make out the glow of artificial light and perhaps the shadow of a seated figure. Every other window in the house is dark.

Rasmussen has been waiting for the signal that will herald the arrival of the perfect moment. Every now and then he lifts the radio to his ear and asks a question: Is he still on? The answer seems to satisfy him.

Finally. Maybe he doesn't say it, actually, but it's what he is thinking. Finally this is happening.

When he leaves the car he closes the door quietly because he doesn't want to make unnecessary noise and because that is the proper, unhurried manner with which he operates. The others follow his cue.

Seven well-dressed people fan across the wet lawns and gardens. Two steal through the backyard of the house and approach the rear door; two more stand on either side of the house, guarding against possible escapes through windows. The other three walk easily up the front steps.

On the stoop Rasmussen pats the gun hanging at his side—a reassuring weight. The next few moments will be the least predictable and most dangerous time in the operations.

Raindrops make tiny wet asterisks on the front windows.

At last Rasmussen will find out for himself what's going on.

He takes a breath and knocks on the door.


Steve Singer's still thinking about getting dressed—he'll do it, but exactly when is up for grabs. It has to be soon, though, because today, for once in his life, he's going shopping. Christmas presents for the family, maybe some computer stuff for himself. Meanwhile he's mooching about the kitchen in his underwear and bathrobe. An actual breakfast would not be out of the question here.

His father should be coming home soon.

Rare is the day that Steve takes off from work. He has serious cash deprivation syndrome—one reason he moved with Matt into his father's house. To stockpile money for tuition, he takes the bus seven days a week to his job in a Computer City north of Portland. He works ten or twelve hours a day, putting him out of sync with the nocturnal schedule of everyone else in the household. When Steve comes home, everyone else is away. His father and his step-mother work the night shift as counselors in a mental hospital. Matt is physically present but mentally inside the computer.

Someone raps sharply on the door.

His father must have forgotten his keys.

Drawing the bathrobe closed, Steve opens the door.

On the stoop are two men and a woman. Beneath their over-coats, the men wear dark, conservative suits; the woman is wearing a dark ensemble. Steve squints at them in surprise, trying to figure out who they could possibly be.

The short, neatly combed hair of the men gives him a clue.

Incredible, he thinks. Eight in the morning, two days before Christmas, and the Jehovah's Witnesses are pounding the streets.

Then he sees the badges. And the guns.


Rasmussen must get to Singer while he's still on the computer—grab him before he has a chance to lock up his computer or delete damning evidence. When the brother opens the door, he flips the badge, shows the warrant, and shoulders through. All softly, politely —he doesn't want a struggle to alert his quarry.

Not that there's going to be a struggle. The brother stands immobile, mouth agape, as Rasmussen leads the party up the stairs.

As they pass, the brother whirls around. He's just discovered that other people have come in behind him, through the kitchen.

Rasmussen moves up the stairs, his hand hovering over the pistol. The door he wants is shut. After so much delay he's at last going to make something happen himself—something physical he can touch. He's going to find out what kind of crazy business is going on. His heart is batting adrenaline into the rest of his body.

Behind him are Mike West, the technician who has been help-ing Rasmussen, and a geek from Washington, D.C., recently arrived with a trunkful of equipment for decoding hard drives.

Rasmussen raises his hand to the door. Got to be ready to duck or draw—this is the moment when FBI agents get shot. Again, he raps on the door. Open up—FBI!

Inside, a shrill, irritated voice croaks back something Rasmus-sen can't understand.

Rasmussen pulls open the door.

His vision needs a moment to adjust to the different level of illumination. And then he can hardly believe his eyes.

Frustrated by his inability to get Matt to stop, Steve had taken to teasing him. In the middle of the night he sometimes rushed up and pounded on the door. Open up! he shouted. It's the FBI! The first few times Matt had shrieked in fear and frantically looked for a place to hide his papers. But then he had realized that it was only Steve, and laughed at him for trying the old scare tactic.

Now it was happening for real.

After the three agents went upstairs, Steve heard the crisp order: Open up—FBI!

And he also heard his brother's response: Shut *up*, Steve! Do you think I'm going to fall for that trick *again*?

There's a terrible smell—Rasmussen cannot imagine its origin. Mov-ing toward him from the center of the smell is a bent, barrel-chested figure whose face and body are wrapped in what looks like an Air Force parka. His hands are up in surprise and the fingers are curi-ously gnarled. The face is a writhing mask of active but uninterpret-able emotions.

For some reason, Rasmussen can't make out his eyes behind the crooked glasses.

The three agents crowd into the room—a more difficult proce-dure than they anticipated, for the floor is covered with dunes of paper, the carcasses of various electronic components, mounds of unwashed clothing, grease-sodden pizza boxes, grimy dinner plates with rotting meat, a pan with pancakes swimming in fetid butter, empty soda cans, and . . . my God, are those misshapen lumps *dog feces*?

Rasmussen has no time to investigate, even if he wanted to. His task is to cut between the suspect and his computer. It's not difficult—Singer is obviously too surprised to consider resisting. The agents shoulder him away from the monitor. For a few seconds the suspect stands motionless in the middle of the room as the agents begin going through his property. Then Rasmussen pulls him to the door. He displays the warrant, which the suspect mechanically examines.

The mess is astonishing. Rasmussen has never seen or imagined its like. It resembles a movie set, the lair of a demented hermit, more than an actual room.

He draws Singer downstairs past his brother and seats him in a kitchen chair. The kitchen is slightly less filth-strewn than the bedroom, but in Rasmussen's opinion *Architectural Digest* is not going to call soon. He thinks he recognizes the pungent odor of cat urine. In what seems like a few seconds technician Mike West appears.

He was on-line, West says. So we caught him red-handed, just like you wanted. But the data on his hard disk is encrypted.

They ask Singer for the key to the code. The stunned Singer agrees to provide it. He responds to other questions with mumbled bursts of technobabble that Rasmussen pretends to understand and West actually does. Upstairs the other agents are disassembling and cataloging the items they plan to seize. Rasmussen notices most of the crew has put on rubber gloves; he's pretty sure that they're not only worried about preserving fingerprints.

Rasmussen and two or three other agents circle Matt in the kitchen, bombarding him with questions. What are you doing? What's on your computer? How come you keep it all encrypted? Who are you working with? Who have you been feeding the information to? They're fishing, of course. But what shell-shocked suspects blurt out in the first moments of a confrontation often makes the case. But it doesn't work with Matt Singer. The suspect doesn't say much at all. As the questions fly, he slumps in his chair, head turned away from his interlocutors. Just shrinking into his seat.

The brother's beside him, not saying a word. Every so often there's a thump from the room upstairs, as the computer expert from Washington, D.C., unloads her equipment. But other than the questions, it's amazingly quiet.

When Rasmussen runs out of general questions, Mike West takes over with the technical stuff. The suspect's thin, bearded face comes partly alive. He likes talking about these things. The same thing occurs when West praises his acumen.

As the conversation sputters on, Rasmussen keeps looking at Singer's fingers, which are bizarrely gnarled. It's as if his fingers have aged five times faster than the rest of his body. Rasmussen guesses he's damaged them by typing on the computer twenty hours a day. And Singer's glasses—they're cocked at a severe angle to the rest of his face. Peering into them, Rasmussen discovers why he hadn't been able to make out the suspect's eyes: the lenses are a grayish mass of fingerprints and oil and dirt. They haven't been cleaned maybe ever, thinks Rasmussen. Maybe ever.

Not your typical white-collar crime.


Steve doesn't understand cause and effect, but it's clear that his phone call to the FBI has finally resulted in action. But why didn't they come when he first called, before Matt had broken into so many places?

Steve's numb with guilt, but at the same time there's a sneaking feeling of excitement. His house is being searched by the FBI. This is not something that everyone can say. The desire to tell the world about it is bursting in his chest.

So he picks up the phone and calls Patrick Humphreys.

• • •

Will Singer, Matt's father, comes in tired from a night with the disturbed and finds half a dozen FBI agents in his house taking away his son. They claim that Matt—Matt!—has been breaking into military computers with top-secret information. It's the most ridiculous thing he's ever heard. He's in the middle of telling off the FBI agent when Steve tells him to back off, because it's true, Matt's a big-time hacker, which is just about the goddamnedest thing Will has ever heard in his life.

In the abstract, Will, who's a bit of a rebel, can appreciate Matt's cleverness. But in the concrete, he is furious. After Steve pulls his father away from the FBI he nearly has to pull him away from Matt, too.

Then the surprise gets to Will—Steve's had months to absorb this while he's just getting the news now—and he just watches, disbelieving, as a parade of neatly dressed FBI agents emerge from Matt's room with boxes of equipment and take it downstairs to their vehicles. Thinking: my son is going to jail.


Patrick roars across town in his new car. The FBI is at the Singers' house! He arrives to find the Bureau on its way out and Will, the father, in a towering rage. Steve says that he was reasonably cool at first, then lost it when the agents began to leave.

It turns out the FBI has been through the place with a vacuum cleaner. Steve has a search warrant and a five-page list of the items they confiscated, which includes his answering machine, a lot of audio CDs, and any loose pieces of cable in the house, even coaxial cable for the television. The FBI walked off with Matt's computer. And because Steve stupidly admitted that Matt might occasionally have used it, they also took Steve's new computer, which is not even two months old.

Steve has just realized that after years of being a computer freak without a computer he finally bought a machine, only to have it taken by the United States government.

Walking around in the mess left by the FBI, Patrick finds himself examining the search warrant and the list of confiscated items.
So he drags Steve to his car, in which they drive to the nearest
photocopy store. There Patrick makes a copy of the warrant.

When Steve asks what the photocopy is for, Patrick says that
he's going to pin it up in the CAT room, next to the dartboard of
Matt.

January 1993

Subpoenas appear at Portland State University, the Massachusetts Institute of Technology, and Texas A&M University two
weeks after the New Year. The subpoenas demand new copies of the
logs previously submitted to the FBI. The logs must be in printed
form, which the sysadmins find infuriating, because it requires
them to print hundreds of pages of documents. They see no reason
for the bother. By confiscating Singer's computer, from their point
of view, the problem has ended.

Jim Settle and Scott Charney have discussed serving CERT,
too, with a subpoena; they are convinced CERT knows about other
break-ins by Singer that involve sensitive installations at business or government. But CERT would resist furiously and the FBI
would end up creating an Internet martyr. Settle can imagine the
on-line denunciations of the government, many of them from the
same sysadmins who demand swift police action against hackers.
He decides to leave CERT alone. The organization may be more
useful as a confidential repository of data than as a prosecutorial
aid, at least for now. This time the FBI can make the case without
them.

Barnett arrived in Portland at about the same time as the subpoenas. She had an appointment with Singer's public defender, a
brassy little man named Schatz who seemed stunned by the piles of
documentation arrayed against his client. In theory, the government

could charge Singer with hundreds of felonies—one for each system
he penetrated illicitly. But such hard-nosed behavior, Schatz told
Barnett, is inappropriate here. She'll understand when she meets
his client.

A day later, Barnett, Rasmussen, and West walked into a room
to meet with the suspect. Singer was there, slumped in his chair
like a tangle of wire. He was wearing a black hooded sweatshirt with
the hood yanked low over his face. Underneath the hood was a
hatchet face surmounted by a shelf of straight hair. Every so often
he curled into himself, his folded arms pressing into his chest. Barnett didn't know that he was hunching over in pain; seeing him hug
himself, she wondered if he were one of those people who are always
cold. Not until long afterward did she learn that Singer suffered
from viral hepatitis, a chronic variety without a well-established
cure. The suspect was accompanied to the interview by Schatz and
Schatz's investigator, a tall ex-cop named Wilson.

Barnett took the lead in questioning. Quickly she established
the main point: Singer had next to no memory of his activities.
It wasn't a pose, Barnett decided. Like all FBI agents, she'd
seen some convenient amnesia in her day. Singer truly could not
remember—something askew in the information-retrieval system
there. Even when he could recall his on-line escapades, he seemed
unaware of their relationship to the real world. When she asked
about his intrusion at, for example, the University of California
at San Francisco, Singer drew a blank. But at the mention of
"ucsf.edu," its Internet address, his face came alight, and he
detailed his break-in there.

The hacker was, in the parlance, a tough interview. His responses were dull, monosyllabic, often not apropos. It was as if he
were bored by a conversation that would determine whether he went
to jail. A spark of interest appeared when Barnett brought out the
datatap transmissions. He paged through them with evident enjoy-
ment; his computer activity, preserved for all time.

An actual smile appeared only once—when the agents asked
him to demonstrate his hacking tools on a computer carried in for

the purpose. Singer was thrilled to discover that the computer contained an exact copy of the data on his hard drive. For a few moments, Barnett thought, he actually caressed the keyboard.

It would be nice, she thought, if she had some idea of what he
really was after, or how this mess got started. But she never learned.

Once again, Rasmussen experienced the dubious pleasure of running a case about computers. He sat in the interrogation room while
Barnett tried to extract information from Singer. Inevitably the dialogue soared over his head and into the celestial realms of bits and
bytes and bauds. According to Settle, Barnett was a major computer
whiz, far beyond a mere technician like West, but it didn't look that
way to Rasmussen. She looked almost as lost as he.

Not that the questioning mattered. One look at Singer twisted
in his chair like an old man laid low by arthritis and it was clear to
Rasmussen that no jury on Earth would vote for a conviction. Maybe
that was justice—prison would be a disaster for Singer. He would
never survive.

Rasmussen wasn't sure whether the kid grasped that he was
in trouble. Only one thing had sunk in—the FBI had taken away his
computer.

All the same, the FBI agents wanted some answers. Barnett
asked repeatedly about the other hackers he knew: Grok, Jsz, No
Means No, and, especially, Rokstar, an Australian hacker who'd
penetrated NASA at about the same time.* The hackers had exchanged messages and programs and data, and it was far from apparent to Rasmussen that this activity should be described as
benign. Or that someone should be excused for stealing information
because he did not profit from it in a monetary sense.

---

* Because they had broken into NASA almost simultaneously, the Bureau naturally
suspected that Info and Rokstar were working together. They weren't, by Info's account; indeed, he had never heard the cracker's name until his interrogation. Rokstar
avoided arrest, stopped breaking into other systems, and became a sysadmin in his
native Australia.

Singer spoke at length only when the discussion veered toward the technical. He enjoyed examining the logs of himself. But his whole posture changed when Barnett brought in the computer. Sitting up straight, he cradled the keyboard like a baby in his lap and inspected the contents of the hard drive. He typed with a curious awkward fluency, his hands seeming to bat at the keys in short, rapid up-and-down motions, as if playing a conga drum.

Only when Singer was touching the computer were his answers longer than a few words. As far as Rasmussen could tell, giving him the machine was the single time the agents managed to hit on something Singer cared about.

To a considerable extent Barnett pitied Singer, whose social, mental, and physical handicaps were all too apparent. The smell issue, for instance. He had not taken a shower for so long that it was physically difficult to remain in the room with him; Rasmussen took a fresh-air break every half hour or so. More distressing was the odd way his mind worked. Sometimes she asked him a question to which he couldn't recall the answer. Then an hour later she would ask him about something else and the answer to the first question would pop up in another context. He seemed utterly unable to imagine the consequences of his actions or why anyone would be upset by them. Which led to interesting questions: If he wasn't conscious of committing crimes, was it wrong to punish him for them? And did his lack of criminal intent mean that he was any less dangerous to his victims?

On a personal level, some parts of the interrogation transcripts gave Settle the willies. Like where Barnett was asking questions about the scope of Singer's activities. She was talking to a kid with brain damage, right? A kid who doesn't go out of the house too much, right, because he gets lost in the neighborhood? And she asked him if he had ever found a system that he couldn't eventually get into.

And Matt Singer paused a long time before giving his considered response: No.

With all the evidence in, Charney and Silverman looked at the Singer case—and blinked. This, they evidently decided, was not the case on which to stake future computer-crime policy. This was not the case to be cited by every hacker's defense attorney for the next twenty years. This was not the case to give to a jury. This was not even a case to plea-bargain with. Who knew what Singer would say when the judge faced him at the sentencing and asked him if he ever intended to break into computers again? Even if the judge let him walk with a suspended sentence, the kid would never stay out of trouble. Either way, he could easily end up having to serve time. He'd last all of fifteen minutes behind bars, and then Charney or Silverman would have to explain to the *Washington Post* why he let a brain-damaged twenty-year-old's life end tragically in prison.

It didn't matter how Settle and Rasmussen or anyone in the FBI felt about it. This one was going into the Twilight Zone. They'd take no action whatsoever. If the kid ever embarrassed them by doing something really serious, they could hold the prosecution over his head as a threat. Who could find fault with that?

A few weeks after the interrogation, Matt moved back to his mother's house—his father was too angry about the FBI. Steve went to visit not long after the move. He went upstairs to his brother's room and saw Matt sitting at his desk, staring out the window.

Steve stared with him for a moment. He saw a fence, and some shrubbery beside the fence, and some rocks at the base of the shrubbery. The rocks—they used to pretend the rocks were computers.

How's it going? Steve eventually asked his brother.

Matt didn't move.

Hey, Matt? You all right?

Matt stared out for another few moments. Then he said, without moving his eyes, When are they going to give it back?

Steve began to speak, but stopped himself. He shrugged, patted Matt on the shoulder, and walked toward the door.

Matt turned after him. They still have my computer, he said. When are they going to give it back?

# EPILOGUE

The Infomaster case served as a training course for many of its protagonists, who went on to careers in the rapidly expanding field of computer security. Paul Mauvais, for instance, went from Portland State to CIAC. Former Portland State student sysadmin Mike Wilson also went to Lawrence Livermore; he left in 1996 to found a computer-security firm. Among his competitors were Jim Settle and Jim Kolouch, who retired from the Federal Bureau of Investigation to become security consultants. Additional members of the crowded field include the sysadmins at Texas A&M, who used their experiences with Infomaster and his friends to develop a suite of security software called Tiger, which is available on the Internet.

Not everyone is in different jobs. Beth Barnett and Levord Burns remain in the FBI, though not with the computer-crime unit, which the Bureau greatly expanded in 1996 and placed under the leadership of Richard Ress, the ex-sniper. Dan Farmer left Sun and went to Silicon Graphics; on his own time, he wrote the Security Analysis Tool for Auditing Networks (SATAN), software that automatically checks for security lapses. Its release in 1996 caused a public furor, because SATAN would let crackers, too, probe networks for security holes. SGI, embarrassed by the flap, fired him; an unembarrassed Sun quickly rehired him.

Responding, in part, to the heavy demand for system administrators, Trent Fisher of Portland and Mike Patton of MIT left their respective universities for private industry; Scott Yelich now heads a small Java-programming firm. Nick Papadakis left MIT in 1996; when last observed, he was puttering through Florida in an RV and hoping that the rest of his midlife crisis was as pleasant as the beginning. Mycroft, by contrast, got a job at MIT. On the West Coast Alvin Cura, Michael Gray, and Patrick Humphreys all work in Silicon Valley. Richard Stallman and the Free Software Foundation are working to release the first complete version of the GNU Project in 1997—although schedules for product release have never been a high priority at the Foundation.

Janaka Jayawardene is still ensconced at the Portland Center for Advanced Technology.

The man whom we call Steve Singer found a well-paying job— he tests video games for one of the large electronics companies in the Silicon Forest. His younger brother is still living on disability payments from Social Security. Borrowing a small amount of money from his family, he has been trying to achieve financial independence by setting up his own business, which he calls Quicknet. It sells access to the Internet.

It may be tempting for the reader to assume that in the interval between the events chronicled in this book and the present, Internet security has sufficiently advanced that such widescale break-ins by inept but determined amateurs could never take place. In the course of researching the story, we consulted a number of computer-security experts. Not one had the slightest doubt that the Internet is as open to crackery now as it was in Infomaster's heyday. Indeed, almost all of them argued that the effective level of security is declining.

As long ago as 1979, Robert M. Morris and Ken Thompson,

two pioneers of networking, issued a widely read warning about the perils of easily guessed passwords; almost two decades later, neither user habits nor sysadmin alertness "have improved much," in the words of William R. Cheswick and Steven M. Bellovin, who designed the security system for Bell Labs. The failure to improve passwords —and, by extension, all security measures—has multiple causes, but one of the most important is that security is a nuisance. Inevitably, security procedures make a network harder to work with, if only because people find it much harder to type (let alone remember) a secure password like "sM$vkqZ!" than a dumb password like "hello." As a result, users actively resist being forced to choose secure passwords. And, as any cracker knows, it takes but one "hello" to render irrelevant all other defenses.

Not only users are ignorant of or resistant to security practices. All too often, system administrators are guilty as well. In many cases they are inexperienced and untrained, a situation fueled by the failure of the supply of top-notch administrators to match the explosive growth of computer networks. In the mid-1980s, the typical sysadmin was a battle-scarred hacker with a head full of code and ten years of Unix expertise. In the mid-1990s, sysadmins are all too often recent graduates whose principal experience consisted of tweaking the Doom games in the college computer center. For every sysadmin like Janaka today, a weary veteran of cracker wars, there are five or ten who are like him in 1991—newly on-line, untrained in security, unequipped to foil intruders. Indeed, having been trained on personal computers, many lack even his strong initial background in Unix-style networking and programming.

Worse, many sysadmins who know better are simply unwilling to practice safe computing. Security is inconvenient; without .rhosts files, hosts.equiv files, and the like, sysadmins have to go through many extra steps every time they perform routine tasks. Indeed, one speaker at a recent National Information Security Systems Security Conference, a leading annual meeting in the field, confessed that he had forgotten to transfer the text of his speech from his office network to his personal laptop, and that the network was so intruder-proof that he couldn't get in to retrieve it. Given the high pressure under which most sysadmins work—how many people wait patiently when their computers crash?—they are understandably reluctant to make their own lives more difficult. Inevitably, windows are left open, doors remain unlatched.

The combination of sysadmin inexperience and intransigence means that the same mistakes keep being made again and again, even in the most sophisticated networks. When part of the network at Bell Labs crashed one holiday weekend, Cheswick and Bellovin sheepishly report, no experienced sysadmin was available. Contacted at home, the backup expert needed a guest account to work on the problem over the phone. Unthinkingly, the frazzled operator at Bell Labs created a passwordless root account; when the problem was solved, the expert, who presumably wanted to hurry back to the festivities, forgot to delete the account. The hole was discovered within a day by crackers. Need one say that the level of expertise and user sophistication at Bell Labs, the birthplace of Unix, is above average?

Hardware and software companies could solve many of these problems by building in security precautions that are difficult to disable. But the vendors are well aware that although their customers claim to want security, they are unwilling to pay the price in convenience. In theory, customers who desire secure networks should not also want preinstalled passwordless root accounts, but in practice they want to be able to call customer support and have a technician dial into the system *right now*, without any nonsense about setting up a new account—and they get sulky if they can't.

Being creatures of the market, computer companies are naturally reluctant to develop products that annoy their client base. Unless facing public humiliation from a widely publicized lapse, vendors are especially reluctant to issue software fixes to security holes, because the patches represent the public admission of a flaw in the product and require extra work to install. And, of course, the time and money invested in developing the fixes don't create any profits. For all these reasons, security is a low priority. Sun Microsystems, the market leader in Internet hardware and software, has as of this writing exactly one full-time employee who works on fixing security flaws.

User resistance, sysadmin inexpertise, vendor foot-dragging— they all combine to make the cracker's job easy. At the end of 1996, Dan Farmer tested almost 2,000 computer networks with obvious security needs—660 banks, 274 credit unions, 312 newspapers, 451 on-line sex clubs (companies that sell pornographic imagery to subscribers, and hence must protect both their stock of pictures and their subscribers' names), and 50 federal sites (congressional, executive, and judicial networks, as well as those belonging to government agencies and the civilian intelligence community). Farmer tested their security quickly and straightforwardly—"The methods used by this survey were *not* rocket science!" as he put it. "I barely electronically breathed on these [systems]"—by running SATAN and checking to see if several important CERT advisories had been heeded. Despite the simplicity of the methods, almost 65 percent had security holes so large that intruders could have entered and seized root or destroyed data in less than a minute. Another 15 percent or so would be instantly vulnerable to the next Sendmail bug (these continue to appear regularly). The sites used both Unix and the various Microsoft operating systems; neither provided better security, although in Farmer's view the various Unix vendors were more willing to admit problems.

As a control, Farmer also tested almost 500 networks randomly chosen from a list of hosts assembled by Network Wizards, a consultant group that annually surveys more than 100,000 Internet sites. Dismayingly, the corporate networks were twice as likely to be easily compromised as the randomly chosen sites. The reason, he argued, is that the relentless commercialization of the Internet is driving companies to offer more and more services on the same network. Because each Internet service has its own security problems, the result is an ever-growing likelihood of failure.

"Businesses and other organizations are coming to the Net, expecting turnkey solutions to their company needs," Farmer wrote. "Unfortunately, the technology for this has not arrived, at least with respect to security." He concluded, "With the ignorance about security combined with the supreme emphasis on functionality and performance, you have a situation like . . . well, a situation that looks almost exactly like what we have today." What we have today, in his view, is a "disaster."

Meanwhile, the bad guys' expertise is growing—or, rather, they are able to penetrate networks in ever more sophisticated ways. Typical intruders remain as inexpert as ever, but they are increasingly equipped with powerful cracker tools. In 1995, for example, networks across the globe were hit by RootKit, a cracker's version of a software suite. To execute RootKit, the cracker need only type "make all install" at the prompt. RootKit then automatically grabs root, installs six Trojan horses, and sets up a sniffer, all the while removing every trace of the attack from network logs, preventing standard sysadmin tools from displaying cracker activity while it is occurring, and ensuring that attempts to look for Trojans will incorrectly report that the Trojaned programs have their original sizes, change times, and mod times.

RootKit is far from the only example. The war-dialer employed by Phantomd has been updated to the point-and-click era; menus now let crackers choose among searching for modems, private branch exchanges, or long-distance carriers. Two programs—the Virus Creation Laboratory and Phalcon/Skism Mass-Produced Code Generator—now let the most inexperienced wannabe create a virus from scratch. Still other programs adapt COPS and SATAN to check every computer in a network for vulnerabilities, then use those vulnerabilities as entry points. And so on.

Most crackers can't create such tools, but the small number who can often distribute them freely. They are exchanged informally on countless underground computer bulletin boards like the Apocalypse Now system discovered by Janaka; many are available on the World Wide Web. A two-minute search of the Web at the beginning of 1997 turned up half a dozen locations that purveyed RootKit, including one that disingenuously urged new users, in the orthographically annoying cracker style, to "have fun and don't fuq shit up, all it duz iz get people put in jail."*

A great deal of attention was paid in 1995 to Kevin Mitnick and his apparent assault on the computer system of security expert Tsutomu Shimomura, thanks to front-page coverage in the *New York Times* and other media outlets, as well as a highly publicized book by Shimomura and John Markoff, a *Times* reporter. (A movie is said to be in the works.) In many of these accounts, Mitnick's methods were portrayed as the stuff of genius. In fact, Mitnick's approach—a gambit known as "IP spoofing," in which the target computer is fooled into thinking that commands from an intruder are actually issued by a computer that the target computer is programmed to trust—had been floating around the cracker underground for a few years. Within a year of Mitnick's exploit, it was widely available as an automated tool, employable by any twelve-year-old with a computer, a modem, and a little spare time.

A report from the U.S. General Accounting Office in May of 1996 illustrated the general situation with a simple graph. The horizontal axis of the graph measured time, from about 1980 to about 1995; the vertical axis depicted the level of computer sophistication, going from "low" to "high." The graph had two lines. One, labeled "Sophistication of Attacker Tools," rose from nearly zero around 1980, when the first version of Crack was being put together, to "high" in 1995, when IP spoofing was automated. The second line was labeled "Required Knowledge of Hackers." It went from "high" in 1980 to "low" in 1995. The implication was readily evident. By the late 1990s, attackers with little knowledge of computer systems will be wielding cracker tools of enormous capacity.

Computer-security experts often complain, with reason, that the media has glamorized crackers by portraying them as brilliant

---

* The sniffer in RootKit, incidentally, is descended from two favorite cracker routines, Sunsniff and Solsniff, which are slightly modified versions of the original Sun sniffer used by Info and Jsz. By 1994, this sniffer in its various incarnations had so permeated the Internet that CIAC publicly warned that it had compromised more than 100,000 networks.

wunderkinds, programmers run amok who outwit the grown-ups with their laptops and code. In fact, the peril lies more in very patient people with minimal computer skills and excellent tools. From this perspective, Matt Singer, assiduously installing his sniffers all over the Internet, is a harbinger of the future. The picture is disquieting enough to suggest that in at least one respect the ideas of the Free Software Foundation are correct: people who worry about private property should think twice about being on the Internet.

As automated tools make cracking ever easier and sysadmin inexperience and user distaste for security leave the Internet ever more open, the inevitable outcome will be a large, continuing rise in cracker activity. In fact, it is already occurring. Between 1985 and 1993, according to the American Society for Industrial Security, the rate of theft of proprietary business information from computers rose 260 percent—with much of the increase due to the Internet. In August and September of 1996, more than a dozen Internet service providers were forced off-line by a flood of attacks that swamped their systems; an on-line feminist publication called *Bitch* was taken over and filled with pornographic and misogynistic imagery; CERT issued an advisory on yet another Sendmail bug that gave root access to intruders; an e-mail "bomb"—a massive onslaught of messages—was sent to a dozen journalists and public figures by a cracker who was, perhaps inevitably, dubbed the Unamailer; and the World Wide Web sites of both the Department of Justice and the Central Intelligence Agency were penetrated (indeed, the CIA site was altered to greet visitors with the words "Central Stupidity Agency").

Many of the incidents continue to be adolescent pranks, but the universal consensus of security experts is that the political and financial stakes will rise. The U.S. Department of Defense, to cite an obvious example, has more than 2.1 million computers linked into some ten thousand local networks, which are in turn tied into a

hundred long-distance networks. These networks, crucial to the nation's military capability, are under siege. According to data from
the Defense Information Systems Agency, the military may have
experienced a quarter of a million attacks in 1995, the most recent
year for which figures are available. More than likely, about two
thirds of the attempted intrusions were successful; typically, fewer
than 1 percent were detected. If, as DISA suggests, the number of
incidents is doubling every year, the Department of Defense network
will be attacked a million times in 1997. Even if only one in a thousand attempts is malicious, the number of digital attacks on the
nation's military will easily exceed the number of physical attacks—
in other words, computer crime will soon become the single greatest
ongoing threat to national security.

It will also be a major economic threat. Estimates of the financial impact of computer crime have risen with the number of cracker
incidents. By 1995, the FBI was already estimating that electronic
malfeasance was costing U.S. businesses alone $7.5 billion a year.
That year, according to an annual survey conducted by the Computer Security Institute of San Francisco, about one out of every five
networks on the Internet was penetrated.

In mid-1996, the Computer Security Institute and the FBI announced the results of a joint survey of 428 U.S. corporations, government agencies, financial institutions, and universities. Forty-two
percent had discovered electronic malfeasance in the previous year.
More than half of the incidents came from outside attacks (the rest
were from insiders who abused their privileges). Fearing negative
publicity, less than 17 percent would report those attacks to law
enforcement. Similar numbers were produced in October by the annual survey of businesses performed by Ernst & Young and *Information Week* magazine. Fifty-four percent of the survey's 1,320
participants had been hit by computer crime within the past two
years. (If computer viruses were counted, the proportion of victims
rose to 78 percent.)

Almost 70 percent of the victims admitted they had no idea
how much money they had lost in the incidents; of those able to

provide a figure, the losses ranged from $250,000 to more than $1 million. Extrapolated across the Internet, the surveys confirm the FBI statistic that criminals with modems and automated cracking programs are already costing private enterprise billions of dollars. "Nobody knows the actual toll," Richard Powers of the Computer Security Institute explained. "All we have is estimates, some of them in the hundreds of billions of dollars." The high figure, he said, "is not from La-La Land, in my opinion. Computer crime is already having a major, significant impact."

The explosion of activity on the World Wide Web will continue to increase the stakes. Corporations are already making their most prized marketing, research and development, and financial data available over the Web. Access is limited, of course, to authorized employees with the right passwords—and to the thousands of crackers who make a career out of breaking into systems that are protected with passwords. In the same vein, the banks, retail stores, and government agencies that are providing ever higher levels of network accessibility to their money, goods, and information over the Web are taking huge risks. Vendors such as Netscape assure the public that transactions made with the help of their software are perfectly safe; then, after some clever graduate student finds yet another way to get around the safeguards, claim that *now* their software is really, truly, perfectly safe.

Perhaps the scariest trend, in the view of some computer-security experts, is an increasingly popular type of software used in the World Wide Web, called "applets." When users visit a Web site, their computers receive copies of specially formatted documents from the computer that hosts the Web site. The documents can include applets, small programs that are automatically sent to the visitors' computers and then activated. Typically applets consist of small animated figures that turn or blink amusingly, livening up the static documents on the Web. But how long will it be, security consultants worry, before crackers, who have already proved their ability to penetrate the programs behind Websites almost at will, start loading popular Websites with bogus applets that install Trojan horses, back doors, and viruses? Some Websites receive millions of visitors a month. If such Websites dispensed cracked applets, they could compromise a significant percentage of the world's personal computers in a matter of weeks. In early 1997, as a harbinger of the future, a German computer club demonstrated that applets could be used to trigger automatic cash transfers from people who use electronic banking.

In the way of engineers everywhere, computer scientists argue that the technical problems posed by network security have technical solutions. At present, security specialists tout two principal means for staving off computer crime: firewalls and encryption. Firewalls can be employed with relative ease but are far from universally effective. Encryption is more effective but, as things stand now, almost unusable.

In simple terms, a firewall is a device—a specialized computer or a program—that sits between an organization's network and the outside world. Outsiders who try to tie into the network via phone must make peace with this device before entering the network. Firewalls typically check the origin and type of all incoming data—more exactly, they inspect the "header," or address, of every data packet. In a sense, they are upscale versions of the screening software created by the sysadmins at Portland State, MIT, and Texas A&M to block Matt Singer. Firewalls look for telltale signs of illicit activity, and slam the door when they see them. They can be configured to block all outside requests to use Telnet, for example, or any attempt at all to communicate from computers not on a specific list of approved machines.

Firewalls raise the bar for crackers, a useful, even vital service. But they inevitably limit users' activities as well; if the office firewall has been set up to reject, say, all incoming signals except those associated with electronic mail, then employees cannot fulfill unexpected needs for data by tapping into the World Wide Web. Moreover, the complexity of the Internet and people's desires make firewalls

inevitably difficult to configure—published estimates have suggested that more than half of all firewalls are not set up properly.
Finally, firewalls are always playing catch-up. As Infomaster discovered, there is always the opportunity to bypass them with a newly
discovered bug or tool, flaws in Sendmail being particularly exploit-
able. The possibility is more than theoretical; in the 1995 *Information Week*/Ernst & Young security survey, more than one third of all
reported security incidents occurred in systems protected by firewalls.

Jim Settle has called the blind reliance on this technology the
Myth of the Great American Firewall. "It's a brand new product to
sell," he said in 1996. "You've got a bunch of them and a lot of
managers are looking for the silver bullet—one thing [that] is going
to solve all my problems." Although he strongly endorsed their use,
Settle had "never seen a firewall that a hacker couldn't eventually
get around."

Settle is slightly more positive about the second solution: encryption. Encryption—that is, encoding all transmissions over networks—can stop crackers. Unfortunately, encryption has been the
subject of a bitter dispute between Internet mavens, who wish to use
the most unbreakable forms of encryption, and law-enforcement
agencies, who wish to ensure that encrypted transmissions do not
foil the ability to perform datataps. For years the federal government
has insisted that encryption users must make it possible for the
police to listen in—a step vigorously resisted by Internet mavens,
who believe (doubtless accurately) that such measures will limit
people to comparatively weak forms of encryption, which will effectively prevent the legitimate use of this technology. Because
blocking encryption, in their view, would be illogical, the digerati
has reacted to these proposals with anger—and the stubborn faith
that the government could not ultimately take such an illogical
course. Given the propensity of many Netheads to regard most
forms of government as beyond hope of redemption, their faith that
Uncle Sam will not act foolishly is puzzling.

Assuming that encryption becomes deployable, though, does
not answer a second, more important question: Will people use it?

Encryption, like all other security measures, is inconvenient. When people can't enter a network without an encryption key, the Internet will have lost the ease of access that is one of its most important features. Computer users have already demonstrated, in the firmest manner possible, their dislike of complicated passwords; it seems reasonable to suppose that this dislike will extend to the use of encryption keys, which are still more complex. Indeed, fear of customers dropping off the Net is one reason that Internet service providers are fighting encryption.

In addition, people fear that if something goes wrong in an encrypted system—losing that impossible-to-remember, 300-character decoding key, for instance—their data will be permanently frozen into gibberish. The fear is not merely theoretical. Windows95, the Microsoft operating system, incorporates software that compresses data to save space on hard drives. In compressed form, the data is essentially encrypted. The on-line help services of Microsoft (and the other companies that sell data compression programs) are filled with stories of people who are desperately seeking access to their own files. The word of mouth is so fearsome, according to trade publications, that fewer than 5 percent of Windows95 owners ever turn on the compression software, because they are afraid of losing their encrypted data.

Even in the unlikely prospect that these problems are quickly resolved, the widespread use and deployment of encryption will only turn crackers' attention to beating it. Surprisingly, many popular forms of encryption, even if applied religiously, may not be nearly as unbreakable as their proponents say. According to Padgett Peterson, the security chief at aviation giant Lockheed Martin, a computer built from scratch specifically for the purpose of breaking encryption schemes would be quite capable of decrypting a large percentage of the messages fed into it. Peterson has determined that such computers can be built, from components that are both widely available and relatively inexpensive.

Finally, no matter how sophisticated firewalls and encryption become, they are inherently vulnerable to the simplest forms of intrusion—the kind practiced by Phantomd. As authentication procedures become more complex, it will become more tempting for people with accounts in more than one network to use the same passwords and encryption keys. Or, if they use different passwords and encryption keys, to write them down in little files, so they won't be forgotten. A hardworking, sedulous cracker will always be able to find such carelessly maintained accounts, and always be able to use them to penetrate others. Firewalls and encryption will always help, but cannot make the problem go away.

As networks grow larger—the systems coming on-line from MCI, Sprint, and AT&T, for instance, are expected to have several million members apiece—they will be ever more susceptible to silly mistakes, and ever harder to police. Any network may have careless users who transmit their passwords in e-mail. But a network with a million accounts is almost certain to have them. Sysadmins can police a network of fifty machines for files with names like "my passwords," but even the most alert cannot maintain such scrutiny over a network of five hundred machines, or five thousand, or fifty thousand.

Fundamentally, all security measures are plagued by the very ubiquity and interconnection of the Internet. Individual homeowners can upgrade the locks on their doors with some assurance that the measure will be effective; they need outwit only the local teenagers, who are unlikely to be able to consult an expert lock picker. Even if one neighborhood has a smart kid who learns how to pick the new lock, such upgraded locks will still be useful in other neighborhoods, because the thug who figures it out is unlikely to be in contact with his confreres across the nation. But with the Internet, all the world's burglars have access to all the world's locks. Not only that, they broadcast their successes—witness Grok helping Phantomd, who in turn teaches Jsz, who then teaches Kevin Mitnick. As soon as one clever burglar figures out how to break a new lock, all the other, less clever ones can pick it, too. It's as if every homeowner on every street faces the combined savvy of every burglar on the planet.

Computer-security experts are constantly finding new ways to improve digital locks, of course—but usually after crackers have already found and exploited the flaws in the previous generation of locks, and the damage has been done. Experts can try to be proactive in this regard, by looking for flaws that crackers themselves have not yet discovered. But the enterprising and clever security pros who manage to do so face a dilemma: Do they notify the big Unix vendors, knowing that in all likelihood the vendors will do nothing unless users screaming about cracker attacks force them to fix the problem? Should they spread the word among the security community, knowing that information in this community inevitably, and usually quite rapidly, leaks into the cracker community? (Security experts' computers, as Infomaster and Jsz demonstrated, are a favorite cracker target; in addition, some security experts have strong ties to the cracker community, and may trade information.)

Recognizing this dilemma, some Internauts—especially a rogue outfit in Britain called 8LGM (the name apparently stands for "eight-legged man")—began anonymously filling the Internet with precise descriptions of how to exploit newly discovered software flaws, in an attempt to force computer vendors to act more quickly on security. The companies whose products were thus skewered complained loudly, pointing out that it alerted crackers to new techniques. At the same time, some industry managers privately conceded that such publicity may be the most effective way to get their employers to act.

Inevitably, the future will be a Red Queen's race, a constantly escalating conflict between a small squad of clever security hackers and their opponents, a much larger army of crackers, many armed with the newest techniques, all looking, million-monkey fashion, for the next hole that will let them inside. The good guys—the hackers —are shrewd, able, and dedicated. But the cardinal attribute of a Red Queen's race is that it has no final winner.

The Internet won't drown under a tsunami of hacking attacks. Indeed, it is hard to imagine what could frighten people enough to deprive themselves of the wonderful convenience of electronic mail. After all, everyone still sends postcards, despite knowing that they

can be read by strangers. Nor can one imagine why organizations
that wish to promulgate knowledge would deprive themselves of the
matchlessly open and inexpensive medium of the Internet, no matter what the risk. The Internet will survive its insecurity, in other
words. The question is more whether the world will be able to trans-
act its business on the Net—whether, as the technophiles envision,
the globe will become the site of a single, world-spanning electronic
neighborhood, a blooming, buzzing matrix aglow with commerce
and speedy exchange and human interaction.

Given the ubiquity of hacker/cracker attacks, that neighborhood will inevitably become something akin to an urban neighborhood in a city like San Francisco or St. Louis. In such places, life
goes on as usual, but pedestrians are cautious about how they move
about, businesses put up bars on their windows at night, and frequent crime is an unpleasant but accepted part of existence. Sometimes people choose to avoid those areas altogether, and they decay.
But sometimes the neighborhood prospers anyway, regardless of
exterior circumstances. Witness the shoppers from New Jersey and
Connecticut thronging the formerly seedy streets of SoHo in Manhattan.

The software enthusiasts promise to obviate the problem of
security with technical fixes like firewalls and encryption. Maybe
these truly will furnish protection, but it is worth noting that people
do not always listen to engineers' promises of safety. To this day,
nuclear engineers argue that the difficulties of atomic power can
be readily overcome. Yet in most places the public has decided,
rationally or no, not to have much truck with nuclear plants. On
the other hand, the public has decided to embrace civil aviation,
despite the general fear of plane crashes and the apparent impos-
sibility of eradicating terrorist hijackings. In the end, that is,
whether the Internet grows into that globe-spanning matrix of
commerce will be a social decision, not a technological one. People
will either feel good about placing much of their lives on the Net,
or they won't.

It is hard to identify what makes people feel good about some
neighborhoods and bad about others—the causes are too various

and ineffable. But one can say that the wired, interconnected city-world that the Internauts envision will never come into existence unless its advocates stop pretending that it has no security problems, or that it can be made perfectly safe in the future by buying fancy new boxes and typing in a few lines of code.

# A  NOTE  ON
# SOURCES  AND
# TECHNIQUES

This book is based on dozens of personal interviews and hundreds of megabytes of computer logs. We attempted to speak with all of the protagonists in the Phantomd affair, interviewing most at length and many repeatedly. Indeed, so many people took time to help us that it is easier here to list those who did not. Two FBI agents, Dennis Kintigh and Levord Burns, rebuffed months of entreaties. Contacted through the computer underground, the cracker Jsz did not answer our many requests to hear his side of the story. We were unable to find Grok, who disappeared from circulation after the incidents recounted here. With those exceptions, we interviewed every individual who is mentioned in this book for more than a few paragraphs.

All interviews but one—with a somewhat suspicious Reed sysadmin—were on the record; citing Justice Department policy, Joshua Silverman and Scott Charney refused to discuss the Singer case in detail, although they freely answered questions about procedures and methods that pertained to it. We were lucky enough to be able to fill in most gaps with other interviews; in addition, we were able to examine many long sessions of recorded chitchat among the crackers. These logs also gave us detailed, fly-on-the-screen views of individual computer break-ins.

Naturally, many interviewees' memories were hazy about events of years past. Indeed, our efforts to assemble a chronology were initially confused by one interviewee's adamant insistence that he would "never, ever forget" the date on which a particular life-altering event occurred—a date that proved to be thirteen months off. As a result, putting together the exact order in which events occurred was a process of weighing separate accounts, comparing memories to written sources, and exercising the authors' best judgment. It would be folly to think that the results were in every case successful.

Because we wished to communicate something of the feel of our story's peculiar venue—the crepuscular foundations of the wired society that lies in our future—we tried to portray the flavor of individual conversations, as relayed to us in interviews. The indirectly quoted results should not be viewed as efforts to reconstruct actual dialogue so much as attempts to give the gist of longer, presumably less focused interactions. Again, it would be foolish to think that in every case we hit exactly the right note. We hope that the gain to the reader in overall understanding is worth the possibility of small errors.

At the same time, we should confess our inventions. The short section in the last chapter describing the reasoning by which Charney and Silverman left the case unprosecuted is our speculation, but we believe it is strongly informed. And the exact details of the early interactions between Phantomd and Grok at the Free Software Foundation and Portland State being the subject of hazy and mutually inconsistent first- and secondhand accounts, we have proposed a course of events that seems logically consistent. As with everything else we learned about the Phantom Dialer incident, the full story of those interactions, should it ever come to light, will doubtless be more complex, harder to believe, and more dismaying.

# FOR FURTHER
# READING

To write this book, we spent considerable time researching on-line and read a whole shelf of computer books. Material on the Internet changes location too rapidly to be usefully cited, but we can list the books that we found of most use.

Cheswick, William R., and Steven M. Bellovin, *Firewalls and Internet Security: Repelling the Wily Hacker* (Reading, Mass.: Addison-Wesley, 1994).

Frisch, Æleen, *Essential Systems Administration*, 2d ed. (Sebastopol, Cal.: O'Reilly & Assocs., 1995).

Garfinkel, Simson, and Eugene Spafford, *Practical UNIX and Internet Security* (Sebastopol, Cal.: O'Reilly & Assocs., 1996).

Gilly, Daniel, et al., *Unix in a Nutshell*, 2d ed. (Sebastopol, Cal.: O'Reilly & Assocs., 1992).

Hafner, Katie, and Matthew Lyon, *Where Wizards Stay Up Late: The Origins of the Internet* (New York: Simon & Schuster, 1996).

Hafner, Katie, and John Markoff, *Cyberpunk: Outlaws and Hackers on the Computer Frontier* (New York: Simon & Schuster, 1991).

Levy, Steven, *Hackers: Heroes of the Computer Revolution* (New York: Dell, 1984).

Platt, Charles, *Anarchy Online* (New York: Black Sheep Books, 1996).

Raymond, Eric, ed., *The New Hacker's Dictionary* (Cambridge, Mass.: MIT Press, 1993).

Salus, Peter H., *Casting the Net: From ARPANET to INTERNET and Beyond . . .* (Reading, Mass.: Addison-Wesley, 1995).

———, *A Quarter-Century of Unix* (Reading, Mass.: Addison-Wesley, 1994).

Slatalla, Michelle, and Joshua Quittner, *Masters of Deception: The Gang that Ruled Cyberspace* (New York: HarperCollins, 1995).

Stoll, Cliff, *The Cuckoo's Egg: Tracking a Spy Through the Maze of Computer Espionage* (New York: Simon & Schuster, 1990).

# ACKNOWLEDGMENTS

Many people helped the authors write this book, most evidently the people involved in the events depicted here who allowed us to speak with them. We thank them for taking the time to help us. In the same way, we are grateful to the many experts in security and Unix who took time away from their busy schedules to give two authors what amounted to a tutorial in networking. Although many of their names do not appear in this book, we could not have written *At Large* without them.

Special appreciation is due our research assistant Sarah Schafer, a talented journalist whose diligence, resourcefulness, critical eye, and attention to detail lent considerable luster to many pages of this book.

We are indeed fortunate to have landed as our editor Bob Bender, who lavished unusual care on our manuscript. We thank him—and Johanna Li, in Bob's office—for patience with dilatory authors. Rick Balkin, our most excellent agent, adviser, and friend, helped guide us through every twist and turn of the project. We must also express our gratitude to colleagues at other publications, who offered their support even on those occasions when our work on this book impinged on our obligations to them: Corby Kummer, Cullen Murphy, and William Whitworth at *The Atlantic Monthly,* Tim Appenzeller and John Benditt at *Science,* Fred Guterl at *Discover,* and George Gendron at *Inc.* Thanks to Charles Platt, for allowing us to borrow a quote from his book, and to Steve Levy, for another quote and for several other favors. We are grateful to Rick Balkin, Gwenda Blair, Ray Kinoshita, Steve Mann, June Peoples, Gene Spafford, Deb Triant, Thea Singer, and Jeff Seglin for reading portions of earlier drafts of the manuscript and to Faith D'Aluisio, Carl Doumani, Pam Hunter, George Johnson, Peter Menzel, and Thanos Triant for hospitality and advice on the road.

Last, but far from least, personal thanks to the people in our lives who are our touchstones: Jason, Alex, Rachel, and Laurie; and Newell, Sasha, and Ray.

# INDEX